TRANSLATED
Translated Language Learning

Siddhartha
سيدهارتا

An Indian Poem
قصيدة هندية

Hermann Hesse
هيرمان هيسه

English / العربية

Copyright © 2024 Tranzlaty
All rights reserved
Published by Tranzlaty
Siddhartha – Eine Indische Dichtung
ISBN: 978-1-83566-673-9
Original text by Hermann Hesse
First published in German in 1922
www.tranzlaty.com

The Son of the Brahman
ابن البراهمان

In the shade of the house

في ظل البيت

in the sunshine of the riverbank

في ضوء الشمس على ضفة النهر

near the boats

بالقرب من القوارب

in the shade of the Sal-wood forest

في ظل غابة سالوود

in the shade of the fig tree

في ظل شجرة التين

this is where Siddhartha grew up

هذا هو المكان الذي نشأ فيه سيدهارثا

he was the handsome son of a Brahman, the young falcon

كان الابن الوسيم لبراهمان، الصقر الشاب

he grew up with his friend Govinda

لقد نشأ مع صديقه جوفيندا

Govinda was also the son of a Brahman

كان جوفيندا أيضًا ابنًا لبراهمان

by the banks of the river the sun tanned his light shoulders

على ضفاف النهر كانت الشمس تحرق كتفيه الخفيفتين

bathing, performing the sacred ablutions, making sacred offerings

الاغتسال، أداء الوضوء المقدس، تقديم القرابين المقدسة

In the mango garden, shade poured into his black eyes

في حديقة المانجو، كان الظل يتدفق إلى عينيه السوداء

when playing as a boy, when his mother sang

عندما كان يلعب وهو صغير، عندما كانت والدته تغني

when the sacred offerings were made

عندما تم تقديم القرابين المقدسة

when his father, the scholar, taught him

عندما علمه والده العالم

when the wise men talked

عندما تحدث الحكماء

For a long time, Siddhartha had been partaking in the discussions of the wise men

لفترة طويلة، كان سيدهارتا يشارك في مناقشات الحكماء

he practiced debating with Govinda

لقد تدرب على المناظرة مع جوفيندا

he practiced the art of reflection with Govinda

لقد مارس فن التأمل مع جوفيندا

and he practiced meditation

ومارس التأمل

He already knew how to speak the Om silently

لقد كان يعرف بالفعل كيفية التحدث بالأوم بصمت

he knew the word of words

لقد عرف كلمة الكلمات

he spoke it silently into himself while inhaling

قالها بصمت في نفسه أثناء الاستنشاق

he spoke it silently out of himself while exhaling

لقد قالها بصمت من نفسه أثناء الزفير

he did this with all the concentration of his soul

لقد فعل هذا بكل تركيز روحه

his forehead was surrounded by the glow of the clear-thinking spirit

كانت جبهته محاطة بتوهج الروح ذات التفكير الواضح

He already knew how to feel Atman in the depths of his being

لقد كان يعرف بالفعل كيف يشعر بالأتمان في أعماق كيانه

he could feel the indestructible

كان بإمكانه أن يشعر باللا يمكن تدميره

he knew what it was to be at one with the universe

لقد عرف ما معنى أن يكون المرء واحداً مع الكون

Joy leapt in his father's heart

قفز الفرح في قلب والده

because his son was quick to learn

لأن ابنه كان سريع التعلم

he was thirsty for knowledge

كان متعطشًا للمعرفة

his father could see him growing up to become a great wise man
كان والده يرى أنه يكبر ليصبح رجلاً حكيماً عظيماً
he could see him becoming a priest
كان بإمكانه أن يرى نفسه يصبح كاهنًا
he could see him becoming a prince among the Brahmans
كان بإمكانه أن يرى نفسه يصبح أميرًا بين البراهمة
Bliss leapt in his mother's breast when she saw him walking
قفز بليس في صدر أمه عندما رأته يمشي
Bliss leapt in her heart when she saw him sit down and get up
قفزت النعيم في قلبها عندما رأته يجلس وينهض
Siddhartha was strong and handsome
كان سيدهارتا قويا ووسيمًا
he, who was walking on slender legs
هو الذي كان يمشي على ساقين نحيلتين
he greeted her with perfect respect
لقد استقبلها بكل احترام
Love touched the hearts of the Brahmans' young daughters
لقد لامس الحب قلوب بنات البراهمة الصغار
they were charmed when Siddhartha walked through the lanes of the town
لقد سُحِروا عندما سار سيدهارثا في أزقة المدينة
his luminous forehead, his eyes of a king, his slim hips
جبهته المضيئة، عيناه الملكتان، ووركاه النحيفتان
But most of all he was loved by Govinda
ولكن أكثر من كل هذا كان محبوبًا من قبل جوفيندا
Govinda, his friend, the son of a Brahman
جوفيندا، صديقه، ابن أحد البراهمة
He loved Siddhartha's eye and sweet voice
لقد أحب عين سيدهارتا وصوته الجميل
he loved the way he walked
لقد أحب الطريقة التي يمشي بها
and he loved the perfect decency of his movements
وكان يحب اللياقة المثالية لحركاته
he loved everything Siddhartha did and said

لقد أحب كل ما فعله وقاله سيدهارثا

but what he loved most was his spirit

لكن ما أحبه أكثر هو روحه

he loved his transcendent, fiery thoughts

لقد أحب أفكاره السامية والنارية

he loved his ardent will and high calling

لقد أحب إرادته القوية ودعوته السامية

Govinda knew he would not become a common Brahman

كان جوفيندا يعلم أنه لن يصبح براهمانًا عاديًا

no, he would not become a lazy official

لا، لن يصبح مسؤولاً كسولاً

no, he would not become a greedy merchant

لا، لن يصبح تاجرًا جشعًا

not a vain, vacuous speaker

ليس متحدثًا مغرورًا أو فارغًا

nor a mean, deceitful priest

ولا كاهنًا حقيرًا مخادعًا

and he also would not become a decent, stupid sheep

ولن يصبح أيضًا خروفًا لائقًا غبيًا

a sheep in the herd of the many

شاة في قطيع الكثيرين

and he did not want to become one of those things

ولم يكن يريد أن يصبح واحدا من تلك الأشياء

he did not want to be one of those tens of thousands of Brahmans

لم يكن يريد أن يكون واحدا من هؤلاء العشرات الآلاف من البراهمة

He wanted to follow Siddhartha; the beloved, the splendid

أراد أن يتبع سيدهارتا؛ الحبيب، الرائع

in days to come, when Siddhartha would become a god, he would be there

في الأيام القادمة، عندما يصبح سيدهارثا إلهًا، سيكون هناك

when he would join the glorious, he would be there

عندما ينضم إلى المجيد، سيكون هناك

Govinda wanted to follow him as his friend

أراد جوفيندا أن يتبعه كصديق له

he was his companion and his servant

وكان رفيقه وخادمه
he was his spear-carrier and his shadow
كان حامل رمحه وظله
Siddhartha was loved by everyone
كان سيدهارتا محبوبا من الجميع
He was a source of joy for everybody
لقد كان مصدر فرح للجميع
he was a delight for them all
لقد كان مصدر سعادة لهم جميعا
But he, Siddhartha, was not a source of joy for himself
ولكنه، سيدهارتا، لم يكن مصدر فرح لنفسه
he found no delight in himself
لم يجد متعة في نفسه
he walked the rosy paths of the fig tree garden
كان يسير في المسارات الوردية لحديقة شجرة التين
he sat in the bluish shade in the garden of contemplation
جلس في الظل الأزرق في حديقة التأمل
he washed his limbs daily in the bath of repentance
كان يغسل أعضاءه يوميا في حمام التوبة
he made sacrifices in the dim shade of the mango forest
لقد قدم تضحياته في الظل الخافت لغابة المانجو
his gestures were of perfect decency
كانت تصرفاته لائقة تماما
he was everyone's love and joy
لقد كان حب الجميع وفرحهم
but he still lacked all joy in his heart
ولكنه ما زال يفتقر إلى كل الفرح في قلبه
Dreams and restless thoughts came into his mind
جاءت الأحلام والأفكار المضطربة إلى ذهنه
his dreams flowed from the water of the river
أحلامه تدفقت من مياه النهر
his dreams sparked from the stars of the night
أحلامه أشرقت من نجوم الليل
his dreams melted from the beams of the sun
ذابت أحلامه من أشعة الشمس

dreams came to him, and a restlessness of the soul came to him

أتته الأحلام، وأتته رعشة النفس

his soul was fuming from the sacrifices

كانت روحه تغلي من التضحيات

he breathed forth from the verses of the Rig-Veda

لقد تنفس من آيات الريج فيدا

the verses were infused into him, drop by drop

لقد تم غرس الآيات فيه قطرة قطرة

the verses from the teachings of the old Brahmans

أبيات من تعاليم البراهمة القدماء

Siddhartha had started to nurse discontent in himself

بدأ سيدهارتا يشعر بالاستياء في نفسه

he had started to feel doubt about the love of his father

لقد بدأ يشعر بالشك في حب والده

he doubted the love of his mother

لقد شك في حب أمه

and he doubted the love of his friend, Govinda

وشكك في حب صديقه جوفيندا

he doubted if their love could bring him joy forever and ever

لقد شك في أن حبهم يمكن أن يجلب له السعادة إلى الأبد

their love could not nurse him

لم يستطع حبهم أن يرضعه

their love could not feed him

حبهم لم يستطع أن يطعمه

their love could not satisfy him

حبهم لم يرضيه

he had started to suspect his father's teachings

لقد بدأ يشك في تعاليم والده

perhaps he had shown him everything he knew

ربما أظهر له كل ما يعرفه

there were his other teachers, the wise Brahmans

وكان هناك معلمين آخرين، البراهمة الحكماء

perhaps they had already revealed to him the best of their wisdom

ربما كانوا قد كشفوا له بالفعل أفضل حكمتهم

he feared that they had already filled his expecting vessel
كان يخشى أن يكونوا قد ملأوا بالفعل وعاء انتظاره

despite the richness of their teachings, the vessel was not full
على الرغم من ثراء تعاليمهم، إلا أن الإناء لم يكن ممتلئًا

the spirit was not content
الروح لم تكن راضية

the soul was not calm
الروح لم تكن هادئة

the heart was not satisfied
لم يشبع القلب

the ablutions were good, but they were water
كانت الوضوءات جيدة ولكنها كانت مياه

the ablutions did not wash off the sin
الوضوء لم يغسل الذنب

they did not heal the spirit's thirst
لم يشفوا عطش الروح

they did not relieve the fear in his heart
لم يزيلوا الخوف من قلبه

The sacrifices and the invocation of the gods were excellent
وكانت التضحيات واستدعاء الآلهة ممتازة

but was that all there was?
ولكن هل كان هذا كل ما كان هناك؟

did the sacrifices give a happy fortune?
هل أعطت التضحيات ثروة سعيدة؟

and what about the gods?
وماذا عن الآلهة؟

Was it really Prajapati who had created the world?
هل كان براجاباتي حقا هو الذي خلق العالم؟

Was it not the Atman who had created the world?
أليس الأتمان هو الذي خلق العالم؟

Atman, the only one, the singular one
الأتمان، الوحيد، المفرد

Were the gods not creations?
أليس الآلهة مخلوقات؟

were they not created like me and you?

ألم يخلقوا مثلي ومثلك؟

were the Gods not subject to time?

هل الآلهة غير خاضعة للزمن؟

were the Gods mortal? Was it good?

هل كان الآلهة بشر؟ هل كان ذلك جيدا؟

was it right? was it meaningful?

هل كان ذلك صحيحا؟ هل كان ذا معنى؟

was it the highest occupation to make offerings to the gods?

هل كانت أعلى مهنة هي تقديم القرابين للآلهة؟

For whom else were offerings to be made?

لمن يجب أن تقدم القرابين الأخرى؟

who else was to be worshipped?

من غيره كان ينبغي أن يُعبَد؟

who else was there, but Him?

من كان هناك غيره؟

The only one, the Atman

الوحيد، الأتمان

And where was Atman to be found?

وأين يمكن العثور على أتمان؟

where did He reside?

أين كان يقيم؟

where did His eternal heart beat?

أين كان ينبض قلبه الأبدي؟

where else but in one's own self?

أين يمكن للمرء أن يجد نفسه إلا في نفسه؟

in its innermost indestructible part

في الجزء الداخلي الذي لا يمكن تدميره

could he be that which everyone had in himself?

هل يمكن أن يكون هو ذلك الذي يمتلكه كل شخص في داخله؟

But where was this self?

ولكن أين كانت هذه الذات؟

where was this innermost part?

أين كان هذا الجزء الأعمق؟

where was this ultimate part?

أين كان هذا الجزء النهائي؟

It was not flesh and bone
لم يكن لحمًا وعظامًا

it was neither thought nor consciousness
لم يكن فكرا ولا وعيا

this is what the wisest ones taught
هذا ما علمه الحكماء

So where was it?
فأين كان؟

the self, myself, the Atman
الذات، نفسي، الأتمان

To reach this place, there was another way
للوصول إلى هذا المكان، كانت هناك طريقة أخرى

was this other way worth looking for?
هل كان هذا الطريق الآخر يستحق البحث عنه؟

Alas, nobody showed him this way
للأسف، لم يرشده أحد إلى هذا الطريق

nobody knew this other way
لا أحد يعرف هذا بطريقة أخرى

his father did not know it
والده لم يعلم بذلك

and the teachers and wise men did not know it
ولم يعلمه المعلمون والحكماء

They knew everything, the Brahmans
لقد عرفوا كل شيء، البراهمة

and their holy books knew everything
وكتبهم المقدسة تعرف كل شيء

they had taken care of everything
لقد اعتنوا بكل شيء

they took care of the creation of the world
لقد اهتموا بخلق العالم

they described origin of speech, food, inhaling, exhaling
لقد وصفوا أصل الكلام، والطعام، والاستنشاق، والزفير

they described the arrangement of the senses
لقد وصفوا ترتيب الحواس

they described the acts of the gods
لقد وصفوا أفعال الآلهة

their books knew infinitely much

كتبهم عرفت الكثير

but was it valuable to know all of this?

ولكن هل كان من المفيد معرفة كل هذا؟

was there not only one thing to be known?

هل كان هناك شيء واحد فقط يجب معرفته؟

was there still not the most important thing to know?

هل لا يزال هناك الشيء الأكثر أهمية الذي يتعين معرفته؟

many verses of the holy books spoke of this innermost, ultimate thing

وقد تحدثت آيات كثيرة من الكتب المقدسة عن هذا الأمر الأعمق والأسمى.

it was spoken of particularly in the Upanishades of Samaveda

وقد تم الحديث عنه بشكل خاص في الأوبنشادات في سامافيدا

they were wonderful verses

لقد كانت أبيات رائعة

"Your soul is the whole world", this was written there

"روحك هي العالم كله" هذا ما كتب هناك

and it was written that man in deep sleep would meet with his innermost part

وقد كتب أن الإنسان في نومه العميق يلتقي بأعماقه.

and he would reside in the Atman

وكان يقيم في الأتمان

Marvellous wisdom was in these verses

لقد كانت الحكمة رائعة في هذه الآيات

all knowledge of the wisest ones had been collected here in magic words

لقد تم جمع كل معرفة الحكماء هنا في كلمات سحرية

it was as pure as honey collected by bees

لقد كان نقيا مثل العسل الذي يجمعه النحل

No, the verses were not to be looked down upon

لا، لا ينبغي الاستخفاف بالآيات

they contained tremendous amounts of enlightenment

لقد احتوت على كميات هائلة من التنوير

they contained wisdom which lay collected and preserved

لقد احتوت على الحكمة التي تم جمعها وحفظها

wisdom collected by innumerable generations of wise Brahmans

الحكمة التي جمعها أجيال لا حصر لها من البراهمة الحكماء

But where were the Brahmans?

ولكن أين كان البراهمة؟

where were the priests?

أين كان الكهنة؟

where the wise men or penitents?

أين الحكماء أو التائبون؟

where were those that had succeeded?

أين الذين نجحوا؟

where were those who knew more than deepest of all knowledge?

أين أولئك الذين عرفوا أكثر من أعمق المعرفة؟

where were those that also lived out the enlightened wisdom?

أين أولئك الذين عاشوا الحكمة المستنيرة؟

Where was the knowledgeable one who brought Atman out of his sleep?

أين العارف الذي أخرج أتمان من نومه؟

who had brought this knowledge into the day?

من الذي جلب هذه المعرفة إلى هذا اليوم؟

who had taken this knowledge into their life?

من الذي أخذ هذه المعرفة إلى حياته؟

who carried this knowledge with every step they took?

من حمل هذه المعرفة مع كل خطوة اتخذها؟

who had married their words with their deeds?

من الذي قرن أقواله بأفعاله؟

Siddhartha knew many venerable Brahmans

عرف سيدهارتا العديد من البراهمة الموقرين

his father, the pure one

والده الطاهر

the scholar, the most venerable one

العالم هو الأعظم

His father was worthy of admiration

وكان والده يستحق الإعجاب

quiet and noble were his manners

كانت أخلاقه هادئة ونبيلة

pure was his life, wise were his words

كانت حياته نقية وكلماته حكيمة

delicate and noble thoughts lived behind his brow

كانت الأفكار الرقيقة والنبيلة تسكن خلف جبينه

but even though he knew so much, did he live in blissfulness?

ولكن مع أنه كان يعلم كل هذا، هل عاش في سعادة؟

despite all his knowledge, did he have peace?

رغم كل ما لديه من علم، هل كان لديه السلام؟

was he not also just a searching man?

ألم يكن أيضًا مجرد رجل باحث؟

was he still not a thirsty man?

فهل كان لا يزال رجلاً عطشاناً؟

Did he not have to drink from holy sources again and again?

ألم يكن عليه أن يشرب من الينابيع المقدسة مرارا وتكرارا؟

did he not drink from the offerings?

ألم يشرب من القرابين؟

did he not drink from the books?

ولم يشرب من الكتب؟

did he not drink from the disputes of the Brahmans?

ألم يشرب من جدالات البراهمة؟

Why did he have to wash off sins every day?

لماذا كان عليه أن يغسل ذنوبه كل يوم؟

must he strive for a cleansing every day?

هل يجب عليه أن يسعى إلى التطهير كل يوم؟

over and over again, every day

مرارا وتكرارا، كل يوم

Was Atman not in him?

هل لم يكن فيه أتمان؟

did not the pristine source spring from his heart?

ألم ينبع النبع النقي من قلبه؟

the pristine source had to be found in one's own self

كان لابد من العثور على المصدر الأصلي في الذات

the pristine source had to be possessed!

كان لا بد من امتلاك المصدر البكر!

doing anything else else was searching

القيام بأي شيء آخر كان البحث

taking any other pass is a detour

إن اتخاذ أي قرار آخر هو بمثابة تحويلة

going any other way leads to getting lost

الذهاب في أي طريق آخر يؤدي إلى الضياع

These were Siddhartha's thoughts

كانت هذه أفكار سيدهارتا

this was his thirst, and this was his suffering

هذا كان عطشه وهذا كان معاناته

Often he spoke to himself from a Chandogya-Upanishad:

وكان غالبًا ما يتحدث إلى نفسه من تشاندوجيا-أوبانيشاد:

"Truly, the name of the Brahman is Satyam"

"إن اسم البراهمان هو ساتيام"

"he who knows such a thing, will enter the heavenly world every day"

"من يعرف مثل هذا الأمر فإنه يدخل العالم السماوي كل يوم"

Often the heavenly world seemed near

في كثير من الأحيان يبدو العالم السماوي قريبًا

but he had never reached the heavenly world completely

ولكنه لم يصل إلى العالم السماوي بشكل كامل

he had never quenched the ultimate thirst

لم يروِ عطشه النهائي أبدًا

And among all the wise and wisest men, none had reached it

ومن بين جميع الحكماء والحكماء لم يصل إليها أحد

he received instructions from them

لقد تلقى منهم التعليمات

but they hadn't completely reached the heavenly world

لكنهم لم يصلوا إلى العالم السماوي بشكل كامل

they hadn't completely quenched their thirst

لم يروا عطشهم بالكامل

because this thirst is an eternal thirst

لأن هذا العطش هو عطش أبدي

"Govinda" Siddhartha spoke to his friend

تحدث "جوفيندا" سيدهارثا إلى صديقه
"Govinda, my dear, come with me under the Banyan tree"
"جوفيندا، يا عزيزي، تعال معي تحت شجرة البانيان"
"let's practise meditation"
"دعونا نمارس التأمل"
They went to the Banyan tree
ذهبوا إلى شجرة البانيان
under the Banyan tree they sat down
تحت شجرة البانيان جلسوا
Siddhartha was right here
كان سيدهارتا هنا
Govinda was twenty paces away
كان جوفيندا على بعد عشرين خطوة
Siddhartha seated himself and he repeated murmuring the verse
جلس سيدهارتا وراح يردد الآية بصوت هامس
Om is the bow, the arrow is the soul
أوم هو القوس، والسهم هو الروح
The Brahman is the arrow's target
البراهمان هو هدف السهم
the target that one should incessantly hit
الهدف الذي يجب على المرء أن يضربه باستمرار
the usual time of the exercise in meditation had passed
لقد مر الوقت المعتاد لممارسة التأمل
Govinda got up, the evening had come
استيقظ جوفيندا، لقد جاء المساء
it was time to perform the evening's ablution
لقد حان وقت أداء الوضوء المسائي
He called Siddhartha's name, but Siddhartha did not answer
نادى باسم سيدهارثا، لكن سيدهارثا لم يجب.
Siddhartha sat there, lost in thought
جلس سيدهارثا هناك، غارقًا في التفكير
his eyes were rigidly focused towards a very distant target
كانت عيناه مركزة بشكل صارم نحو هدف بعيد جدًا
the tip of his tongue was protruding a little between the teeth

كان طرف لسانه بارزًا قليلاً بين الأسنان

he seemed not to breathe

يبدو أنه لا يتنفس

Thus sat he, wrapped up in contemplation

وهكذا جلس منغمسا في التأمل

he was deep in thought of the Om

كان مستغرقًا في التفكير في أوم

his soul sent after the Brahman like an arrow

روحه أرسلت وراء البراهمان مثل السهم

Once, Samanas had travelled through Siddhartha's town

ذات مرة، سافر ساماناس عبر بلدة سيدهارثا

they were ascetics on a pilgrimage

كانوا زاهدين في الحج

three skinny, withered men, neither old nor young

ثلاثة رجال نحيفين، ذابلين، ليسوا كبارًا ولا صغارًا

dusty and bloody were their shoulders

كانت أكتافهم مغبرة وملطخة بالدماء

almost naked, scorched by the sun, surrounded by loneliness

عارية تقريبًا، محروقة من الشمس، محاطة بالوحدة

strangers and enemies to the world

الغرباء والأعداء للعالم

strangers and jackals in the realm of humans

الغرباء والذئاب في عالم البشر

Behind them blew a hot scent of quiet passion

خلفهم نفخت رائحة حارة من العاطفة الهادئة

a scent of destructive service

رائحة الخدمة المدمرة

a scent of merciless self-denial

رائحة الحرمان الذاتي بلا رحمة

the evening had come

لقد جاء المساء

after the hour of contemplation, Siddhartha spoke to Govinda

بعد ساعة من التأمل، تحدث سيدهارثا إلى جوفيندا

"Early tomorrow morning, my friend, Siddhartha will go to the Samanas"

"غدًا في الصباح الباكر، سيذهب صديقي سيدهارثا إلى ساماناس"

"He will become a Samana"

"سوف يصبح سامانا"

Govinda turned pale when he heard these words

شحب جوفيندا عندما سمع هذه الكلمات

and he read the decision in the motionless face of his friend

وقرأ القرار على وجه صديقه الجامد

the determination was unstoppable, like the arrow shot from the bow

كان التصميم لا يمكن إيقافه، مثل السهم الذي انطلق من القوس

Govinda realized at first glance; now it is beginning

أدرك جوفيندا من النظرة الأولى؛ والآن بدأ الأمر

now Siddhartha is taking his own way

الآن سيدهارثا يأخذ طريقه الخاص

now his fate is beginning to sprout

الآن بدأ مصيره يتكشف

and because of Siddhartha, Govinda's fate is sprouting too

وبسبب سيدهارتا، فإن مصير جوفيندا يتطور أيضًا

he turned pale like a dry banana-skin

أصبح شاحبًا مثل قشرة الموز الجافة

"Oh Siddhartha," he exclaimed

"أوه سيدهارتا" هتف

"will your father permit you to do that?"

"هل والدك يسمح لك بذلك؟"

Siddhartha looked over as if he was just waking up

نظر سيدهارثا وكأنه كان يستيقظ للتو

like an Arrow he read Govinda's soul

مثل السهم قرأ روح جوفيندا

he could read the fear and the submission in him

كان بإمكانه قراءة الخوف والخضوع بداخله

"Oh Govinda," he spoke quietly, "let's not waste words"

"أوه جوفيندا"، تحدث بهدوء، "دعنا لا نضيع الكلمات"

"Tomorrow at daybreak I will begin the life of the Samanas"

"غدًا عند شروق الشمس سأبدأ حياة الساماناس"

"let us speak no more of it"

"لا داعي للحديث عن هذا الأمر أكثر"

Siddhartha entered the chamber where his father was sitting

دخل سيدهارثا الغرفة التي كان يجلس فيها والده

his father was was on a mat of bast

كان والده على حصيرة من اللحاء

Siddhartha stepped behind his father

خطى سيدهارثا خلف والده

and he remained standing behind him

وبقي واقفا خلفه

he stood until his father felt that someone was standing behind him

وقف حتى شعر والده أن هناك من يقف خلفه

Spoke the Brahman: "Is that you, Siddhartha?"

تكلم البراهمان: "هل هذا أنت، سيدهارتا؟"

"Then say what you came to say"

"ثم قل ما جئت لتقوله"

Spoke Siddhartha: "With your permission, my father"

تكلم سيدهارتا: "بإذنك يا والدي"

"I came to tell you that it is my longing to leave your house tomorrow"

"جئت لأخبرك أن شوقي هو أن أترك منزلك غدًا"

"I wish to go to the ascetics"

"أريد أن أذهب إلى الزاهدين"

"My desire is to become a Samana"

"رغبتي هي أن أصبح سامانا"

"May my father not oppose this"

"لا يعترض والدي على هذا"

The Brahman fell silent, and he remained so for long

فسكت البراهمان، وظل على هذا الحال لفترة طويلة.

the stars in the small window wandered

تجولت النجوم في النافذة الصغيرة

and they changed their relative positions

وغيروا مواقعهم النسبية

Silent and motionless stood the son with his arms folded

كان الابن يقف صامتًا بلا حراك وذراعيه مطويتان
silent and motionless sat the father on the mat
جلس الأب صامتًا بلا حراك على الحصيرة
and the stars traced their paths in the sky
والنجوم تتبع مساراتها في السماء
Then spoke the father
ثم تحدث الأب
"it is not proper for a Brahman to speak harsh and angry words"
"ليس من اللائق أن يتكلم البراهمان بكلمات قاسية وغاضبة"
"But indignation is in my heart"
"ولكن السخط في قلبي"
"I wish not to hear this request for a second time"
"أتمنى أن لا أسمع هذا الطلب مرة ثانية"
Slowly, the Brahman rose
ببطء، ارتفع البراهمان
Siddhartha stood silently, his arms folded
وقف سيدهارتا بصمت، وذراعيه مطويتان
"What are you waiting for?" asked the father
"ماذا تنتظر؟" سأل الأب
Spoke Siddhartha, "You know what I'm waiting for"
قال سيدهارتا "أنت تعرف ما أنتظره"
Indignant, the father left the chamber
غاضبًا، غادر الأب الغرفة
indignant, he went to his bed and lay down
غاضبًا، ذهب إلى سريره واستلقى
an hour passed, but no sleep had come over his eyes
مرت ساعة ولم ينام في عينيه
the Brahman stood up and he paced to and fro
وقف البراهمان وراح يمشي ذهابا وإيابا
and he left the house in the night
وخرج من البيت في الليل
Through the small window of the chamber he looked back inside
من خلال النافذة الصغيرة للغرفة نظر إلى الداخل
and there he saw Siddhartha standing

وهناك رأى سيدهارثا واقفًا
his arms were folded and he had not moved from his spot
كانت ذراعيه مطويتين ولم يتحرك من مكانه
Pale shimmered his bright robe
شاحب يلمع ردائه المشرق
With anxiety in his heart, the father returned to his bed
وعاد الأب إلى فراشه وهو قلق في قلبه
another sleepless hour passed
لقد مرت ساعة أخرى بلا نوم
since no sleep had come over his eyes, the Brahman stood up again
وبما أن النوم لم يطل عينيه، وقف البراهمان مرة أخرى
he paced to and fro, and he walked out of the house
كان يمشي ذهابا وإيابا، ثم خرج من المنزل
and he saw that the moon had risen
ورأى أن القمر قد طلع
Through the window of the chamber he looked back inside
من خلال نافذة الغرفة نظر إلى الداخل مرة أخرى
there stood Siddhartha, unmoved from his spot
كان سيدهارتا يقف هناك، دون أن يتحرك من مكانه
his arms were folded, as they had been
كانت ذراعيه مطويتين كما كانا
moonlight was reflecting from his bare shins
كان ضوء القمر ينعكس من ساقيه العاريتين
With worry in his heart, the father went back to bed
ومع القلق في قلبه، عاد الأب إلى السرير
he came back after an hour
لقد عاد بعد ساعة
and he came back again after two hours
وعاد مرة أخرى بعد ساعتين
he looked through the small window
كان ينظر من خلال النافذة الصغيرة
he saw Siddhartha standing in the moon light
لقد رأى سيدهارتا واقفًا في ضوء القمر
he stood by the light of the stars in the darkness
كان واقفاً على ضوء النجوم في الظلام

And he came back hour after hour
وعاد ساعة بعد ساعة

silently, he looked into the chamber
بصمت، نظر إلى الغرفة

he saw him standing in the same place
لقد رآه واقفا في نفس المكان

it filled his heart with anger
لقد امتلأ قلبه بالغضب

it filled his heart with unrest
لقد ملأ قلبه بالقلق

it filled his heart with anguish
لقد ملأ قلبه بالألم

it filled his heart with sadness
لقد ملئ قلبه بالحزن

the night's last hour had come
لقد حانت الساعة الأخيرة من الليل

his father returned and stepped into the room
عاد والده ودخل الغرفة

he saw the young man standing there
رأى الشاب واقفا هناك

he seemed tall and like a stranger to him
لقد بدا طويل القامة وكأنه غريب بالنسبة له

"Siddhartha," he spoke, "what are you waiting for?"
"سيدهارتا"، تحدث، "ماذا تنتظر؟"

"You know what I'm waiting for"
"أنت تعرف ما أنتظره"

"Will you always stand that way and wait?
"هل ستظل واقفًا بهذه الطريقة وتنتظر دائمًا؟

"I will always stand and wait"
"سوف أقف وأنتظر دائمًا"

"will you wait until it becomes morning, noon, and evening?"
"هل ستنتظر حتى يصبح الصباح والظهر والمساء؟"

"I will wait until it become morning, noon, and evening"
"سأنتظر حتى يصبح الصباح والظهيرة والمساء"

"You will become tired, Siddhartha"

"سوف تتعب يا سيدهارتا"
"I will become tired"
"سوف اتعب"
"You will fall asleep, Siddhartha"
"سوف تنام يا سيدهارتا"
"I will not fall asleep"
"لن أنام"
"You will die, Siddhartha"
"سوف تموت يا سيدهارثا"
"I will die," answered Siddhartha
"سأموت" أجاب سيدهارثا
"And would you rather die, than obey your father?"
"وهل تفضل الموت على طاعة والدك؟"
"Siddhartha has always obeyed his father"
"سيدارثا كان يطيع والده دائمًا"
"So will you abandon your plan?"
"فهل ستتخلى عن خطتك؟"
"Siddhartha will do what his father will tell him to do"
"سيفعل سيدهارثا ما يطلب منه والده أن يفعله"
The first light of day shone into the room
أشرق ضوء النهار الأول في الغرفة
The Brahman saw that Siddhartha knees were softly trembling
رأى البراهمان أن ركبتي سيدهارتا كانتا ترتعشان بهدوء
In Siddhartha's face he saw no trembling
لم ير أي ارتعاش في وجه سيدهارتا
his eyes were fixed on a distant spot
كانت عيناه مثبتتين على مكان بعيد
This was when his father realized
كان هذا عندما أدرك والده
even now Siddhartha no longer dwelt with him in his home
حتى الآن لم يعد سيدهارثا يقيم معه في منزله
he saw that he had already left him
رأى أنه قد تركه بالفعل
The Father touched Siddhartha's shoulder
لمس الأب كتف سيدهارتا

"You will," he spoke, "go into the forest and be a Samana"
"سوف"، قال، "تذهب إلى الغابة وتصبح سامانا"
"When you find blissfulness in the forest, come back"
"عندما تجد النعيم في الغابة، عد"
"come back and teach me to be blissful"
"عد وعلمني كيف أكون سعيدًا"
"If you find disappointment, then return"
"إذا وجدت خيبة أمل فارجع"
"return and let us make offerings to the gods together, again"
"ارجع ولنقدم القرابين للآلهة معًا مرة أخرى"
"Go now and kiss your mother"
"اذهب الآن وقبّل أمك"
"tell her where you are going"
"أخبرها إلى أين أنت ذاهب"
"But for me it is time to go to the river"
"ولكن بالنسبة لي حان الوقت للذهاب إلى النهر"
"it is my time to perform the first ablution"
"لقد حان وقت الوضوء الأول"

He took his hand from the shoulder of his son, and went outside
فأخذ يده من كتف ابنه وخرج.

Siddhartha wavered to the side as he tried to walk
انحنى سيدهارثا إلى الجانب وهو يحاول المشي

He put his limbs back under control and bowed to his father
أعاد السيطرة على أطرافه وانحنى لأبيه

he went to his mother to do as his father had said
ذهب إلى أمه ليفعل كما قال له والده

As he slowly left on stiff legs a shadow rose near the last hut
وبينما كان يغادر ببطء على ساقيه المتصلبتين، ارتفع ظل بالقرب من الكوخ الأخير

who had crouched there, and joined the pilgrim?
من كان جالساً هناك وانضم إلى الحاج؟

"Govinda, you have come" said Siddhartha and smiled
"جوفيندا، لقد أتيت" قال سيدهارثا وابتسم

"I have come," said Govinda
"لقد جئت" قال جوفيندا

With the Samanas
مع الساماناس

In the evening of this day they caught up with the ascetics
وفي مساء هذا اليوم لحقوا بالزاهدين
the ascetics; the skinny Samanas
الزاهدون؛ السامانا النحيفون
they offered them their companionship and obedience
لقد عرضوا عليهم صحبتهم وطاعتهم
Their companionship and obedience were accepted
وقد تم قبول صحبتهم وطاعتهم
Siddhartha gave his garments to a poor Brahman in the street
أعطى سيدهارتا ملابسه لبراهمان فقير في الشارع
He wore nothing more than a loincloth and earth-coloured, unsown cloak
لم يكن يرتدي أكثر من مئزر وعباءة بلون الأرض غير مخيطة
He ate only once a day, and never anything cooked
كان يأكل مرة واحدة فقط في اليوم، ولم يكن يطبخ أي شيء على الإطلاق
He fasted for fifteen days, he fasted for twenty-eight days
صام خمسة عشر يوما، صام ثمانية وعشرين يوما
The flesh waned from his thighs and cheeks
لقد تلاشى اللحم من فخذيه وخديه
Feverish dreams flickered from his enlarged eyes
تومض الأحلام المحمومة من عينيه المتوسعتين
long nails grew slowly on his parched fingers
نمت أظافر طويلة ببطء على أصابعه الجافة
and a dry, shaggy beard grew on his chin
ونبتت على ذقنه لحية جافة أشعثاء
His glance turned to ice when he encountered women
تحولت نظراته إلى الجليد عندما واجه النساء
he walked through a city of nicely dressed people
كان يتجول في مدينة من الناس الذين يرتدون ملابس أنيقة
his mouth twitched with contempt for them
ارتجف فمه ازدراءً لهم
He saw merchants trading and princes hunting

رأى التجار يتاجرون والأمراء يصطادون
he saw mourners wailing for their dead
رأى المعزين ينتحبون على موتاهم
and he saw whores offering themselves
ورأى عاهرات يعرضن أنفسهن
physicians trying to help the sick
الأطباء يحاولون مساعدة المرضى
priests determining the most suitable day for seeding
الكهنة يحددون اليوم الأنسب للبذر
lovers loving and mothers nursing their children
العشاق المحبين والأمهات المرضعات لأطفالهن
and all of this was not worthy of one look from his eyes
وكل هذا لم يكن يستحق نظرة واحدة من عينيه
it all lied, it all stank, it all stank of lies
كل هذا كذب، كل هذا كريه، كل هذا كريه بسبب الكذب
it all pretended to be meaningful and joyful and beautiful
لقد تظاهر كل شيء بأنه ذو معنى ومبهج وجميل
and it all was just concealed putrefaction
وكان كل ذلك مجرد تعفن مخفي
the world tasted bitter; life was torture
لقد كان العالم مذاقه مرّا، وكانت الحياة عذابًا

A single goal stood before Siddhartha
كان هناك هدف واحد يقف أمام سيدهارتا
his goal was to become empty
كان هدفه أن يصبح فارغا
his goal was to be empty of thirst
كان هدفه أن يكون خاليا من العطش
empty of wishing and empty of dreams
خالي من التمنيات و خالي من الأحلام
empty of joy and sorrow
خالي من الفرح والحزن
his goal was to be dead to himself
كان هدفه أن يموت لنفسه
his goal was not to be a self any more
لم يكن هدفه أن يكون ذاتا بعد الآن

his goal was to find tranquillity with an emptied heart
كان هدفه أن يجد السكينة بقلب فارغ
his goal was to be open to miracles in unselfish thoughts
كان هدفه أن يكون منفتحًا على المعجزات في الأفكار غير الأنانية
to achieve this was his goal
وكان تحقيق هذا هو هدفه
when all of his self was overcome and had died
عندما تغلبت كل ذاته ومات
when every desire and every urge was silent in the heart
عندما كانت كل رغبة وكل دافع صامت في القلب
then the ultimate part of him had to awake
ثم كان على الجزء الأخير منه أن يستيقظ
the innermost of his being, which is no longer his self
أعمق ما في كيانه، والذي لم يعد هو ذاته
this was the great secret
هذا كان السر العظيم

Silently, Siddhartha exposed himself to the burning rays of the sun
في صمت، عرّض سيدارتا نفسه لأشعة الشمس الحارقة
he was glowing with pain and he was glowing with thirst
كان يتوهج بالألم وكان يتوهج بالعطش
and he stood there until he neither felt pain nor thirst
ووقف هناك حتى لم يشعر بألم ولا عطش
Silently, he stood there in the rainy season
ووقف هناك بصمت في موسم الأمطار
from his hair the water was dripping over freezing shoulders
من شعره كان الماء يتساقط على الكتفين المتجمدين
the water was dripping over his freezing hips and legs
كان الماء يتساقط فوق وركيه وساقيه المتجمدتين
and the penitent stood there
والتائب وقف هناك
he stood there until he could not feel the cold any more
وقف هناك حتى لم يعد يشعر بالبرد
he stood there until his body was silent

he stood there until his body was quiet

وقف هناك حتى صمت جسده

Silently, he cowered in the thorny bushes

وقف هناك حتى هدأ جسده

blood dripped from the burning skin

بصمت، كان يختبئ في الشجيرات الشائكة

blood dripped from festering wounds

الدم يسيل من الجلد المحترق

and Siddhartha stayed rigid and motionless

الدماء تتساقط من الجروح المتقيحة

he stood until no blood flowed any more

وظل سيدهارتا جامدًا بلا حراك

he stood until nothing stung any more

وقف حتى لم يسيل الدم بعد الآن

he stood until nothing burned any more

وقف حتى لم يعد هناك أي شيء يلدغه

Siddhartha sat upright and learned to breathe sparingly

وقف حتى لم يعد هناك شيء يحترق

he learned to get along with few breaths

جلس سيدهارتا منتصبًا وتعلم التنفس بشكل معتدل

he learned to stop breathing

لقد تعلم أن يتعايش مع القليل من الأنفاس

He learned, beginning with the breath, to calm the beating of his heart

لقد تعلم التوقف عن التنفس

he learned to reduce the beats of his heart

لقد تعلم، بدءًا من التنفس، تهدئة دقات قلبه

he meditated until his heartbeats were only a few

لقد تعلم كيفية تقليل ضربات قلبه

and then his heartbeats were almost none

فتأمل حتى أصبحت نبضات قلبه قليلة

Instructed by the oldest of the Samanas, Siddhartha practised self-denial

ثم أصبحت نبضات قلبه شبه معدومة

he practised meditation, according to the new Samana rules

تحت إشراف أقدم الساماناس، مارس سيدهارتا إنكار الذات

لقد مارس التأمل وفقًا لقواعد سامانا الجديدة

A heron flew over the bamboo forest

طار طائر البلشون فوق غابة الخيزران

Siddhartha accepted the heron into his soul

لقد قبل سيدهارتا البلشون في روحه

he flew over forest and mountains

طار فوق الغابات والجبال

he was a heron, he ate fish

كان طائر بلشون، كان يأكل السمك

he felt the pangs of a heron's hunger

لقد شعر بآلام جوع البلشون

he spoke the heron's croak

لقد تكلم بنقيق البلشون

he died a heron's death

لقد مات موتة البلشون

A dead jackal was lying on the sandy bank

كان هناك ابن آوى ميت ملقى على الضفة الرملية

Siddhartha's soul slipped inside the body of the dead jackal

انزلقت روح سيدهارتا داخل جسد ابن آوى الميت

he was the dead jackal laying on the banks and bloated

كان مثل ابن آوى الميت ملقى على ضفاف النهر منتفخا

he stank and decayed and was dismembered by hyenas

لقد كان رائحته كريهة وتحلل وتم تقطيعه بواسطة الضباع

he was skinned by vultures and turned into a skeleton

لقد سلخه النسور وتحول إلى هيكل عظمي

he was turned to dust and blown across the fields

لقد تحول إلى غبار وطار عبر الحقول

And Siddhartha's soul returned

وعادت روح سيدهارتا

it had died, decayed, and was scattered as dust

لقد ماتت وتحللت وتناثرت كالغبار

it had tasted the gloomy intoxication of the cycle

لقد ذاقت طعم التسمم الكئيب للدورة

it awaited with a new thirst, like a hunter in the gap

لقد انتظر بعطش جديد، مثل الصياد في الفجوة

in the gap where he could escape from the cycle

في الفجوة حيث يمكنه الهروب من الدورة
in the gap where an eternity without suffering began
في الفجوة حيث بدأت الأبدية بدون معاناة
he killed his senses and his memory
لقد قتل حواسه وذاكرته
he slipped out of his self into thousands of other forms
لقد انزلق من ذاته إلى آلاف الأشكال الأخرى
he was an animal, a carrion, a stone
كان حيوانًا، جيفة، حجرًا
he was wood and water
كان خشبا وماء
and he awoke every time to find his old self again
وكان يستيقظ في كل مرة ليجد نفسه القديم مرة أخرى
whether sun or moon, he was his self again
سواء كان الشمس أو القمر، كان هو نفسه مرة أخرى
he turned round in the cycle
لقد استدار في الدورة
he felt thirst, overcame the thirst, felt new thirst
شعر بالعطش، تغلب على العطش، شعر بعطش جديد

Siddhartha learned a lot when he was with the Samanas
لقد تعلم سيدهارثا الكثير عندما كان مع الساماناس
he learned many ways leading away from the self
لقد تعلم العديد من الطرق التي تؤدي إلى الابتعاد عن الذات
he learned how to let go
لقد تعلم كيف يتخلى
He went the way of self-denial by means of pain
لقد سلك طريق إنكار الذات عن طريق الألم
he learned self-denial through voluntarily suffering and overcoming pain
لقد تعلم إنكار الذات من خلال المعاناة طوعاً والتغلب على الألم
he overcame hunger, thirst, and tiredness
تغلب على الجوع والعطش والتعب
He went the way of self-denial by means of meditation
لقد سلك طريق إنكار الذات عن طريق التأمل

he went the way of self-denial through imagining the mind to be void of all conceptions

لقد سلك طريق إنكار الذات من خلال تصور العقل خاليا من كل المفاهيم

with these and other ways he learned to let go

بهذه الطرق وغيرها تعلم كيف يتخلى عن كل شيء

a thousand times he left his self

ألف مرة ترك نفسه

for hours and days he remained in the non-self

لساعات وأيام بقي في اللاذات

all these ways led away from the self

كل هذه الطرق تؤدي بعيدا عن الذات

but their path always led back to the self

لكن طريقهم كان دائمًا يؤدي إلى الذات

Siddhartha fled from the self a thousand times

لقد فر سيدهارتا من الذات ألف مرة

but the return to the self was inevitable

لكن العودة إلى الذات كانت حتمية

although he stayed in nothingness, coming back was inevitable

رغم بقائه في العدم إلا أن العودة كانت حتمية

although he stayed in animals and stones, coming back was inevitable

رغم أنه بقي في الحيوانات والأحجار إلا أن العودة كانت حتمية

he found himself in the sunshine or in the moonlight again

وجد نفسه في ضوء الشمس أو في ضوء القمر مرة أخرى

he found himself in the shade or in the rain again

وجد نفسه في الظل أو تحت المطر مرة أخرى

and he was once again his self; Siddhartha

وعاد إلى ذاته مرة أخرى؛ سيدهارتا

and again he felt the agony of the cycle which had been forced upon him

وشعر مرة أخرى بألم الدورة التي فرضت عليه

by his side lived Govinda, his shadow

بجانبه عاش جوفيندا، ظله

Govinda walked the same path and undertook the same efforts

سار جوفيندا على نفس الطريق وبذل نفس الجهود

they spoke to one another no more than the exercises required

لم يتحدثوا مع بعضهم البعض أكثر من التمارين المطلوبة

occasionally the two of them went through the villages

في بعض الأحيان كان الاثنان يمران عبر القرى

they went to beg for food for themselves and their teachers

ذهبوا لطلب الطعام لأنفسهم ولمعلميهم

"How do you think we have progressed, Govinda" he asked

"كيف تعتقد أننا تقدمنا، جوفيندا" سأل

"Did we reach any goals?" Govinda answered

"هل حققنا أي أهداف؟" أجاب جوفيندا

"We have learned, and we'll continue learning"

"لقد تعلمنا وسنستمر في التعلم"

"You'll be a great Samana, Siddhartha"

"ستكون سامانا عظيمة، سيدهارتا"

"Quickly, you've learned every exercise"

"بسرعة، لقد تعلمت كل التمارين"

"often, the old Samanas have admired you"

"في كثير من الأحيان، كان السامانا العجوز معجبًا بك"

"One day, you'll be a holy man, oh Siddhartha"

"في يوم من الأيام، سوف تصبح رجلاً مقدسًا، يا سيدهارتا"

Spoke Siddhartha, "I can't help but feel that it is not like this, my friend"

قال سيدهارتا، "لا أستطيع إلا أن أشعر أن الأمر ليس كذلك، يا صديقي"

"What I've learned being among the Samanas could have been learned more quickly"

"ما تعلمته من خلال وجودي بين السامانا كان من الممكن أن أتعلمه بسرعة أكبر"

"it could have been learned by simpler means"

"كان من الممكن أن يتم تعلمه بوسائل أبسط"

"it could have been learned in any tavern"

"كان من الممكن أن يتم تعلمه في أي حانة"

"it could have been learned where the whorehouses are"

"كان من الممكن معرفة مكان بيوت الدعارة"
"I could have learned it among carters and gamblers"
"لقد كان بإمكاني أن أتعلم ذلك بين سائقي العربات والمقامرين"
Spoke Govinda, "Siddhartha is joking with me"
قال جوفيندا "سيدهارثا يمزح معي"
"How could you have learned meditation among wretched people?"
"كيف كان بإمكانك أن تتعلم التأمل بين الناس البائسين؟"
"how could whores have taught you about holding your breath?"
"كيف يمكن للعاهرات أن يعلموك حبس أنفاسك؟"
"how could gamblers have taught you insensitivity against pain?"
"كيف يمكن للمقامرين أن يعلموك عدم الحساسية تجاه الألم؟"
Siddhartha spoke quietly, as if he was talking to himself
تحدث سيدهارثا بهدوء، وكأنه يتحدث إلى نفسه
"What is meditation?"
"ما هو التأمل؟"
"What is leaving one's body?"
"ما الذي يخرج من الجسم؟"
"What is fasting?"
ما هو الصيام؟
"What is holding one's breath?"
"ما هو حبس الأنفاس؟"
"It is fleeing from the self"
"إنه الهروب من الذات"
"it is a short escape of the agony of being a self"
"إنه هروب قصير من عذاب كونك ذاتًا"
"it is a short numbing of the senses against the pain"
"إنه تخدير قصير للحواس ضد الألم"
"it is avoiding the pointlessness of life"
"إنه تجنب عدم جدوى الحياة"
"The same numbing is what the driver of an ox-cart finds in the inn"
"نفس التخدير هو ما يجده سائق عربة الثيران في النزل"

"drinking a few bowls of rice-wine or fermented coconut-milk"

"شرب بضعة أوعية من نبيذ الأرز أو حليب جوز الهند المخمر"

"Then he won't feel his self anymore"

"ثم لن يشعر بنفسه بعد الآن"

"then he won't feel the pains of life anymore"

"ثم لن يشعر بآلام الحياة بعد الآن"

"then he finds a short numbing of the senses"

"ثم يجد خدرًا قصيرًا في الحواس"

"When he falls asleep over his bowl of rice-wine, he'll find the same what we find"

"عندما ينام فوق وعاء نبيذ الأرز، سيجد نفس ما وجدناه"

"he finds what we find when we escape our bodies through long exercises"

"يجد ما نجده عندما نهرب من أجسادنا من خلال تمارين طويلة"

"all of us are staying in the non-self"

"نحن جميعا نبقى في اللاذات"

"This is how it is, oh Govinda"

"هكذا هو الحال، أوه جوفيندا"

Spoke Govinda, "You say so, oh friend"

قال جوفيندا "أنت تقول ذلك يا صديقي"

"and yet you know that Siddhartha is no driver of an ox-cart"

"ومع ذلك فأنت تعلم أن سيدهارثا ليس سائق عربة يجرها ثور"

"and you know a Samana is no drunkard"

"وأنت تعرف أن سامانا ليس سكيرًا"

"it's true that a drinker numbs his senses"

"صحيح أن من يشرب يخدر حواسه"

"it's true that he briefly escapes and rests"

"صحيح أنه يهرب لفترة وجيزة ويستريح"

"but he'll return from the delusion and finds everything to be unchanged"

"لكنّه سيعود من الوهم ليجد أنّ كلّ شيء لم يتغير"

"he has not become wiser"

"لم يصبح أكثر حكمة"

"he has gathered any enlightenment"

"لقد جمع أي تنوير"

"he has not risen several steps"
"لم يرتفع عدة خطوات"
And Siddhartha spoke with a smile
وتحدث سيدهارثا بابتسامة
"I do not know, I've never been a drunkard"
"لا أعلم، لم أكن سكيرًا أبدًا"
"I know that I find only a short numbing of the senses"
"أعلم أنني لا أجد سوى خدر قصير في الحواس"
"I find it in my exercises and meditations"
"أجد ذلك في تماريني وتأملاتي"
"and I find I am just as far removed from wisdom as a child in the mother's womb"
"وأنا أجد نفسي بعيدًا عن الحكمة كطفل في بطن أمه"
"this I know, oh Govinda"
"هذا ما أعرفه يا جوفيندا"

And once again, another time, Siddhartha began to speak
ومرة أخرى، في وقت آخر، بدأ سيدهارثا في التحدث
Siddhartha had left the forest, together with Govinda
لقد غادر سيدهارتا الغابة برفقة جوفيندا
they left to beg for some food in the village
لقد ذهبوا للتسول للحصول على بعض الطعام في القرية
he said, "What now, oh Govinda?"
قال، "ماذا الآن يا جوفيندا؟"
"are we on the right path?"
هل نحن على الطريق الصحيح؟
"are we getting closer to enlightenment?"
هل نحن نقترب من التنوير؟
"are we getting closer to salvation?"
هل نحن نقترب من الخلاص؟
"Or do we perhaps live in a circle?"
"أم أننا نعيش في دائرة؟"
"we, who have thought we were escaping the cycle"
"نحن الذين ظننا أننا نهرب من الدائرة"
Spoke Govinda, "We have learned a lot"
وقال جوفيندا "لقد تعلمنا الكثير"

"Siddhartha, there is still much to learn"
"سيدهارتا، لا يزال هناك الكثير لنتعلمه"
"We are not going around in circles"
"نحن لا ندور في حلقات مفرغة"
"we are moving up; the circle is a spiral"
"نحن نتحرك إلى الأعلى؛ الدائرة عبارة عن حلزوني"
"we have already ascended many levels"
"لقد صعدنا بالفعل إلى مستويات عديدة"
Siddhartha answered, "How old would you think our oldest Samana is?"
أجاب سيدهارتا، "كم تعتقد أن عمر سامانا الكبرى هو؟"
"how old is our venerable teacher?"
"كم عمر معلمنا الجليل؟"
Spoke Govinda, "Our oldest one might be about sixty years of age"
قال جوفيندا "قد يكون أكبر أبنائنا في الستين من عمره"
Spoke Siddhartha, "He has lived for sixty years"
قال سيدهارتا "لقد عاش ستين عامًا"
"and yet he has not reached the nirvana"
"ولكنه لم يصل إلى النيرفانا"
"He'll turn seventy and eighty"
"سيصبح عمره سبعين وثمانين"
"you and me, we will grow just as old as him"
"أنت وأنا سوف نكبر مثله تمامًا"
"and we will do our exercises"
"وسوف نقوم بتمارينا"
"and we will fast, and we will meditate"
"وسوف نصوم ونتأمل"
"But we will not reach the nirvana"
"ولكننا لن نصل إلى النيرفانا"
"he won't reach nirvana and we won't"
"لن يصل إلى النيرفانا ولن نصل نحن"
"there are uncountable Samanas out there"
"هناك عدد لا يحصى من الساماناس هناك"
"perhaps not a single one will reach the nirvana"
"ربما لن يصل أحد إلى النيرفانا"

"We find comfort, we find numbness, we learn feats"

"نجد الراحة، نجد الخدر، نتعلم المآثر"

"we learn these things to deceive others"

"نحن نتعلم هذه الأشياء لخداع الآخرين"

"But the most important thing, the path of paths, we will not find"

"ولكن الأهم من ذلك، طريق المسارات، لن نجده"

Spoke Govinda "If you only wouldn't speak such terrible words, Siddhartha!"

قال جوفيندا "لو لم تقل مثل هذه الكلمات الرهيبة يا سيدهارثا!"

"there are so many learned men"

"هناك الكثير من الرجال المتعلمين"

"how could not one of them not find the path of paths?"

"كيف لا يجد أحدهم طريق السبل؟"

"how can so many Brahmans not find it?"

"كيف يمكن للعديد من البراهمة أن لا يجدوها؟"

"how can so many austere and venerable Samanas not find it?"

"كيف يمكن للعديد من الساماناس المتزمتين والموقرين ألا يجدوها؟"

"how can all those who are searching not find it?"

"كيف يمكن لجميع الذين يبحثون عنه أن لا يجدوه؟"

"how can the holy men not find it?"

"كيف لا يستطيع القديسون العثور عليه؟"

But Siddhartha spoke with as much sadness as mockery

لكن سيدهارثا تحدث بقدر من الحزن والسخرية

he spoke with a quiet, a slightly sad, a slightly mocking voice

تحدث بصوت هادئ، حزين قليلاً، ساخر قليلاً

"Soon, Govinda, your friend will leave the path of the Samanas"

"قريبًا، جوفيندا، سيترك صديقك طريق السامانا"

"he has walked along your side for so long"

"لقد سار بجانبك لفترة طويلة"

"I'm suffering of thirst"

"أنا أعاني من العطش"

"on this long path of a Samana, my thirst has remained as strong as ever"

"على هذا الطريق الطويل لسامانا، ظل عطشي قويًا كما كان دائمًا"

"I always thirsted for knowledge"

"كنت متعطشًا دائمًا للمعرفة"

"I have always been full of questions"

"لقد كنت دائمًا مليئًا بالأسئلة"

"I have asked the Brahmans, year after year"

"لقد طلبت من البراهمة سنة بعد سنة"

"and I have asked the holy Vedas, year after year"

"ولقد طلبت من الفيدا المقدسة سنة بعد سنة"

"and I have asked the devoted Samanas, year after year"

"ولقد طلبت من الساماناس المخلصين، سنة بعد سنة"

"perhaps I could have learned it from the hornbill bird"

"ربما كان بإمكاني أن أتعلم ذلك من طائر أبو قرن"

"perhaps I should have asked the chimpanzee"

"ربما كان ينبغي لي أن أسأل الشمبانزي"

"It took me a long time"

"لقد استغرق الأمر مني وقتا طويلا"

"and I am not finished learning this yet"

"ولم أنتهي من تعلم هذا بعد"

"oh Govinda, I have learned that there is nothing to be learned!"

"أوه جوفيندا، لقد تعلمت أنه ليس هناك شيء يمكن تعلمه!"

"There is indeed no such thing as learning"

"لا يوجد شيء اسمه التعلم"

"There is just one knowledge"

"هناك معرفة واحدة فقط"

"this knowledge is everywhere, this is Atman"

"هذه المعرفة موجودة في كل مكان، هذه هي الأتمان"

"this knowledge is within me and within you"

"هذه المعرفة موجودة في داخلي وفي داخلك"

"and this knowledge is within every creature"

"وهذه المعرفة موجودة في كل مخلوق"

"this knowledge has no worse enemy than the desire to know it"

"إن هذه المعرفة ليس لها عدو أسوأ من الرغبة في معرفتها"

"that is what I believe"

"هذا ما أؤمن به"

At this, Govinda stopped on the path

عند هذا، توقف جوفيندا على الطريق

he rose his hands, and spoke

رفع يديه وتكلم

"If only you would not bother your friend with this kind of talk"

"لو أنك لم تزعج صديقك بهذا النوع من الحديث"

"Truly, your words stir up fear in my heart"

"حقا، كلامك يثير الخوف في قلبي"

"consider, what would become of the sanctity of prayer?"

"فكر ماذا سيحدث لقدسية الصلاة؟"

"what would become of the venerability of the Brahmans' caste?"

"ماذا سيحدث لتبجيل طبقة البراهمة؟"

"what would happen to the holiness of the Samanas?

"ماذا سيحدث لقداسة الساماناس؟

"What would then become of all of that is holy"

"ما سيحدث بعد ذلك لكل هذا هو أمر مقدس"

"what would still be precious?"

"ما الذي لا يزال ثمينًا؟"

And Govinda mumbled a verse from an Upanishad to himself

وتذمر جوفيندا بآية من الأوبانيشاد لنفسه

"He who ponderingly, of a purified spirit, loses himself in the meditation of Atman"

"من يتأمل بروح نقية يفقد نفسه في تأمل الأتمان"

"inexpressible by words is the blissfulness of his heart"

"لا يمكن التعبير عن سعادة قلبه بالكلمات"

But Siddhartha remained silent

لكن سيدهارثا بقي صامتا

He thought about the words which Govinda had said to him

لقد فكر في الكلمات التي قالها له جوفيندا

and he thought the words through to their end

وفكر في الكلمات حتى نهايتها

he thought about what would remain of all that which seemed holy

كان يفكر فيما سيبقى من كل ما يبدو مقدسًا

What remains? What can stand the test?

ماذا تبقى؟ ما الذي يستطيع الصمود أمام الاختبار؟

And he shook his head

وهز رأسه

the two young men had lived among the Samanas for about three years

كان الشابان يعيشان بين السامانا لمدة ثلاث سنوات تقريبًا

some news, a rumour, a myth reached them

وصلت إليهم بعض الأخبار أو الإشاعات أو الأسطورة

the rumour had been retold many times

وقد تم إعادة نشر الشائعة عدة مرات

A man had appeared, Gotama by name

لقد ظهر رجل اسمه جوتاما

the exalted one, the Buddha

الواحد العظيم، بوذا

he had overcome the suffering of the world in himself

لقد تغلب على معاناة العالم في نفسه

and he had halted the cycle of rebirths

وقد أوقف دورة الولادات الجديدة

He was said to wander through the land, teaching

وقيل إنه كان يتجول في الأرض ويعلم

he was said to be surrounded by disciples

قيل أنه كان محاطًا بالتلاميذ

he was said to be without possession, home, or wife

قيل أنه كان بلا ممتلكات أو منزل أو زوجة

he was said to be in just the yellow cloak of an ascetic

قيل أنه كان يرتدي فقط عباءة صفراء زاهدة

but he was with a cheerful brow

ولكنه كان ذو جبين مرح

and he was said to be a man of bliss

وقيل عنه أنه رجل سعيد

Brahmans and princes bowed down before him

انحنى أمامه البراهمة والأمراء

and they became his students

وأصبحوا طلابه

This myth, this rumour, this legend resounded

هذه الأسطورة، هذه الشائعة، هذه الأسطورة ترددت

its fragrance rose up, here and there, in the towns

ارتفع عطرها هنا وهناك في المدن

the Brahmans spoke of this legend

وتحدث البراهمة عن هذه الأسطورة

and in the forest, the Samanas spoke of it

وفي الغابة تحدث عنها الساماناس

again and again, the name of Gotama the Buddha reached the ears of the young men

مرة بعد مرة، وصل اسم غوتاما بوذا إلى آذان الشباب

there was good and bad talk of Gotama

كان هناك حديث جيد وسيئ عن جوتاما

some praised Gotama, others defamed him

بعضهم أشاد بغوتاما والبعض الآخر شوه سمعته

It was as if the plague had broken out in a country

كان الأمر كما لو أن الطاعون انتشر في بلد ما

news had been spreading around that in one or another place there was a man

انتشرت أخبار مفادها أنه في مكان أو آخر يوجد رجل

a wise man, a knowledgeable one

رجل حكيم، عالم

a man whose word and breath was enough to heal everyone

رجل كانت كلمته ونفسه كافيين لشفاء الجميع

his presence could heal anyone who had been infected with the pestilence

كان وجوده قادرًا على شفاء أي شخص مصاب بالطاعون

such news went through the land, and everyone would talk about it

انتشرت مثل هذه الأخبار في جميع أنحاء البلاد، وكان الجميع يتحدثون عنها

many believed the rumours, many doubted them

كثيرون صدقوا الشائعات، وكثيرون شككوا فيها

but many got on their way as soon as possible

لكن كثيرين منهم انطلقوا في طريقهم في أسرع وقت ممكن

they went to seek the wise man, the helper

ذهبوا للبحث عن الرجل الحكيم والمساعد

the wise man of the family of Sakya

حكيم عائلة ساقية

He possessed, so the believers said, the highest enlightenment

لقد كان يمتلك، كما قال المؤمنون، أعلى درجات التنوير

he remembered his previous lives; he had reached the nirvana

تذكر حياته السابقة، لقد وصل إلى النيرفانا

and he never returned into the cycle

ولم يعد إلى الدورة أبدًا

he was never again submerged in the murky river of physical forms

لم يعد يغرق مرة أخرى في النهر الموحل للأشكال المادية

Many wonderful and unbelievable things were reported of him

وقد قيل عنه أشياء كثيرة عجيبة لا تصدق

he had performed miracles

لقد صنع المعجزات

he had overcome the devil

لقد تغلب على الشيطان

he had spoken to the gods

لقد تحدث إلى الآلهة

But his enemies and disbelievers said Gotama was a vain seducer

لكن أعداءه وكفاره قالوا أن غوتاما كان مغويًا مغرورًا

they said he spent his days in luxury

قالوا أنه قضى أيامه في رفاهية

they said he scorned the offerings

قالوا إنه احتقر العروض

they said he was without learning

قالوا أنه كان بلا تعليم

they said he knew neither meditative exercises nor self-castigation

قالوا إنه لا يعرف تمارين التأمل ولا تأنيب الذات

The myth of Buddha sounded sweet

أسطورة بوذا بدت حلوة

The scent of magic flowed from these reports

رائحة السحر تتدفق من هذه التقارير

After all, the world was sick, and life was hard to bear

بعد كل شيء، كان العالم مريضًا، وكانت الحياة صعبة التحمل

and behold, here a source of relief seemed to spring forth

وهنا بدا وكأن مصدرًا للارتياح ينبثق

here a messenger seemed to call out

هنا بدا وكأن الرسول ينادي

comforting, mild, full of noble promises

مُريح، لطيف، مليء بالوعود النبيلة

Everywhere where the rumour of Buddha was heard, the young men listened up

في كل مكان سمعت فيه شائعة بوذا، كان الشباب يستمعون

everywhere in the lands of India they felt a longing

في كل مكان في أراضي الهند شعروا بالشوق

everywhere where the people searched, they felt hope

في كل مكان بحث فيه الناس شعروا بالأمل

every pilgrim and stranger was welcome when he brought news of him

كان كل حاج وغريب موضع ترحيب عندما كان يحمل أخبارًا عنه

the exalted one, the Sakyamuni

العظيم، الساكياموني

The myth had also reached the Samanas in the forest

وصلت الأسطورة أيضًا إلى الساماناس في الغابة

and Siddhartha and Govinda heard the myth too

وسمعت سيدهارتا وجوفيندا الأسطورة أيضًا

slowly, drop by drop, they heard the myth

ببطء، قطرة قطرة، سمعوا الأسطورة

every drop was laden with hope

كل قطرة كانت محملة بالأمل

every drop was laden with doubt

كل قطرة كانت محملة بالشك

They rarely talked about it

نادرا ما تحدثوا عن ذلك

because the oldest one of the Samanas did not like this myth

لأن أقدم أفراد عائلة سامانا لم يعجبه هذا الأسطورة

he had heard that this alleged Buddha used to be an ascetic

لقد سمع أن هذا بوذا المزعوم كان زاهدًا

he heard he had lived in the forest

سمع أنه عاش في الغابة

but he had turned back to luxury and worldly pleasures

ولكنه عاد إلى الترف والملذات الدنيوية

and he had no high opinion of this Gotama

ولم يكن لديه رأي كبير في هذا غوتاما

"Oh Siddhartha," Govinda spoke one day to his friend

"أوه سيدهارتا،" تحدث جوفيندا ذات يوم إلى صديقه

"Today, I was in the village"

"اليوم كنت في القرية"

"and a Brahman invited me into his house"

"ودعاني أحد البراهمة إلى منزله"

"and in his house, there was the son of a Brahman from Magadha"

"وكان في بيته ابن أحد البراهمة من ماجادها"

"he has seen the Buddha with his own eyes"

"لقد رأى بوذا بأم عينيه"

"and he has heard him teach"

"وسمعه يعلم"

"Verily, this made my chest ache when I breathed"

"إن هذا كان يجعل صدري يوجعني حين أتنفس"

"and I thought this to myself:"

"وقلت لنفسي هذا:"

"if only we heard the teachings from the mouth of this perfected man!"

"لو سمعنا تعاليم هذا الرجل الكامل!"

"Speak, friend, wouldn't we want to go there too"

"تكلم يا صديقي، ألا نرغب في الذهاب إلى هناك أيضًا؟"

"wouldn't it be good to listen to the teachings from the Buddha's mouth?"

"ألا يكون من الجيد الاستماع إلى التعاليم من فم بوذا؟"

Spoke Siddhartha, "I had thought you would stay with the Samanas"

تحدث سيدهارتا، "لقد كنت أعتقد أنك ستبقى مع عائلة سامانا"

"I always had believed your goal was to live to be seventy"

"لقد اعتقدت دائمًا أن هدفك هو أن تعيش حتى سن السبعين"

"I thought you would keep practising those feats and exercises"

"اعتقدت أنك ستستمر في ممارسة هذه المآثر والتمارين"

"and I thought you would become a Samana"

"وكنت أعتقد أنك ستصبح سامانا"

"But behold, I had not known Govinda well enough"

"لكن انظر، لم أكن أعرف جوفيندا جيدًا بما فيه الكفاية"

"I knew little of his heart"

"لم أكن أعرف إلا القليل عن قلبه"

"So now you want to take a new path"

"لذا الآن تريد أن تأخذ مسارًا جديدًا"

"and you want to go there where the Buddha spreads his teachings"

"وأنت تريد أن تذهب إلى هناك حيث ينشر بوذا تعاليمه"

Spoke Govinda, "You're mocking me"

قال جوفيندا "أنت تسخر مني"

"Mock me if you like, Siddhartha!"

"استهزئ بي إذا أردت يا سيدهارثا!"

"But have you not also developed a desire to hear these teachings?"

"ولكن هل لم تتطور لديك أيضًا الرغبة في سماع هذه التعاليم؟"

"have you not said you would not walk the path of the Samanas for much longer?"

"ألم تقل أنك لن تسير على طريق السامانا لفترة أطول؟"

At this, Siddhartha laughed in his very own manner

عند هذا، ضحك سيدهارتا بطريقته الخاصة

the manner in which his voice assumed a touch of sadness

الطريقة التي كان صوته يحمل لمسة من الحزن

but it still had that touch of mockery

لكنها لا تزال تحمل لمسة من السخرية

Spoke Siddhartha, "Govinda, you've spoken well"

تحدث سيدهارتا قائلاً: "جوفيندا، لقد تحدثت بشكل جيد"

"you've remembered correctly what I said"

"لقد تذكرت بشكل صحيح ما قلته"

"If only you remembered the other thing you've heard from me"

"لو تذكرت الشيء الآخر الذي سمعته مني"

"I have grown distrustful and tired against teachings and learning"

"لقد أصبحت غير واثق ومتعب من التعاليم والتعلم"

"my faith in words, which are brought to us by teachers, is small"

"إيماني بالكلمات التي يقدمها لنا المعلمون ضئيل"

"But let's do it, my dear"

"ولكن دعونا نفعل ذلك يا عزيزتي"

"I am willing to listen to these teachings"

"أنا على استعداد للاستماع إلى هذه التعاليم"

"though in my heart I do not have hope"

"على الرغم من أنني لا أملك أملا في قلبي"

"I believe that we've already tasted the best fruit of these teachings"

"أعتقد أننا قد تذوقنا بالفعل أفضل ثمار هذه التعاليم"

Spoke Govinda, "Your willingness delights my heart"

قال جوفيندا "استعدادك يسعد قلبي"

"But tell me, how should this be possible?"

"ولكن قل لي، كيف يمكن أن يكون هذا ممكنا؟"

"How can the Gotama's teachings have already revealed their best fruit to us?"

"كيف يمكن لتعاليم غوتاما أن تكشف لنا بالفعل أفضل ثمارها؟"

"we have not heard his words yet"

"لم نسمع كلامه بعد"

Spoke Siddhartha, "Let us eat this fruit"

قال سيدهارتا "دعونا نأكل هذه الفاكهة"

"and let us wait for the rest, oh Govinda!"

"دعونا ننتظر الباقي، أوه جوفيندا!"
"But this fruit consists in him calling us away from the Samanas"
"ولكن هذه الثمرة تتلخص في دعوته لنا بعيدًا عن الساماناس"
"and we have already received it thanks to the Gotama!"
"وقد حصلنا عليه بالفعل بفضل غوتاما!"
"Whether he has more, let us await with calm hearts"
"إن كان لديه المزيد، فلننتظر بقلوب هادئة"

On this very same day Siddhartha spoke to the oldest Samana
في هذا اليوم نفسه تحدث سيدهارتا إلى سامانا الأكبر سناً
he told him of his decision to leaves the Samanas
أخبره بقراره بمغادرة ساماناس
he informed the oldest one with courtesy and modesty
فأخبر الأكبر سنا بكل أدب وتواضع
but the Samana became angry that the two young men wanted to leave him
لكن سامانا غضب لأن الشابين أرادا أن يتركاه
and he talked loudly and used crude words
وكان يتحدث بصوت مرتفع ويستخدم كلمات بذيئة
Govinda was startled and became embarrassed
لقد انزعج جوفيندا وأصبح محرجًا
But Siddhartha put his mouth close to Govinda's ear
لكن سيدهارتا وضع فمه بالقرب من أذن جوفيندا
"Now, I want to show the old man what I've learned from him"
"الآن أريد أن أظهر للرجل العجوز ما تعلمته منه"
Siddhartha positioned himself closely in front of the Samana
وضع سيدهارتا نفسه بشكل وثيق أمام سامانا
with a concentrated soul, he captured the old man's glance
بروح مركزة، استولى على نظرة الرجل العجوز
he deprived him of his power and made him mute
حرمه من قوته وجعله أخرس
he took away his free will

لقد سلب منه إرادته الحرة

he subdued him under his own will, and commanded him

فأخضعه بإرادته وأمره

his eyes became motionless, and his will was paralysed

أصبحت عيناه بلا حراك، وإرادته مشلولة

his arms were hanging down without power

كانت ذراعيه تتدلى إلى أسفل دون قوة

he had fallen victim to Siddhartha's spell

لقد وقع ضحية لتعويذة سيدهارتا

Siddhartha's thoughts brought the Samana under their control

لقد أدت أفكار سيدهارتا إلى إخضاع السامانا لسيطرتهم

he had to carry out what they commanded

كان عليه أن ينفذ ما أمروه به .

And thus, the old man made several bows

وهكذا صنع الرجل العجوز عدة أقواس

he performed gestures of blessing

لقد قام بحركات البركة

he spoke stammeringly a godly wish for a good journey

تحدث بتلعثم عن تمنياته الطيبة برحلة سعيدة

the young men returned the good wishes with thanks

رد الشباب التحيات الطيبة بالشكر

they went on their way with salutations

واصلوا طريقهم مع التحية

On the way, Govinda spoke again

وفي الطريق تحدث جوفيندا مرة أخرى

"Oh Siddhartha, you have learned more from the Samanas than I knew"

"أوه سيدهارتا، لقد تعلمت من الساماناس أكثر مما كنت أعرف"

"It is very hard to cast a spell on an old Samana"

"من الصعب جدًا إلقاء تعويذة على سامانا القديمة"

"Truly, if you had stayed there, you would soon have learned to walk on water"

"حقا لو بقيت هناك لتعلمت المشي على الماء قريبا"

"I do not seek to walk on water" said Siddhartha

"أنا لا أسعى إلى المشي على الماء" قال سيدهارتا

"Let old Samanas be content with such feats!"
"فليكن السامانا العجوز راضيًا بمثل هذه الأعمال!"

Gotama
جوتاما

In Savathi, every child knew the name of the exalted Buddha
في سافاتي، كان كل طفل يعرف اسم بوذا العظيم

every house was prepared for his coming
كان كل بيت مستعدا لمجيئه

each house filled the alms-dishes of Gotama's disciples
كل بيت ملأ صحون الصدقات لتلاميذ جوتاما

Gotama's disciples were the silently begging ones
كان تلاميذ غوتاما هم الذين يتوسلون بصمت

Near the town was Gotama's favourite place to stay
كان مكان الإقامة المفضل لدى جوتاما بالقرب من المدينة

he stayed in the garden of Jetavana
لقد بقي في حديقة جيتافانا

the rich merchant Anathapindika had given the garden to Gotama
كان التاجر الغني أناتابينديكا قد أعطى الحديقة إلى جوتاما

he had given it to him as a gift
لقد أعطاه له كهدية

he was an obedient worshipper of the exalted one
وكان عابداً لله تعالى مطيعاً

the two young ascetics had received tales and answers
لقد تلقى الشابان الزاهدتان حكايات وأجوبة

all these tales and answers pointed them to Gotama's abode
كل هذه الحكايات والأجوبة أشارت بهم إلى مسكن جوتاما

they arrived in the town of Savathi
وصلوا إلى مدينة سافاتي

they went to the very first door of the town
ذهبوا إلى أول باب للمدينة

and they begged for food at the door

وكانوا يطلبون الطعام عند الباب
a woman offered them food
عرضت عليهم امرأة الطعام
and they accepted the food
فقبلوا الطعام
Siddhartha asked the woman
سأل سيدهارتا المرأة
"oh charitable one, where does the Buddha dwell?"
"يا أيها الخير، أين يسكن بوذا؟"
"we are two Samanas from the forest"
"نحن سامانا من الغابة"
"we have come to see the perfected one"
"لقد جئنا لنرى الكامل"
"we have come to hear the teachings from his mouth"
"لقد جئنا لنسمع تعاليمه من فمه"
Spoke the woman, "you Samanas from the forest"
تكلمت المرأة "أنت سامانا من الغابة"
"you have truly come to the right place"
"لقد وصلت بالفعل إلى المكان الصحيح"
"you should know, in Jetavana, there is the garden of Anathapindika"
"يجب أن تعلم أنه في جيتافانا توجد حديقة أناثابينديكا"
"that is where the exalted one dwells"
"هناك حيث يسكن المرتفع"
"there you pilgrims shall spend the night"
"هناك سوف تقضيون الليل أيها الحجاج"
"there is enough space for the innumerable, who flock here"
"هناك مساحة كافية لعدد لا يحصى من الناس الذين يتوافدون هنا"
"they too come to hear the teachings from his mouth"
"هم أيضًا يأتون ليسمعوا تعاليم فمه"
This made Govinda happy, and full of joy
وهذا جعل جوفيندا سعيدًا ومليئًا بالبهجة
he exclaimed, "we have reached our destination"
هتف قائلا "لقد وصلنا إلى وجهتنا"
"our path has come to an end!"
"لقد انتهى طريقنا!"

"But tell us, oh mother of the pilgrims"

"ولكن أخبرينا يا أم الحجاج"

"do you know him, the Buddha?"

هل تعرفه ، بوذا؟

"have you seen him with your own eyes?"

هل رأيته بأم عينيك؟

Spoke the woman, "Many times I have seen him, the exalted one"

قالت المرأة: لقد رأيته مرات عديدة، وهو المرتفع.

"On many days I have seen him"

"لقد رأيته في كثير من الأيام"

"I have seen him walking through the alleys in silence"

"لقد رأيته يمشي في الأزقة في صمت"

"I have seen him wearing his yellow cloak"

"لقد رأيته يرتدي عباءته الصفراء"

"I have seen him presenting his alms-dish in silence"

"لقد رأيته يقدم صحن صدقته في صمت"

"I have seen him at the doors of the houses"

"لقد رأيته على أبواب البيوت"

"and I have seen him leaving with a filled dish"

"ورأيته يخرج بطبق ممتلئ"

Delightedly, Govinda listened to the woman

استمع جوفيندا إلى المرأة بسرور

and he wanted to ask and hear much more

وأراد أن يسأل ويسمع أكثر

But Siddhartha urged him to walk on

لكن سيدهارثا حثه على المضي قدمًا

They thanked the woman and left

شكروا المرأة وغادروا

they hardly had to ask for directions

لم يكن عليهم أن يسألوا عن الاتجاهات

many pilgrims and monks were on their way to the Jetavana

وكان العديد من الحجاج والرهبان في طريقهم إلى جيتافانا

they reached it at night, so there were constant arrivals

لقد وصلوا إليها ليلاً، لذا كان هناك وصول مستمر

and those who sought shelter got it

والذين طلبوا المأوى حصلوا عليه

The two Samanas were accustomed to life in the forest

لقد اعتادت السمانتان على الحياة في الغابة

so without making any noise they quickly found a place to stay

لذلك، وبدون إحداث أي ضوضاء، وجدوا بسرعة مكانًا للإقامة.

and they rested there until the morning

فاستراحوا هناك حتى الصباح

At sunrise, they saw with astonishment the size of the crowd

عند شروق الشمس، رأوا بدهشة حجم الحشد

a great many number of believers had come

لقد جاء عدد كبير من المؤمنين

and a great number of curious people had spent the night here

وقد أمضى عدد كبير من الفضوليين الليل هنا

On all paths of the marvellous garden, monks walked in yellow robes

في جميع مسارات الحديقة الرائعة، كان الرهبان يسيرون بأردية صفراء

under the trees they sat here and there, in deep contemplation

تحت الأشجار جلسوا هنا وهناك، في تأمل عميق

or they were in a conversation about spiritual matters

أو كانوا في محادثة حول الأمور الروحية

the shady gardens looked like a city

بدت الحدائق الظليلة وكأنها مدينة

a city full of people, bustling like bees

مدينة مليئة بالناس، تعج بالنشاط مثل النحل

The majority of the monks went out with their alms-dish

خرج أغلب الرهبان مع صحن الصدقات الخاص بهم

they went out to collect food for their lunch

خرجوا لجمع الطعام لوجبة الغداء

this would be their only meal of the day

ستكون هذه هي وجبتهم الوحيدة في اليوم

The Buddha himself, the enlightened one, also begged in the mornings

كان بوذا نفسه، المستنير، يتوسل أيضًا في الصباح

Siddhartha saw him, and he instantly recognised him

لقد رآه سيدهارثا، وتعرف عليه على الفور

he recognised him as if a God had pointed him out

لقد تعرف عليه وكأن إلهًا أشار إليه

He saw him, a simple man in a yellow robe

لقد رآه رجلاً بسيطاً يرتدي ثوباً أصفر

he was bearing the alms-dish in his hand, walking silently

كان يحمل طبق الصدقات في يده، ويمشي بصمت

"Look here!" Siddhartha said quietly to Govinda

"انظر هنا!" قال سيدهارثا بهدوء لجوفيندا

"This one is the Buddha"

"هذا هو بوذا"

Attentively, Govinda looked at the monk in the yellow robe

نظر جوفيندا باهتمام إلى الراهب الذي يرتدي الرداء الأصفر

this monk seemed to be in no way different from any of the others

يبدو أن هذا الراهب لم يكن مختلفًا بأي حال من الأحوال عن أي من الآخرين

but soon, Govinda also realized that this is the one

لكن سرعان ما أدرك جوفيندا أيضًا أن هذا هو

And they followed him and observed him

فتبعوه وراقبوه

The Buddha went on his way, modestly and deep in his thoughts

واصل بوذا طريقه متواضعًا وعميقًا في أفكاره

his calm face was neither happy nor sad

وجهه الهادئ لم يكن سعيدا ولا حزينا

his face seemed to smile quietly and inwardly

يبدو أن وجهه يبتسم بهدوء وداخليًا

his smile was hidden, quiet and calm

كانت ابتسامته مخفية وهادئة وهادئة

the way the Buddha walked somewhat resembled a healthy child

كانت طريقة مشية بوذا تشبه إلى حد ما طريقة مشية طفل سليم

he walked just as all of his monks did

كان يمشي كما يفعل كل رهبانه

he placed his feet according to a precise rule

وضع قدميه وفقًا لقاعدة دقيقة

his face and his walk, his quietly lowered glance

وجهه ومشيته ونظرته المنخفضة الهادئة

his quietly dangling hand, every finger of it

يده المتدلية بهدوء، كل إصبع منها

all these things expressed peace

كل هذه الأشياء تعبر عن السلام

all these things expressed perfection

كل هذه الأشياء تعبر عن الكمال

he did not search, nor did he imitate

لم يبحث ولم يقلد

he softly breathed inwardly an unwhithering calm

تنفس بهدوء في داخله هدوء لا يهدأ

he shone outwardly an unwhithering light

أشرق في الخارج ضوء لا يذبل

he had about him an untouchable peace

كان لديه سلام لا يمكن المساس به

the two Samanas recognised him solely by the perfection of his calm

لقد تعرف عليه السامانا فقط من خلال هدوئه المثالي.

they recognized him by the quietness of his appearance

عرفوه من هدوء مظهره

the quietness in his appearance in which there was no searching

الهدوء في مظهره حيث لم يكن هناك أي تفتيش

there was no desire, nor imitation

لم تكن هناك رغبة ولا تقليد

there was no effort to be seen

لم يكن هناك أي جهد ليتم رؤيته

only light and peace was to be seen in his appearance

لم يكن هناك من يرى في مظهره إلا النور والسلام

"Today, we'll hear the teachings from his mouth" said Govinda

"اليوم سوف نسمع التعاليم من فمه" قال جوفيندا

Siddhartha did not answer

لم يجب سيدهارثا

He felt little curiosity for the teachings

لقد شعر بقليل من الفضول تجاه التعاليم

he did not believe that they would teach him anything new

لم يكن يعتقد أنهم سيعلمونه أي شيء جديد

he had heard the contents of this Buddha's teachings again and again

لقد سمع محتويات تعاليم بوذا هذه مرارا وتكرارا

but these reports only represented second hand information

لكن هذه التقارير لم تمثل سوى معلومات من جهة ثانية

But attentively he looked at Gotama's head

ولكنه نظر باهتمام إلى رأس جوتاما

his shoulders, his feet, his quietly dangling hand

كتفيه، قدميه، يده المتدلية بهدوء

it was as if every finger of this hand was of these teachings

وكأن كل إصبع من أصابع هذه اليد كان من هذه التعاليم

his fingers spoke of truth

أصابعه تحدثت عن الحقيقة

his fingers breathed and exhaled the fragrance of truth

تنفست أصابعه وزفر عطر الحقيقة

his fingers glistened with truth

أصابعه كانت تتلألأ بالحقيقة

this Buddha was truthful down to the gesture of his last finger

كان هذا بوذا صادقًا حتى في لفتة إصبعه الأخيرة

Siddhartha could see that this man was holy

كان سيدهارتا قادرًا على رؤية أن هذا الرجل كان مقدسًا

Never before, Siddhartha had venerated a person so much

لم يسبق لسيدهارتا أن كان يحترم شخصًا بهذا القدر من الاحترام

he had never before loved a person as much as this one

لم يحب شخصًا من قبل بقدر هذا الشخص

They both followed the Buddha until they reached the town

لقد تبعا بوذا حتى وصلا إلى المدينة

and then they returned to their silence

ثم عادوا إلى صمتهم

they themselves intended to abstain on this day
لقد عزموا على الامتناع عن التصويت في هذا اليوم
They saw Gotama returning the food that had been given to him
لقد رأوا غوتاما يعيد الطعام الذي أعطي له
what he ate could not even have satisfied a bird's appetite
ما أكله لم يكن ليشبع حتى شهية طائر
and they saw him retiring into the shade of the mango-trees
ورأوه متقاعدًا في ظل أشجار المانجو

in the evening the heat had cooled down
في المساء انخفضت الحرارة
everyone in the camp started to bustle about and gathered around
بدأ الجميع في المخيم في التحرك والتجمع حول بعضهم البعض
they heard the Buddha teaching, and his voice
لقد سمعوا تعاليم بوذا، وصوته
and his voice was also perfected
وكان صوته أيضا مثاليا
his voice was of perfect calmness
كان صوته هادئا تماما
his voice was full of peace
كان صوته مليئا بالسلام
Gotama taught the teachings of suffering
لقد علم غوتاما تعاليم المعاناة
he taught of the origin of suffering
لقد علم عن أصل المعاناة
he taught of the way to relieve suffering
لقد علم عن كيفية تخفيف المعاناة
Calmly and clearly his quiet speech flowed on
كان حديثه الهادئ يتدفق بهدوء ووضوح.
Suffering was life, and full of suffering was the world
كانت المعاناة هي الحياة، وكان العالم مليئًا بالمعاناة
but salvation from suffering had been found
ولكن الخلاص من المعاناة كان قد تم العثور عليه

salvation was obtained by him who would walk the path of the Buddha

لقد تم الحصول على الخلاص من خلال من سار على طريق بوذا.

With a soft, yet firm voice the exalted one spoke

بصوت هادئ وحازم تحدث الرجل العظيم

he taught the four main doctrines

لقد قام بتدريس العقائد الأربع الرئيسية

he taught the eight-fold path

لقد علم الطريق الثماني

patiently he went the usual path of the teachings

لقد سار بصبر على الطريق المعتاد للتعاليم

his teachings contained the examples

كانت تعاليمه تحتوي على الأمثلة

his teaching made use of the repetitions

لقد استخدم في تعليمه التكرار

brightly and quietly his voice hovered over the listeners

كان صوته يحوم فوق المستمعين بهدوء وإشراق.

his voice was like a light

كان صوته مثل الضوء

his voice was like a starry sky

كان صوته مثل السماء المرصعة بالنجوم

When the Buddha ended his speech, many pilgrims stepped forward

عندما أنهى بوذا خطابه، تقدم العديد من الحجاج إلى الأمام

they asked to be accepted into the community

لقد طلبوا القبول في المجتمع

they sought refuge in the teachings

لقد لجأوا إلى التعاليم

And Gotama accepted them by speaking

وقبلهم غوتاما بالكلام

"You have heard the teachings well"

"لقد سمعت التعاليم جيدا"

"join us and walk in holiness"

"انضم إلينا وامش في القداسة"

"put an end to all suffering"

"وضع حد لكل المعاناة"

Behold, then Govinda, the shy one, also stepped forward and spoke

انظر، إذن، جوفيندا، الخجول، تقدم أيضًا إلى الأمام وتحدث

"I also take my refuge in the exalted one and his teachings"

"وألجأ أيضًا إلى العالم وتعاليمه"

and he asked to be accepted into the community of his disciples

وطلب أن يتم قبوله في جماعة تلاميذه

and he was accepted into the community of Gotama's disciples

وتم قبوله في جماعة تلاميذ جوتاما

the Buddha had retired for the night

كان بوذا قد تقاعد ليلًا

Govinda turned to Siddhartha and spoke eagerly

التفت جوفيندا إلى سيدهارثا وتحدث بلهفة

"Siddhartha, it is not my place to scold you"

"سيدهارتا، ليس من حقي أن أوبخك"

"We have both heard the exalted one"

"لقد سمعنا العلي"

"we have both perceived the teachings"

"لقد فهمنا كلينا التعاليم"

"Govinda has heard the teachings"

"لقد سمع جوفيندا التعاليم"

"he has taken refuge in the teachings"

"لقد لجأ إلى التعاليم"

"But, my honoured friend, I must ask you"

"ولكن يا صديقي العزيز، يجب أن أسألك"

"don't you also want to walk the path of salvation?"

"ألا تريد أنت أيضًا أن تسير في طريق الخلاص؟"

"Would you want to hesitate?"

"هل تريد أن تتردد؟"

"do you want to wait any longer?"

هل تريد الانتظار لفترة أطول؟

Siddhartha awakened as if he had been asleep

استيقظ سيدهارتا وكأنه كان نائما

For a long time, he looked into Govinda's face
لفترة طويلة، نظر إلى وجه جوفيندا
Then he spoke quietly, in a voice without mockery
ثم تحدث بهدوء وبصوتٍ خالٍ من السخرية
"Govinda, my friend, now you have taken this step"
"جوفيندا، صديقي، لقد اتخذت هذه الخطوة الآن"
"now you have chosen this path"
"لقد اخترت هذا الطريق الآن"
"Always, oh Govinda, you've been my friend"
"دائمًا، يا جوفيندا، لقد كنت صديقي"
"you've always walked one step behind me"
"لقد كنت دائمًا تمشي خطوة واحدة خلفي"
"Often I have thought about you"
"لقد فكرت فيك كثيرًا"
"'Won't Govinda for once also take a step by himself'"
"لن يتخذ جوفيندا خطوة بمفرده مرة أخرى"
"'won't Govinda take a step without me?'"
"هل سيتخذ جوفيندا خطوة بدوني؟"
"'won't he take a step driven by his own soul?'"
"فهل يخطو خطوة مدفوعة بروحه؟"
"Behold, now you've turned into a man"
"ها أنت الآن قد تحولت إلى رجل"
"you are choosing your path for yourself"
"أنت تختار طريقك لنفسك"
"I wish that you would go it up to its end"
"أتمنى أن تصل إلى نهايتها"
"oh my friend, I hope that you shall find salvation!"
"يا صديقي، أتمنى أن تجد الخلاص!"
Govinda, did not completely understand it yet
جوفيندا، لم يفهم الأمر بشكل كامل بعد
he repeated his question in an impatient tone
كرر سؤاله بنبرة غير صبورة
"Speak up, I beg you, my dear!"
"تكلمي، أتوسل إليك يا عزيزتي!"
"Tell me, since it could not be any other way"
"أخبرني، لأنه لا يمكن أن يكون هناك أي طريقة أخرى"

"won't you also take your refuge with the exalted Buddha?"

"ألا يمكنك أيضًا أن تلجأ إلى بوذا العظيم؟"

Siddhartha placed his hand on Govinda's shoulder

وضع سيدهارثا يده على كتف جوفيندا

"You failed to hear my good wish for you"

"لقد فشلت في سماع أمنياتي الطيبة لك"

"I'm repeating my wish for you"

"أنا أكرر أمنيتي لك"

"I wish that you would go this path"

"أتمنى أن تسلك هذا الطريق"

"I wish that you would go up to this path's end"

"أتمنى أن تصل إلى نهاية هذا الطريق"

"I wish that you shall find salvation!"

"أتمنى أن تجد الخلاص!"

In this moment, Govinda realized that his friend had left him

في هذه اللحظة أدرك جوفيندا أن صديقه قد تركه

when he realized this he started to weep

عندما أدرك ذلك بدأ بالبكاء

"Siddhartha!" he exclaimed lamentingly

"سيدهارتا!" هتف بحسرة

Siddhartha kindly spoke to him

تحدث إليه سيدهارثا بلطف

"don't forget, Govinda, who you are"

"لا تنسى يا جوفيندا من أنت"

"you are now one of the Samanas of the Buddha"

"أنت الآن أحد سامانا بوذا"

"You have renounced your home and your parents"

"لقد تخليت عن منزلك ووالديك"

"you have renounced your birth and possessions"

"لقد تخليت عن ميلادك وممتلكاتك"

"you have renounced your free will"

"لقد تخليت عن إرادتك الحرة"

"you have renounced all friendship"

"لقد تخليت عن كل الصداقة"

"This is what the teachings require"

"this is what the exalted one wants"
"هذا ما تتطلبه التعاليم"

"This is what you wanted for yourself"
"هذا ما يريده العلي"

"هذا ما اردته لنفسك"

"Tomorrow, oh Govinda, I will leave you"
"غدًا، يا جوفيندا، سأتركك"

For a long time, the friends continued walking in the garden
لفترة طويلة، واصل الأصدقاء المشي في الحديقة

for a long time, they lay there and found no sleep
ظلوا هناك لفترة طويلة ولم يجدوا أي نوم

And over and over again, Govinda urged his friend
ومرة أخرى، حث جوفيندا صديقه

"why would you not want to seek refuge in Gotama's teachings?"
"لماذا لا تريد اللجوء إلى تعاليم غوتاما؟"

"what fault could you find in these teachings?"
"ما الخطأ الذي تجده في هذه التعاليم؟"

But Siddhartha turned away from his friend
لكن سيدهارثا ابتعد عن صديقه

every time he said, "Be content, Govinda!"
في كل مرة قال: "كن راضيًا، جوفيندا!"

"Very good are the teachings of the exalted one"
"حسنة جداً هي تعاليم العلي"

"how could I find a fault in his teachings?"
"كيف يمكنني أن أجد خطأ في تعاليمه؟"

it was very early in the morning
لقد كان ذلك في الصباح الباكر جدًا

one of the oldest monks went through the garden
أحد أقدم الرهبان مر بالحديقة

he called to those who had taken their refuge in the teachings
ودعا أولئك الذين لجأوا إلى التعاليم

he called them to dress them up in the yellow robe
ودعاهم إلى ارتداء الثوب الأصفر.

and he instruct them in the first teachings and duties of their position
ويعلمهم التعاليم الأولى وواجبات منصبهم
Govinda once again embraced his childhood friend
احتضن جوفيندا صديق طفولته مرة أخرى
and then he left with the novices
ثم غادر مع المبتدئين
But Siddhartha walked through the garden, lost in thought
لكن سيدهارتا سار عبر الحديقة، غارقًا في التفكير
Then he happened to meet Gotama, the exalted one
ثم حدث أن التقى بغوتاما، الشخص الرفيع.
he greeted him with respect
استقبله باحترام
the Buddha's glance was full of kindness and calm
كانت نظرة بوذا مليئة باللطف والهدوء
the young man summoned his courage
استجمع الشاب شجاعته
he asked the venerable one for the permission to talk to him
فطلب من الجليل الإذن بالحديث معه
Silently, the exalted one nodded his approval
في صمت أومأ الرجل الرفيع برأسه موافقًا.
Spoke Siddhartha, "Yesterday, oh exalted one"
تكلم سيدهارتا، "بالأمس، أيها السامي"
"I had been privileged to hear your wondrous teachings"
"لقد كان من حسن حظي أن أسمع تعاليمك الرائعة"
"Together with my friend, I had come from afar, to hear your teachings"
"لقد أتيت مع صديقي من بعيد لسماع تعاليمك"
"And now my friend is going to stay with your people"
"والآن صديقي سوف يبقى مع شعبك"
"he has taken his refuge with you"
"لقد لجأ إليك"
"But I will again start on my pilgrimage"
"ولكن سأبدأ مرة أخرى رحلتي"
"As you please," the venerable one spoke politely
"كما يحلو لك" تحدث الجليل بأدب

"Too bold is my speech," Siddhartha continued
"إن كلامي جريء للغاية"، تابع سيدهارثا
"but I do not want to leave the exalted on this note"
"لكنني لا أريد أن أترك المرتفعات على هذه الملاحظة"
"I want to share with the most venerable one my honest thoughts"
"أريد أن أشارك مع الشخص الأكثر احترامًا أفكاري الصادقة"
"Does it please the venerable one to listen for one moment longer?"
"هل يرضى الجليل أن يستمع ولو للحظة واحدة؟"
Silently, the Buddha nodded his approval
في صمت، أومأ بوذا برأسه موافقًا
Spoke Siddhartha, "oh most venerable one"
قال سيدهارتا "يا أيها الجليل"
"there is one thing I have admired in your teachings most of all"
"هناك شيء واحد أعجبتني في تعاليمك أكثر من أي شيء آخر"
"Everything in your teachings is perfectly clear"
"كل شيء في تعاليمك واضح تمامًا"
"what you speak of is proven"
"ما تتحدث عنه مثبت"
"you are presenting the world as a perfect chain"
"أنت تقدم العالم كسلسلة مثالية"
"a chain which is never and nowhere broken"
"سلسلة لا تنكسر أبدًا ولا في أي مكان"
"an eternal chain the links of which are causes and effects"
"سلسلة أبدية تتكون روابطها من أسباب وتأثيرات"
"Never before, has this been seen so clearly"
"لم يسبق من قبل أن رأينا هذا بوضوح"
"never before, has this been presented so irrefutably"
"لم يتم تقديم هذا من قبل بشكل لا يقبل الجدل"
"truly, the heart of every Brahman has to beat stronger with love"
"في الحقيقة، يجب على قلب كل براهمان أن ينبض بقوة أكبر بالحب"
"he has seen the world through your perfectly connected teachings"

"لقد رأى العالم من خلال تعاليمك المترابطة تمامًا"
"without gaps, clear as a crystal"
"بدون فجوات، واضح كالبلور"
"not depending on chance, not depending on Gods"
"لا تعتمد على الصدفة، لا تعتمد على الآلهة"
"he has to accept it whether it may be good or bad"
"عليه أن يقبل الأمر سواء كان جيدًا أم سيئًا"
"he has to live by it whether it would be suffering or joy"
"عليه أن يعيش بها سواء كان ذلك معاناة أو فرحًا"
"but I do not wish to discuss the uniformity of the world"
"لكنني لا أرغب في مناقشة توحيد العالم"
"it is possible that this is not essential"
"من الممكن أن هذا ليس ضروريا"
"everything which happens is connected"
"كل ما يحدث متصل"
"the great and the small things are all encompassed"
"الأشياء الكبيرة والصغيرة كلها متحدة"
"they are connected by the same forces of time"
"إنهم مرتبطون بنفس قوى الزمن"
"they are connected by the same law of causes"
"إنهم مرتبطون بنفس قانون الأسباب"
"the causes of coming into being and of dying"
"أسباب الوجود والموت"
"this is what shines brightly out of your exalted teachings"
"هذا ما يبرز بوضوح من تعاليمك السامية"
"But, according to your very own teachings, there is a small gap"
"ولكن وفقًا لتعاليمك الخاصة، هناك فجوة صغيرة"
"this unity and necessary sequence of all things is broken in one place"
"هذه الوحدة والتسلسل الضروري لكل الأشياء مكسورة في مكان واحد"
"this world of unity is invaded by something alien"
"هذا العالم الموحد غزاة شيء غريب"
"there is something new, which had not been there before"
"هناك شيء جديد، لم يكن موجودًا من قبل"
"there is something which cannot be demonstrated"

"هناك شيء لا يمكن اثباته"
"there is something which cannot be proven"
"هناك شيء لا يمكن اثباته"
"these are your teachings of overcoming the world"
"هذه هي تعاليمك للتغلب على العالم"
"these are your teachings of salvation"
"هذه هي تعاليمكم للخلاص"
"But with this small gap, the eternal breaks apart again"
"ولكن مع هذه الفجوة الصغيرة، ينكسر الأبدي مرة أخرى"
"with this small breach, the law of the world becomes void"
"مع هذا الخرق الصغير، يصبح قانون العالم باطلاً"
"Please forgive me for expressing this objection"
"أرجو أن تسامحني على التعبير عن هذا الاعتراض"
Quietly, Gotama had listened to him, unmoved
كان غوتاما يستمع إليه بهدوء، دون أن يتأثر
Now he spoke, the perfected one, with his kind and polite clear voice
فتكلم الآن الكامل بصوته اللطيف المهذب الواضح
"You've heard the teachings, oh son of a Brahman"
"لقد سمعت التعاليم يا ابن البراهمان"
"and good for you that you've thought about it this deeply"
"ومن الجيد لك أن تفكر في الأمر بعمق"
"You've found a gap in my teachings, an error"
"لقد وجدت ثغرة في تعاليمي، خطأ"
"You should think about this further"
"ينبغي عليك أن تفكر في هذا الأمر أكثر"
"But be warned, oh seeker of knowledge, of the thicket of opinions"
"ولكن احذر يا طالب العلم من غابة الآراء"
"be warned of arguing about words"
"احذر من الجدال حول الكلمات"
"There is nothing to opinions"
"لا يوجد شيء للآراء"
"they may be beautiful or ugly"
"قد تكون جميلة أو قبيحة"
"opinions may be smart or foolish"

"الآراء قد تكون ذكية أو حمقاء"
"everyone can support opinions, or discard them"
"يمكن للجميع دعم الآراء أو رفضها"
"But the teachings, you've heard from me, are no opinion"
"لكن التعاليم التي سمعتها مني ليست رأيًا"
"their goal is not to explain the world to those who seek knowledge"
"هدفهم ليس شرح العالم لأولئك الذين يسعون إلى المعرفة"
"They have a different goal"
"لديهم هدف مختلف"
"their goal is salvation from suffering"
"هدفهم هو الخلاص من المعاناة"
"This is what Gotama teaches, nothing else"
"هذا ما يعلمه غوتاما، لا شيء آخر"
"I wish that you, oh exalted one, would not be angry with me" said the young man
"أتمنى أن لا تغضب عليّ أيها العظيم" قال الشاب
"I have not spoken to you like this to argue with you"
"لم أتحدث إليك بهذه الطريقة لأجادل معك"
"I do not wish to argue about words"
"لا أريد الجدال حول الكلمات"
"You are truly right, there is little to opinions"
"أنت على حق حقًا، لا يوجد سوى القليل من الآراء"
"But let me say one more thing"
"ولكن دعني أقول شيئًا آخر"
"I have not doubted in you for a single moment"
"لم أشك فيك لحظة واحدة"
"I have not doubted for a single moment that you are Buddha"
"لم أشك للحظة واحدة في أنك بوذا"
"I have not doubted that you have reached the highest goal"
"لم أشك في أنك وصلت إلى الهدف الأعلى"
"the highest goal towards which so many Brahmans are on their way"
"الهدف الأسمى الذي يسعى إليه العديد من البراهمة"
"You have found salvation from death"

"لقد وجدت الخلاص من الموت"
"It has come to you in the course of your own search"
"لقد جاء إليك في سياق بحثك الخاص"
"it has come to you on your own path"
"لقد جاء إليك بطريقك الخاص"
"it has come to you through thoughts and meditation"
"لقد جاء إليك من خلال الأفكار والتأمل"
"it has come to you through realizations and enlightenment"
"لقد جاء إليك من خلال الإدراك والتنوير"
"but it has not come to you by means of teachings!"
"ولكن لم يأتكم عن طريق التعليم!"
"And this is my thought"
"وهذه فكرتي"
"nobody will obtain salvation by means of teachings!"
"لن ينال أحد الخلاص من خلال التعاليم!"
"You will not be able to convey your hour of enlightenment"
"لن تتمكن من نقل ساعة التنوير الخاصة بك"
"words of what has happened to you won't convey the moment!"
"الكلمات التي تصف ما حدث لك لن تنقل اللحظة!"
"The teachings of the enlightened Buddha contain much"
"إن تعاليم بوذا المستنير تحتوي على الكثير"
"it teaches many to live righteously"
"إنه يعلم الكثيرين أن يعيشوا حياة صالحة"
"it teaches many to avoid evil"
"إنه يعلم الكثيرين تجنب الشر"
"But there is one thing which these teachings do not contain"
"ولكن هناك شيء واحد لا تحتويه هذه التعاليم"
"they are clear and venerable, but the teachings miss something"
"إنها واضحة ومحترمة، لكن التعاليم تفتقد شيئًا ما"
"the teachings do not contain the mystery"
"إن التعاليم لا تحتوي على الغموض"
"the mystery of what the exalted one has experienced for himself"
"سر ما شهده المرتفع بنفسه"

"among hundreds of thousands, only he experienced it"
"من بين مئات الآلاف، هو الوحيد الذي اختبر ذلك"
"This is what I have thought and realized, when I heard the teachings"
"هذا ما فكرت فيه وأدركته عندما سمعت التعاليم"
"This is why I am continuing my travels"
"هذا هو السبب الذي يجعلني أواصل سفري"
"this is why I do not to seek other, better teachings"
"لهذا السبب لا أريد أن أبحث عن تعاليم أخرى أفضل"
"I know there are no better teachings"
"أعلم أنه لا يوجد تعاليم أفضل"
"I leave to depart from all teachings and all teachers"
"أود أن أبتعد عن كل التعاليم وكل المعلمين"
"I leave to reach my goal by myself, or to die"
"أرحل للوصول إلى هدفي بنفسي، أو أموت"
"But often, I'll think of this day, oh exalted one"
"لكن في كثير من الأحيان، سأفكر في هذا اليوم، يا صاحب السمو"
"and I'll think of this hour, when my eyes beheld a holy man"
"وسأفكر في هذه الساعة، عندما رأت عيني رجلاً مقدسًا"
The Buddha's eyes quietly looked to the ground
نظرت عيون بوذا بهدوء إلى الأرض
quietly, in perfect equanimity, his inscrutable face was smiling
بهدوء، في اتزان تام، كان وجهه الغامض مبتسمًا
the venerable one spoke slowly
تحدث الجليل ببطء
"I wish that your thoughts shall not be in error"
"أتمنى أن لا تكون أفكارك خاطئة"
"I wish that you shall reach the goal!"
"أتمنى أن تصل إلى الهدف!"
"But there is something I ask you to tell me"
"ولكن هناك شيء أطلب منك أن تخبرني به"
"Have you seen the multitude of my Samanas?"
"هل رأيتم كثرة سامانا؟"
"they have taken refuge in the teachings"

"لقد لجأوا إلى التعاليم"
"do you believe it would be better for them to abandon the teachings?"
هل تعتقد أنه سيكون من الأفضل لهم أن يتخلوا عن التعاليم؟
"should they to return into the world of desires?"
"فهل ينبغي لهم أن يعودوا إلى عالم الرغبات؟"
"Far is such a thought from my mind" exclaimed Siddhartha
"إن مثل هذه الفكرة بعيدة كل البعد عن ذهني" صاح سيدهارثا
"I wish that they shall all stay with the teachings"
"أتمنى أن يظلوا جميعًا على نفس التعاليم"
"I wish that they shall reach their goal!"
"أتمنى أن يصلوا إلى هدفهم!"
"It is not my place to judge another person's life"
"ليس من حقي أن أحكم على حياة شخص آخر"
"I can only judge my own life "
"لا أستطيع الحكم إلا على حياتي"
"I must decide, I must chose, I must refuse"
"يجب أن أقرر، يجب أن أختار، يجب أن أرفض"
"Salvation from the self is what we Samanas search for"
"الخلاص من الذات هو ما نبحث عنه نحن الساماناس"
"oh exalted one, if only I were one of your disciples"
"يا عظيم لو كنت من تلاميذك"
"I'd fear that it might happen to me"
"أخشى أن يحدث لي ذلك"
"only seemingly, would my self be calm and be redeemed"
"ظاهريًا فقط، أريد أن أكون هادئًا وأخلًص"
"but in truth it would live on and grow"
"ولكن في الحقيقة سوف تستمر في العيش والنمو"
"because then I would replace my self with the teachings"
"لأنني حينها سأستبدل نفسي بالتعاليم"
"my self would be my duty to follow you"
"إن من واجبي أن أتبعك"
"my self would be my love for you"
"أنا سوف أكون حبي لك"
"and my self would be the community of the monks!"
"وأنا أريد أن أكون جماعة الرهبان!"

With half of a smile Gotama looked into the stranger's eyes
بابتسامة نصفية نظر غوتاما إلى عيني الغريب
his eyes were unwaveringly open and kind
كانت عيناه مفتوحتين بلا تردد ولطيفتين
he bid him to leave with a hardly noticeable gesture
طلب منه المغادرة بإشارة غير ملحوظة
"You are wise, oh Samana" the venerable one spoke
"أنت حكيمة يا سمانا" قال الجليل
"You know how to talk wisely, my friend"
"أنت تعرف كيف تتحدث بحكمة يا صديقي"
"Be aware of too much wisdom!"
"احذر من كثرة الحكمة!"
The Buddha turned away
ابتعد بوذا
Siddhartha would never forget his glance
لن ينسى سيدهارتا نظرته أبدًا
his half smile remained forever etched in Siddhartha's memory
ظلت ابتسامته النصفية محفورة إلى الأبد في ذاكرة سيدهارتا
Siddhartha thought to himself
فكر سيدهارتا في نفسه
"I have never before seen a person glance and smile this way"
"لم يسبق لي أن رأيت شخصًا ينظر ويبتسم بهذه الطريقة"
"no one else sits and walks like he does"
"لا أحد يجلس ويمشي مثله"
"truly, I wish to be able to glance and smile this way"
"حقا، أتمنى أن أكون قادرا على النظر والابتسام بهذه الطريقة"
"I wish to be able to sit and walk this way, too"
"أتمنى أن أكون قادرًا على الجلوس والمشي بهذه الطريقة أيضًا"
"liberated, venerable, concealed, open, childlike and mysterious"
"محررة، جليلة، مخفية، مفتوحة، طفولية وغامضة"
"he must have succeeded in reaching the innermost part of his self"
"لا بد أنه نجح في الوصول إلى الجزء الأعمق من ذاته"

"only then can someone glance and walk this way"
"فقط حينها يمكن لأحد أن ينظر ويمشي في هذا الطريق"
"I will also seek to reach the innermost part of my self"
"سأسعى أيضًا للوصول إلى الجزء الأعمق من ذاتي"
"I saw a man" Siddhartha thought
"لقد رأيت رجلاً" فكر سيدهارثا
"a single man, before whom I would have to lower my glance"
"رجل واحد، يجب أن أخفض نظري أمامه"
"I do not want to lower my glance before anyone else"
"لا أريد أن أخفض نظري أمام أي شخص آخر"
"No teachings will entice me more anymore"
"لن تجذبني أي تعاليم بعد الآن"
"because this man's teachings have not enticed me"
"لأن تعاليم هذا الرجل لم تقنعني"
"I am deprived by the Buddha" thought Siddhartha
"لقد حرمني بوذا" فكر سيدهارتا
"I am deprived, although he has given so much"
"أنا محروم، على الرغم من أنه أعطى الكثير"
"he has deprived me of my friend"
"لقد حرمني من صديقي"
"my friend who had believed in me"
"صديقي الذي آمن بي"
"my friend who now believes in him"
"صديقي الذي يؤمن به الآن"
"my friend who had been my shadow"
"صديقي الذي كان ظلي"
"and now he is Gotama's shadow"
"والآن هو ظل غوتاما"
"but he has given me Siddhartha"
"لكنّه أعطاني سيدارثا"
"he has given me myself"
"لقد أعطاني نفسي"

Awakening
الصحوة

Siddhartha left the mango grove behind him
ترك سيدهارثا بستان المانجو خلفه
but he felt his past life also stayed behind
ولكنه شعر أن حياته الماضية بقيت خلفه أيضًا
the Buddha, the perfected one, stayed behind
بوذا، الذي تم إكماله، بقي خلفًا
and Govinda stayed behind too
وبقي جوفيندا أيضًا
and his past life had parted from him
وقد فارقته حياته الماضية
he pondered as he was walking slowly
كان يفكر وهو يمشي ببطء
he pondered about this sensation, which filled him completely
فتأمل هذا الإحساس الذي ملأه تماما
He pondered deeply, like diving into a deep water
ففكر بعمق، كأنه يغوص في مياه عميقة
he let himself sink down to the ground of the sensation
لقد سمح لنفسه بالغرق في أرض الإحساس
he let himself sink down to the place where the causes lie
لقد سمح لنفسه بالغرق في المكان الذي تكمن فيه الأسباب
to identify the causes is the very essence of thinking
إن تحديد الأسباب هو جوهر التفكير
this was how it seemed to him
هكذا بدا له
and by this alone, sensations turn into realizations
وبهذا وحده تتحول الأحاسيس إلى تحقيقات.
and these sensations are not lost
وهذه الأحاسيس لم تضيع
but the sensations become entities
لكن الأحاسيس تصبح كيانات
and the sensations start to emit what is inside of them
وتبدأ الأحاسيس في إخراج ما بداخلها

they show their truths like rays of light
إنهم يظهرون حقائقهم مثل أشعة الضوء
Slowly walking along, Siddhartha pondered
كان سيدهارثا يمشي ببطء، وكان يفكر
He realized that he was no youth any more
أدرك أنه لم يعد شابًا بعد الآن
he realized that he had turned into a man
أدرك أنه تحول إلى رجل
He realized that something had left him
أدرك أن شيئا ما قد تركه
the same way a snake is left by its old skin
بنفس الطريقة التي يترك بها الثعبان جلده القديم
what he had throughout his youth no longer existed in him
ما كان عليه طيلة شبابه لم يعد موجودا فيه
it used to be a part of him; the wish to have teachers
لقد كان هذا جزءًا منه؛ الرغبة في وجود معلمين
the wish to listen to teachings
الرغبة في الاستماع إلى التعاليم
He had also left the last teacher who had appeared on his path
كما ترك المعلم الأخير الذي ظهر في طريقه
he had even left the highest and wisest teacher
لقد ترك حتى المعلم الأعلى والأكثر حكمة
he had left the most holy one, Buddha
لقد ترك أقدس شخص، بوذا
he had to part with him, unable to accept his teachings
كان عليه أن يفارقه، غير قادر على قبول تعاليمه
Slower, he walked along in his thoughts
ببطء، سار في أفكاره
and he asked himself, "But what is this?"
فسأل نفسه: "ولكن ما هذا؟"
"what have you sought to learn from teachings and from teachers?"
"ما الذي سعيت إلى تعلمه من التعاليم ومن المعلمين؟"
"and what were they, who have taught you so much?"
"ومن هم هؤلاء الذين علموك هذا القدر؟"

"what are they if they have been unable to teach you?"
"فما هم إذا لم يتمكنوا من تعليمك؟"
And he found, "It was the self"
فوجد "أنها الذات"
"it was the purpose and essence of which I sought to learn"
"لقد كان هذا هو الهدف والجوهر الذي سعيت إلى تعلمه"
"It was the self I wanted to free myself from"
"لقد كانت الذات التي أردت تحرير نفسي منها"
"the self which I sought to overcome"
"الذات التي سعيت للتغلب عليها"
"But I was not able to overcome it"
"ولكن لم أتمكن من التغلب عليها"
"I could only deceive it"
"لا أستطيع إلا أن أخدعه"
"I could only flee from it"
"لم أستطع إلا الفرار منه"
"I could only hide from it"
"لا أستطيع إلا أن أختبئ منه"
"Truly, no thing in this world has kept my thoughts so busy"
"حقاً، لا يوجد شيء في هذا العالم يشغل أفكاري إلى هذا الحد"
"I have been kept busy by the mystery of me being alive"
"لقد ظللت مشغولاً بغموض كوني على قيد الحياة"
"the mystery of me being one"
"سر كوني واحداً"
"the mystery if being separated and isolated from all others"
"الغموض في الانفصال والعزلة عن الآخرين"
"the mystery of me being Siddhartha!"
"سر كوني سيدهارتا!"
"And there is no thing in this world I know less about"
"ولا يوجد شيء في هذا العالم أعرف عنه أقل"
he had been pondering while slowly walking along
لقد كان يفكر بينما كان يسير ببطء
he stopped as these thoughts caught hold of him
توقف عندما سيطرت عليه هذه الأفكار
and right away another thought sprang forth from these thoughts

وعلى الفور خرجت فكرة أخرى من هذه الأفكار

"there's one reason why I know nothing about myself"
"هناك سبب واحد يجعلني لا أعرف شيئًا عن نفسي"

"there's one reason why Siddhartha has remained alien to me"
"هناك سبب واحد يجعل سيدهارثا غريبًا بالنسبة لي"

"all of this stems from one cause"
"كل هذا ينبع من سبب واحد"

"I was afraid of myself, and I was fleeing"
"كنت خائفة من نفسي، وكنت أهرب"

"I have searched for both Atman and Brahman"
"لقد بحثت عن كل من الأتمان والبراهمان"

"for this I was willing to dissect my self"
"لهذا السبب كنت على استعداد لتشريح نفسي"

"and I was willing to peel off all of its layers"
"وكنت على استعداد لتقشير كل طبقاته"

"I wanted to find the core of all peels in its unknown interior"
"أردت أن أجد جوهر كل قشور الفاكهة في داخلها المجهول"

"the Atman, life, the divine part, the ultimate part"
"الأتمان، الحياة، الجزء الإلهي، الجزء النهائي"

"But I have lost myself in the process"
"لكنني فقدت نفسي في هذه العملية"

Siddhartha opened his eyes and looked around
فتح سيدهارثا عينيه ونظر حوله

looking around, a smile filled his face
نظر حوله، ابتسم وملأ وجهه

a feeling of awakening from long dreams flowed through him
لقد تدفق عليه شعور باليقظة من أحلام طويلة

the feeling flowed from his head down to his toes
كان الشعور يتدفق من رأسه إلى أصابع قدميه

And it was not long before he walked again
ولم يمض وقت طويل قبل أن يمشي مرة أخرى

he walked quickly, like a man who knows what he has got to do

كان يمشي بسرعة، مثل رجل يعرف ما يجب عليه فعله

"now I will not let Siddhartha escape from me again!"

"الآن لن أسمح لسيدهارثا بالهروب مني مرة أخرى!"

"I no longer want to begin my thoughts and my life with Atman"

"لم أعد أرغب في أن أبدأ أفكاري وحياتي مع أتمان"

"nor do I want to begin my thoughts with the suffering of the world"

"ولا أريد أن أبدأ أفكاري بمعاناة العالم"

"I do not want to kill and dissect myself any longer"

"لا أريد أن أقتل وأشرح نفسي بعد الآن"

"Yoga-Veda shall not teach me anymore"

"لا ينبغي لليوغا فيدا أن تعلميني بعد الآن"

"nor Atharva-Veda, nor the ascetics"

"ولا الأثارفا فيدا، ولا الزاهدون"

"there will not be any kind of teachings"

"لن يكون هناك أي نوع من التعاليم"

"I want to learn from myself and be my student"

"أريد أن أتعلم من نفسي وأن أكون تلميذي"

"I want to get to know myself; the secret of Siddhartha"

"أريد أن أعرف نفسي؛ سر سيدهارتا"

He looked around, as if he was seeing the world for the first time

نظر حوله وكأنه يرى العالم لأول مرة

Beautiful and colourful was the world

كان العالم جميلا وملونًا

strange and mysterious was the world

كان العالم غريبًا وغامضًا

Here was blue, there was yellow, here was green

هنا كان أزرق، وكان هناك أصفر، وكان هنا أخضر

the sky and the river flowed

السماء والنهر يتدفقان

the forest and the mountains were rigid

كانت الغابة والجبال صلبة

all of the world was beautiful

كان العالم كله جميلا
all of it was mysterious and magical
كان كل ذلك غامضًا وسحريًا
and in its midst was he, Siddhartha, the awakening one
وفي وسطها كان هو، سيدهارتا، المستيقظ
and he was on the path to himself
وكان في طريقه إلى نفسه
all this yellow and blue and river and forest entered Siddhartha
كل هذا الأصفر والأزرق والنهر والغابة دخل سيدهارتا
for the first time it entered through the eyes
لأول مرة دخلت من خلال العيون
it was no longer a spell of Mara
لم يعد تعويذة مارا
it was no longer the veil of Maya
لم يعد حجاب مايا
it was no longer a pointless and coincidental
لم يعد الأمر عديم الجدوى ومصادفة
things were not just a diversity of mere appearances
لم تكن الأشياء مجرد تنوع في المظاهر فقط
appearances despicable to the deeply thinking Brahman
المظاهر حقيرة بالنسبة للبراهمان المفكر العميق
the thinking Brahman scorns diversity, and seeks unity
إن البراهمان المفكر يحتقر التنوع ويسعى إلى الوحدة
Blue was blue and river was river
كان الأزرق أزرقًا وكان النهر نهرًا
the singular and divine lived hidden in Siddhartha
لقد عاش المتفرد والإلهي مخفيًا في سيدهارتا
divinity's way and purpose was to be yellow here, and blue there
كان هدف الإلهية وطريقها أن تكون صفراء هنا وزرقاء هناك
there sky, there forest, and here Siddhartha
هناك السماء، وهناك الغابة، وهنا سيدهارتا
The purpose and essential properties was not somewhere behind the things
الغرض والخصائص الأساسية لم تكن في مكان ما وراء الأشياء

the purpose and essential properties was inside of everything

الغرض والخصائص الأساسية كانت موجودة داخل كل شيء

"How deaf and stupid have I been!" he thought

"كم كنت أصمًا وغبيًا!" فكر

and he walked swiftly along

وكان يمشي بسرعة على طول

"When someone reads a text he will not scorn the symbols and letters"

"عندما يقرأ شخص نصًا، فلن يحتقر الرموز والحروف"

"he will not call the symbols deceptions or coincidences"

"لن يسمي الرموز خداعًا أو مصادفات"

"but he will read them as they were written"

"لكنه سوف يقرأها كما هي مكتوبة"

"he will study and love them, letter by letter"

"سيدرسهم ويحبهم حرفًا بحرف"

"I wanted to read the book of the world and scorned the letters"

"أردت أن أقرأ كتاب العالم، فاحتقرت الحروف"

"I wanted to read the book of myself and scorned the symbols"

"أردت أن أقرأ كتاب نفسي واحتقرت الرموز"

"I called my eyes and my tongue coincidental"

"لقد أسميت عيني ولساني تصادفًا"

"I said they were worthless forms without substance"

"قلت أنها أشكال لا قيمة لها ولا جوهر"

"No, this is over, I have awakened"

"لا، لقد انتهى هذا، لقد استيقظت"

"I have indeed awakened"

"لقد استيقظت بالفعل"

"I had not been born before this very day"

"لم أكن قد ولدت قبل هذا اليوم"

In thinking these thoughts, Siddhartha suddenly stopped once again

وفي أثناء تفكيره بهذه الأفكار، توقف سيدهارثا فجأة مرة أخرى

he stopped as if there was a snake lying in front of him

توقف وكأن هناك ثعبانًا مستلقيًا أمامه

suddenly, he had also become aware of something else

فجأة، أصبح على علم بشيء آخر أيضًا

He was indeed like someone who had just woken up

لقد كان بالفعل مثل شخص استيقظ للتو

he was like a new-born baby starting life anew

كان مثل طفل حديث الولادة يبدأ حياته من جديد

and he had to start again at the very beginning

وكان عليه أن يبدأ من جديد من البداية

in the morning he had had very different intentions

في الصباح كانت لديه نوايا مختلفة تماما

he had thought to return to his home and his father

كان يفكر في العودة إلى منزله وأبيه

But now he stopped as if a snake was lying on his path

ولكنه توقف الآن وكأن ثعبانًا كان مستلقيًا في طريقه

he made a realization of where he was

لقد أدرك مكانه

"I am no longer the one I was"

"أنا لم أعد كما كنت"

"I am no ascetic anymore"

"أنا لم أعد زاهدًا"

"I am not a priest anymore"

"أنا لم أعد كاهنًا"

"I am no Brahman anymore"

"أنا لم أعد براهمانًا بعد الآن"

"Whatever should I do at my father's place?"

"ماذا ينبغي لي أن أفعل في منزل والدي؟"

"Study? Make offerings? Practise meditation?"

"الدراسة؟ تقديم القرابين؟ ممارسة التأمل؟"

"But all this is over for me"

"لكن كل هذا انتهى بالنسبة لي"

"all of this is no longer on my path"

"كل هذا لم يعد في طريقي"

Motionless, Siddhartha remained standing there

بقي سيدهارتا واقفًا هناك بلا حراك

and for the time of one moment and breath, his heart felt cold

وللحظة ونفس واحد شعر ببرودة في قلبه

he felt a coldness in his chest

شعر ببرودة في صدره

the same feeling a small animal feels when it sees how alone it is

نفس الشعور الذي يشعر به الحيوان الصغير عندما يرى مدى شعوره بالوحدة

For many years, he had been without home and had felt nothing

لقد كان بلا منزل لسنوات عديدة ولم يشعر بأي شيء

Now, he felt he had been without a home

الآن شعر أنه كان بلا منزل

Still, even in the deepest meditation, he had been his father's son

ومع ذلك، حتى في أعمق التأمل، كان ابنًا لأبيه

he had been a Brahman, of a high caste

لقد كان براهمانيًا، من طبقة عليا

he had been a cleric

لقد كان رجل دين

Now, he was nothing but Siddhartha, the awoken one

الآن، لم يكن سوى سيدهارتا، الشخص المستيقظ

nothing else was left of him

لم يبق منه شيء آخر

Deeply, he inhaled and felt cold

استنشق بعمق وشعر بالبرد

a shiver ran through his body

سرت قشعريرة في جسده

Nobody was as alone as he was

لم يكن أحد وحيدًا مثله

There was no nobleman who did not belong to the noblemen

لم يكن هناك نبيل لا ينتمي إلى النبلاء

there was no worker that did not belong to the workers

لم يكن هناك عامل لا ينتمي إلى العمال

they had all found refuge among themselves
لقد وجدوا جميعا ملجأً فيما بينهم
they shared their lives and spoke their languages
لقد تقاسموا حياتهم وتحدثوا لغاتهم
there are no Brahman who would not be regarded as Brahmans
لا يوجد براهمان لا يمكن اعتبارهم براهمان
and there are no Brahmans that didn't live as Brahmans
ولا يوجد براهمانيون لم يعيشوا كبراهمانيين
there are no ascetic who could not find refuge with the Samanas
لا يوجد زاهد لم يجد ملجأً في الساماناس
and even the most forlorn hermit in the forest was not alone
وحتى الناسك الأكثر حزنًا في الغابة لم يكن وحيدًا
he was also surrounded by a place he belonged to
وكان محاطًا أيضًا بالمكان الذي ينتمي إليه
he also belonged to a caste in which he was at home
كان ينتمي أيضًا إلى الطبقة التي كان يعيش فيها
Govinda had left him and became a monk
لقد تركه جوفيندا وأصبح راهبًا
and a thousand monks were his brothers
وكان معه ألف راهب من إخوته
they wore the same robe as him
كانوا يرتدون نفس الرداء الذي كان يرتديه
they believed in his faith and spoke his language
لقد آمنوا بإيمانه وتكلموا لغته
But he, Siddhartha, where did he belong to?
ولكن، سيدهارتا، إلى أين ينتمي؟
With whom would he share his life?
مع من سيشارك حياته؟
Whose language would he speak?
من هي اللغة التي سيتكلم بها؟
the world melted away all around him
لقد ذاب العالم من حوله
he stood alone like a star in the sky
لقد وقف وحيدا مثل نجم في السماء

cold and despair surrounded him

كان البرد واليأس يحيطان به

but Siddhartha emerged out of this moment

لكن سيدهارتا خرج من هذه اللحظة

Siddhartha emerged more his true self than before

ظهر سيدهارتا أكثر حقيقته من ذي قبل

he was more firmly concentrated than he had ever been

لقد كان أكثر تركيزًا مما كان عليه من قبل

He felt; "this had been the last tremor of the awakening"

شعر أن "هذه كانت الهزة الأخيرة للصحوة"

"the last struggle of this birth"

"النضال الأخير في هذه الولادة"

And it was not long until he walked again in long strides

ولم يمض وقت طويل حتى عاد يمشي بخطوات طويلة

he started to proceed swiftly and impatiently

بدأ في التحرك بسرعة وبفارغ الصبر

he was no longer going home

لم يعد يذهب إلى المنزل

he was no longer going to his father

لم يعد يذهب إلى والده

Part Two
الجزء الثاني

***

Kamala
كامالا

Siddhartha learned something new on every step of his path

لقد تعلم سيدهارثا شيئًا جديدًا في كل خطوة من خطواته

because the world was transformed and his heart was enchanted

لأن العالم تحول وقلبه سحر

He saw the sun rising over the mountains

رأى الشمس تشرق فوق الجبال

and he saw the sun setting over the distant beach

ورأى الشمس تغرب على الشاطئ البعيد

At night, he saw the stars in the sky in their fixed positions

وفي الليل رأى النجوم في السماء في مواقعها الثابتة

and he saw the crescent of the moon floating like a boat in the blue

ورأى هلال القمر يطفو كالقارب في البحر الأزرق.

He saw trees, stars, animals, and clouds

لقد رأى الأشجار والنجوم والحيوانات والسحب

rainbows, rocks, herbs, flowers, streams and rivers

قوس قزح، الصخور، الأعشاب، الزهور، الجداول والأنهار

he saw the glistening dew in the bushes in the morning

لقد رأى الندى المتلألئ في الشجيرات في الصباح

he saw distant high mountains which were blue

رأى جبالاً عالية بعيدة كانت زرقاء اللون

wind blew through the rice-field

هبت الرياح عبر حقل الأرز

all of this, a thousand-fold and colourful, had always been there

كل هذا، ألف ضعف وملون، كان موجودًا دائمًا

the sun and the moon had always shone

كانت الشمس والقمر يشرقان دائمًا

rivers had always roared and bees had always buzzed

كانت الأنهار تزأر دائمًا وكان النحل يطن دائمًا

but in former times all of this had been a deceptive veil

ولكن في الأزمنة السابقة كان كل هذا حجابًا خادعًا

to him it had been nothing more than fleeting

بالنسبة له لم يكن الأمر أكثر من مجرد عابر

it was supposed to be looked upon in distrust

كان من المفترض أن ينظر إليه بعدم ثقة

it was destined to be penetrated and destroyed by thought

لقد كان مقدراً له أن يخترقه الفكر ويدمره

since it was not the essence of existence

لأنه لم يكن جوهر الوجود

since this essence lay beyond, on the other side of, the visible

لأن هذا الجوهر يكمن وراء الجانب الآخر من المرئي

But now, his liberated eyes stayed on this side

لكن الآن، عيناه المحررتان بقيتا على هذا الجانب

he saw and became aware of the visible

لقد رأى وأصبح على علم بالمرئي

he sought to be at home in this world

كان يسعى إلى أن يكون في بيته في هذا العالم

he did not search for the true essence

لم يبحث عن الجوهر الحقيقي

he did not aim at a world beyond

لم يكن يهدف إلى عالم أبعد من ذلك

this world was beautiful enough for him

كان هذا العالم جميلا بما فيه الكفاية بالنسبة له

looking at it like this made everything childlike

النظر إليه بهذه الطريقة يجعل كل شيء يبدو طفوليًا

Beautiful were the moon and the stars

كان القمر والنجوم جميلين

beautiful was the stream and the banks

كان النهر والضفاف جميلين

the forest and the rocks, the goat and the gold-beetle

الغابة والصخور والماعز والخنفساء الذهبية

the flower and the butterfly; beautiful and lovely it was
الزهرة والفراشة؛ كانت جميلة ورائعة

to walk through the world was childlike again
كان المشي في العالم طفوليا مرة أخرى

this way he was awoken
بهذه الطريقة تم إيقاظه

this way he was open to what is near
بهذه الطريقة كان منفتحًا على ما هو قريب

this way he was without distrust
بهذه الطريقة كان بلا شك

differently the sun burnt the head
بطريقة مختلفة أحرقت الشمس الرأس

differently the shade of the forest cooled him down
على نحو مختلف، كان ظل الغابة يبرده

differently the pumpkin and the banana tasted
طعم اليقطين والموز مختلفان

Short were the days, short were the nights
كانت الأيام قصيرة، وكانت الليالي قصيرة

every hour sped swiftly away like a sail on the sea
كل ساعة مرت بسرعة مثل الشراع في البحر

and under the sail was a ship full of treasures, full of joy
وتحت الشراع كانت هناك سفينة مليئة بالكنوز، مليئة بالفرح

Siddhartha saw a group of apes moving through the high canopy
رأى سيدهارثا مجموعة من القردة تتحرك عبر مظلة عالية

they were high in the branches of the trees
كانوا عاليا في أغصان الأشجار

and he heard their savage, greedy song
وسمع أغنيتهم الوحشية الجشعة

Siddhartha saw a male sheep following a female one and mating with her
رأى سيدهارثا خروفًا ذكرًا يتبع خروفًا أنثى ويتزاوج معها

In a lake of reeds, he saw the pike hungrily hunting for its dinner
في بحيرة القصب، رأى سمكة البايك تبحث بشغف عن عشائها

young fish were propelling themselves away from the pike
كانت الأسماك الصغيرة تدفع نفسها بعيدًا عن سمكة البايك
they were scared, wiggling and sparkling
كانوا خائفين، يتمايلون ويتألقون
the young fish jumped in droves out of the water
قفزت الأسماك الصغيرة بأعداد كبيرة من الماء
the scent of strength and passion came forcefully out of the water
خرجت رائحة القوة والعاطفة بقوة من الماء
and the pike stirred up the scent
والرماح حركت الرائحة
All of this had always existed
كل هذا كان موجودا دائما
and he had not seen it, nor had he been with it
ولم يكن قد رآه ولم يكن معه
Now he was with it and he was part of it
الآن كان معها وكان جزءًا منها
Light and shadow ran through his eyes
كان الضوء والظل يمران عبر عينيه
stars and moon ran through his heart
كانت النجوم والقمر يمران عبر قلبه

Siddhartha remembered everything he had experienced in the Garden Jetavana
تذكر سيدهارثا كل ما مر به في حديقة جيتافانا
he remembered the teaching he had heard there from the divine Buddha
تذكر التعاليم التي سمعها هناك من بوذا الإلهي
he remembered the farewell from Govinda
تذكر وداع جوفيندا
he remembered the conversation with the exalted one
فتذكر الحديث مع العالي
Again he remembered his own words that he had spoken to the exalted one
فتذكر مرة أخرى كلامه الذي قاله للواحد العظيم
he remembered every word

لقد تذكر كل كلمة

he realized he had said things which he had not really known

أدرك أنه قال أشياء لم يكن يعرفها حقًا

he astonished himself with what he had said to Gotama

لقد اندهش من ما قاله لجوتاما

the Buddha's treasure and secret was not the teachings

لم يكن كنز بوذا وسرّه هو التعاليم

but the secret was the inexpressible and not teachable

لكن السر كان غير قابل للتعبير عنه ولا يمكن تعليمه

the secret which he had experienced in the hour of his enlightenment

السر الذي اختبره في ساعة تنويره

the secret was nothing but this very thing which he had now gone to experience

لم يكن السر سوى هذا الشيء الذي ذهب الآن لتجربته

the secret was what he now began to experience

كان السر هو ما بدأ يشعر به الآن

Now he had to experience his self

الآن كان عليه أن يختبر نفسه

he had already known for a long time that his self was Atman

لقد كان يعرف منذ فترة طويلة أن ذاته هي أتمان

he knew Atman bore the same eternal characteristics as Brahman

لقد عرف أن الأتمان يحمل نفس الخصائص الأبدية مثل براهمان

But he had never really found this self

ولكنه لم يجد هذه الذات حقًا أبدًا

because he had wanted to capture the self in the net of thought

لأنه أراد أن يأسر الذات في شبكة الفكر

but the body was not part of the self

ولكن الجسد لم يكن جزءًا من الذات

it was not the spectacle of the senses

لم يكن مشهدًا للحواس

so it also was not the thought, nor the rational mind

لذلك لم يكن الفكر ولا العقل العقلاني كذلك
it was not the learned wisdom, nor the learned ability
لم تكن الحكمة المكتسبة ولا القدرة المكتسبة
from these things no conclusions could be drawn
ومن هذه الأشياء لم يمكن التوصل إلى أي استنتاجات
No, the world of thought was also still on this side
لا، عالم الفكر كان أيضًا لا يزال على هذا الجانب
Both, the thoughts as well as the senses, were pretty things
كانت كل من الأفكار والحواس أشياء جميلة
but the ultimate meaning was hidden behind both of them
لكن المعنى النهائي كان مخفيًا وراء كليهما
both had to be listened to and played with
كان لابد من الاستماع إلى كليهما واللعب بهما
neither had to be scorned nor overestimated
لم يكن من الضروري الاستهزاء به أو المبالغة في تقديره
there were secret voices of the innermost truth
كانت هناك أصوات سرية للحقيقة الأعمق
these voices had to be attentively perceived
كان لابد من إدراك هذه الأصوات باهتمام
He wanted to strive for nothing else
لم يكن يريد أن يسعى إلى أي شيء آخر
he would do what the voice commanded him to do
كان سيفعل ما يأمره به الصوت
he would dwell where the voices advised him to
كان يسكن حيث تنصحه الأصوات
Why had Gotama sat down under the Bodhi tree?
لماذا جلس غوتاما تحت شجرة بودي؟
He had heard a voice in his own heart
لقد سمع صوتا في قلبه
a voice which had commanded him to seek rest under this tree
صوت أمره بالبحث عن الراحة تحت هذه الشجرة
he could have gone on to make offerings
كان بإمكانه أن يستمر في تقديم العروض
he could have performed his ablutions
كان بإمكانه أن يتوضأ

he could have spent that moment in prayer
كان بإمكانه أن يقضي تلك اللحظة في الصلاة
he had chosen not to eat or drink
لقد اختار عدم الأكل أو الشرب
he had chosen not to sleep or dream
لقد اختار عدم النوم أو الحلم
instead, he had obeyed the voice
بدلا من ذلك، كان قد أطاع الصوت
To obey like this was good
أن نطيع هكذا كان أمرا جيدا
it was good not to obey to an external command
كان من الجيد عدم الانصياع لأمر خارجي
it was good to obey only the voice
كان من الجيد أن نطيع الصوت فقط
to be ready like this was good and necessary
أن نكون مستعدين بهذه الطريقة كان أمراً جيداً وضرورياً
there was nothing else that was necessary
لم يكن هناك أي شيء آخر ضروري

in the night Siddhartha got to a river
في الليل وصل سيدهارثا إلى النهر
he slept in the straw hut of a ferryman
كان ينام في كوخ القش الخاص بصاحب العبارة
this night Siddhartha had a dream
في هذه الليلة كان لدى سيدهارثا حلم
Govinda was standing in front of him
وكان جوفيندا واقفا أمامه
he was dressed in the yellow robe of an ascetic
كان يرتدي رداءً أصفر اللون لزاهد
Sad was how Govinda looked
كان مظهر جوفيندا حزينًا
sadly he asked, "Why have you forsaken me?"
فسألها بحزن: لماذا تركتيني؟
Siddhartha embraced Govinda, and wrapped his arms around him
احتضن سيدهارثا جوفيندا، ولف ذراعيه حوله

he pulled him close to his chest and kissed him
جذبه إلى صدره وقبله
but it was not Govinda anymore, but a woman
لكنها لم تعد جوفيندا، بل امرأة
a full breast popped out of the woman's dress
صدر ممتلئ خرج من ثوب المرأة
Siddhartha lay and drank from the breast
استلقى سيدهارثا وشرب من الثدي
sweetly and strongly tasted the milk from this breast
تذوقت الحليب من هذا الثدي بشكل حلو وقوي
It tasted of woman and man
لقد كان طعمه امرأة ورجل
it tasted of sun and forest
لقد كان طعمه مثل الشمس والغابة
it tasted of animal and flower
لقد كان طعمه حيوانًا وزهرة
it tasted of every fruit and every joyful desire
ذاقت كل فاكهة وكل رغبة بهيجة
It intoxicated him and rendered him unconscious
لقد أدى إلى سكره وإغمائه
Siddhartha woke up from the dream
استيقظ سيدهارثا من الحلم
the pale river shimmered through the door of the hut
كان النهر الشاحب يتلألأ عبر باب الكوخ
a dark call of an owl resounded deeply through the forest
صدى صوت البومة المظلم عميقًا في الغابة
Siddhartha asked the ferryman to get him across the river
طلب سيدهارتا من صاحب العبارة أن ينقله عبر النهر
The ferryman got him across the river on his bamboo-raft
لقد نقله القارب عبر النهر على طوافه المصنوع من الخيزران
the water shimmered reddish in the light of the morning
كان الماء يتلألأ باللون الأحمر في ضوء الصباح
"This is a beautiful river," he said to his companion
"هذا نهر جميل" قال لرفيقه
"Yes," said the ferryman, "a very beautiful river"
"نعم،" قال القارب، "نهر جميل جدًا"

"I love it more than anything"

"أنا أحبه أكثر من أي شيء"

"Often I have listened to it"

"لقد استمعت إليها كثيرًا"

"often I have looked into its eyes"

"لقد نظرت في عينيه في كثير من الأحيان"

"and I have always learned from it"

"ولقد تعلمت منه دائمًا"

"Much can be learned from a river"

"يمكن تعلم الكثير من النهر"

"I thank you, my benefactor" spoke Siddhartha

"أشكرك يا محسني" قال سيدهارتا

he disembarked on the other side of the river

نزل على الجانب الآخر من النهر

"I have no gift I could give you for your hospitality, my dear"

"ليس لدي هدية أستطيع أن أقدمها لك مقابل حسن ضيافتك يا عزيزتي"

"and I also have no payment for your work"

"وأنا أيضا ليس لدي أي أجر مقابل عملك"

"I am a man without a home"

"أنا رجل بلا منزل"

"I am the son of a Brahman and a Samana"

"أنا ابن براهمان وسامانا"

"I did see it," spoke the ferryman

"لقد رأيته" قال صاحب العبارة

"I did not expect any payment from you"

"لم أتوقع أي مبلغ منك"

"it is custom for guests to bear a gift"

"من المعتاد أن يحمل الضيوف هدية"

"but I did not expect this from you either"

"ولكنني لم أتوقع هذا منك أيضًا"

"You will give me the gift another time"

"سوف تعطيني الهدية في وقت آخر"

"Do you think so?" asked Siddhartha, bemusedly

"هل تعتقد ذلك؟" سأل سيدهارثا في حيرة

"I am sure of it," replied the ferryman

"أنا متأكد من ذلك" أجاب العبّار
"This too, I have learned from the river"
"هذا أيضًا تعلمته من النهر"
"everything that goes comes back!"
"كل ما يذهب يعود!"
"You too, Samana, will come back"
"أنت أيضًا، سامانا، ستعود"
"Now farewell! Let your friendship be my reward"
"الآن وداعا! دع صداقتك تكون مكافأتي"
"Commemorate me, when you make offerings to the gods"
"اذكروني عندما تقدمون القرابين للآلهة"
Smiling, they parted from each other
ابتسموا وافترقا عن بعضهما البعض
Smiling, Siddhartha was happy about the friendship
ابتسم سيدهارثا وكان سعيدًا بالصداقة
and he was happy about the kindness of the ferryman
وكان سعيدا بلطف العبّارة
"He is like Govinda," he thought with a smile
"إنه مثل جوفيندا" فكر وهو يبتسم
"all I meet on my path are like Govinda"
"كل من أقابله في طريقي هم مثل جوفيندا"
"All are thankful for what they have"
"الجميع شاكرون لما لديهم"
"but they are the ones who would have a right to receive thanks"
"ولكنهم هم الذين يستحقون الشكر"
"all are submissive and would like to be friends"
"الجميع خاضعون ويرغبون في أن يكونوا أصدقاء"
"all like to obey and think little"
"الجميع يحبون الطاعة والتفكير القليل"
"all people are like children"
"كل الناس مثل الاطفال"

At about noon, he came through a village
وفي حوالي الظهر، مر عبر قرية

In front of the mud cottages, children were rolling about in the street

أمام الأكواخ الطينية، كان الأطفال يتدحرجون في الشارع

they were playing with pumpkin-seeds and sea-shells

كانوا يلعبون ببذور اليقطين وأصداف البحر

they screamed and wrestled with each other

لقد صرخوا وتصارعوا مع بعضهم البعض

but they all timidly fled from the unknown Samana

لكنهم جميعا فروا بخجل من سامانا المجهولة

In the end of the village, the path led through a stream

في نهاية القرية، كان الطريق يؤدي عبر مجرى مائي

by the side of the stream, a young woman was kneeling

على جانب النهر كانت هناك امرأة شابة راكعة

she was washing clothes in the stream

كانت تغسل الملابس في النهر

When Siddhartha greeted her, she lifted her head

عندما استقبلها سيدهارثا، رفعت رأسها

and she looked up to him with a smile

ونظرت إليه بابتسامة

he could see the white in her eyes glistening

كان بإمكانه أن يرى اللون الأبيض في عينيها اللامعة

He called out a blessing to her

نادى عليها بالبركة

this was the custom among travellers

كانت هذه العادة بين المسافرين

and he asked how far it was to the large city

وسأل كم المسافة إلى المدينة الكبيرة

Then she got up and came to him

ثم قامت وجاءت إليه

beautifully her wet mouth was shimmering in her young face

كان فمها الرطب يلمع بشكل جميل في وجهها الشاب

She exchanged humorous banter with him

تبادلت معه المزاح المضحك

she asked whether he had eaten already

سألته هل كان قد أكل بالفعل

and she asked curious questions

وسألت أسئلة فضولية

"is it true that the Samanas slept alone in the forest at night?"

"هل صحيح أن الساماناس كانوا ينامون لوحدهم في الغابة في الليل؟"

"is it true Samanas are not allowed to have women with them"

"هل صحيح أن الساماناس لا يسمح لهم باصطحاب النساء معهم"

While talking, she put her left foot on his right one

أثناء حديثها وضعت قدمها اليسرى على قدمه اليمنى

the movement of a woman who would want to initiate sexual pleasure

حركة المرأة التي تريد أن تبدأ المتعة الجنسية

the textbooks call this "climbing a tree"

تسمي الكتب المدرسية هذا "تسلق شجرة"

Siddhartha felt his blood heating up

شعر سيدهارثا بارتفاع درجة حرارة دمه

he had to think of his dream again

كان عليه أن يفكر في حلمه مرة أخرى

he bend slightly down to the woman

انحنى قليلا نحو المرأة

and he kissed with his lips the brown nipple of her breast

وقبل بشفتيه حلمة ثديها البنية

Looking up, he saw her face smiling

نظر إلى الأعلى فرأى وجهها مبتسما

and her eyes were full of lust

وكانت عيناها مليئة بالشهوة

Siddhartha also felt desire for her

شعر سيدهارثا أيضًا بالرغبة فيها

he felt the source of his sexuality moving

شعر أن مصدر جنسيته يتحرك

but he had never touched a woman before

ولكنه لم يلمس امرأة من قبل

so he hesitated for a moment

فتردد للحظة

his hands were already prepared to reach out for her

كانت يداه مستعدة بالفعل للوصول إليها

but then he heard the voice of his innermost self
ولكن بعد ذلك سمع صوت نفسه الداخلية
he shuddered with awe at his voice
لقد ارتجف من الرهبة عند سماع صوته
and this voice told him no
وهذا الصوت قال له لا
all charms disappeared from the young woman's smiling face
اختفت كل السحر من وجه الشابة المبتسم
he no longer saw anything else but a damp glance
لم يعد يرى شيئا آخر سوى نظرة رطبة
all he could see was female animal in heat
كل ما استطاع رؤيته هو حيوان أنثى في حالة شبق
Politely, he petted her cheek
بكل أدب، قام بمداعبة خدها
he turned away from her and disappeared away
ابتعد عنها واختفى
he left from the disappointed woman with light steps
غادر من أمام المرأة الخائبة بخطوات خفيفة
and he disappeared into the bamboo-wood
واختفى في غابة الخيزران

he reached the large city before the evening
وصل إلى المدينة الكبيرة قبل المساء
and he was happy to have reached the city
وكان سعيدا لأنه وصل إلى المدينة
because he felt the need to be among people
لأنه شعر بالحاجة إلى التواجد بين الناس
or a long time, he had lived in the forests
أو لفترة طويلة، كان يعيش في الغابات
for first time in a long time he slept under a roof
لأول مرة منذ فترة طويلة نام تحت سقف
Before the city was a beautifully fenced garden
قبل أن تكون المدينة عبارة عن حديقة مسيجة بشكل جميل
the traveller came across a small group of servants
صادف المسافر مجموعة صغيرة من الخدم

the servants were carrying baskets of fruit
وكان الخدم يحملون سلال الفاكهة
four servants were carrying an ornamental sedan-chair
كان أربعة من الخدم يحملون كرسيًا مزخرفًا
on this chair sat a woman, the mistress
على هذا الكرسي جلست امرأة، العشيقة
she was on red pillows under a colourful canopy
كانت على وسائد حمراء تحت مظلة ملونة
Siddhartha stopped at the entrance to the pleasure-garden
توقف سيدهارتا عند مدخل حديقة المتعة
and he watched the parade go by
وشاهد العرض يمر
he saw saw the servants and the maids
لقد رأى الخدم والخادمات
he saw the baskets and the sedan-chair
رأى السلال وكرسي المحفة
and he saw the lady on the chair
ورأى السيدة على الكرسي
Under her black hair he saw a very delicate face
تحت شعرها الأسود رأى وجهًا رقيقًا للغاية
a bright red mouth, like a freshly cracked fig
فم أحمر لامع، مثل التين الطازج المتشقق
eyebrows which were well tended and painted in a high arch
الحواجب التي تم العناية بها جيدًا ورسمها بقوس مرتفع
they were smart and watchful dark eyes
لقد كانوا أذكياء وذوي عيون داكنة يقظة
a clear, tall neck rose from a green and golden garment
رقبة طويلة وواضحة تبرز من ثوب أخضر وذهبي
her hands were resting, long and thin
كانت يداها مستريحتين، طويلتين ورقيقتين
she had wide golden bracelets over her wrists
كانت ترتدي أساور ذهبية عريضة حول معصميها
Siddhartha saw how beautiful she was, and his heart rejoiced
رأى سيدهارتا مدى جمالها، وفرح قلبه

He bowed deeply, when the sedan-chair came closer
انحنى بعمق عندما اقترب الكرسي المتحرك
straightening up again, he looked at the fair, charming face
استقام مرة أخرى، ونظر إلى الوجه الجميل الساحر
he read her smart eyes with the high arcs
قرأ عينيها الذكيتين بالأقواس العالية
he breathed in a fragrance of something he did not know
استنشق رائحة شيء لم يعرفه
With a smile, the beautiful woman nodded for a moment
مع ابتسامة، أومأت المرأة الجميلة برأسها للحظة
then she disappeared into the garden
ثم اختفت في الحديقة
and then the servants disappeared as well
ثم اختفى الخدم أيضا
"I am entering this city with a charming omen" Siddhartha thought
"سأدخل هذه المدينة بفأل ساحر" فكر سيدهارتا
He instantly felt drawn into the garden
لقد شعر على الفور بالانجذاب إلى الحديقة
but he thought about his situation
لكنه فكر في وضعه
he became aware of how the servants and maids had looked at him
لقد أدرك كيف نظر إليه الخدم والخادمات
they thought him despicable, distrustful, and rejected him
اعتبروه حقيرًا، وغير جدير بالثقة، ورفضوه
"I am still a Samana" he thought
"أنا لا أزال سامانا" كان يفكر
"I am still an ascetic and beggar"
"أنا لا أزال زاهدًا ومتسولًا"
"I must not remain like this"
"لا يجب أن أبقى هكذا"
"I will not be able to enter the garden like this," he laughed
"لن أتمكن من دخول الحديقة بهذه الطريقة" ضحك
he asked the next person who came along the path about the garden

- 95 -

سأل الشخص التالي الذي جاء على طول الطريق عن الحديقة
and he asked for the name of the woman
وسأل عن اسم المرأة
he was told that this was the garden of Kamala, the famous courtesan
قيل له أن هذه حديقة كامالا، العاهرة الشهيرة
and he was told that she also owned a house in the city
وقيل لها أنها تملك بيتاً في المدينة أيضاً
Then, he entered the city with a goal
ثم دخل المدينة بهدف
Pursuing his goal, he allowed the city to suck him in
في سعيه لتحقيق هدفه، سمح للمدينة أن تستحوذ عليه
he drifted through the flow of the streets
لقد انجرف عبر تدفق الشوارع
he stood still on the squares in the city
كان واقفا في ساحات المدينة
he rested on the stairs of stone by the river
كان يستريح على الدرج الحجري بجانب النهر
When the evening came, he made friends with a barber's assistant
عندما جاء المساء أصبح صديقا لمساعد الحلاق
he had seen him working in the shade of an arch
لقد رآه يعمل في ظل قوس
and he found him again praying in a temple of Vishnu
فوجدته يصلي مرة أخرى في معبد فيشنو
he told about stories of Vishnu and the Lakshmi
لقد روى قصصًا عن فيشنو ولاكشمي
Among the boats by the river, he slept this night
بين القوارب على النهر نام هذه الليلة
Siddhartha came to him before the first customers came into his shop
جاء سيدهارثا إليه قبل أن يأتي العملاء الأوائل إلى متجره
he had the barber's assistant shave his beard and cut his hair
لقد طلب من مساعد الحلاق أن يحلق لحيته ويقص شعره
he combed his hair and anointed it with fine oil
فقام بتمشيط شعره ودهنه بزيت ناعم

Then he went to take his bath in the river
ثم ذهب للاستحمام في النهر

late in the afternoon, beautiful Kamala approached her garden
في وقت متأخر من بعد الظهر، اقتربت كامالا الجميلة من حديقتها

Siddhartha was standing at the entrance again
كان سيدهارثا واقفًا عند المدخل مرة أخرى

he made a bow and received the courtesan's greeting
انحنى وتلقى تحية العاهرة

he got the attention of one of the servant
لقد لفت انتباه أحد الخدم

he asked him to inform his mistress
طلب منه أن يخبر عشيقته

"a young Brahman wishes to talk to her"
"شاب براهماني يرغب في التحدث معها"

After a while, the servant returned
وبعد فترة عاد الخادم

the servant asked Siddhartha to follow him
طلب الخادم من سيدهارثا أن يتبعه

Siddhartha followed the servant into a pavilion
تبع سيدهارتا الخادم إلى الجناح

here Kamala was lying on a couch
هنا كانت كامالا مستلقية على الأريكة

and the servant left him alone with her
وتركته الخادمة معها وحدها

"Weren't you also standing out there yesterday, greeting me?" asked Kamala
"ألم تكن واقفًا هناك أيضًا بالأمس، لتحييني؟" سألت كامالا

"It's true that I've already seen and greeted you yesterday"
"صحيح أنني رأيتك واستقبلتك بالأمس"

"But didn't you yesterday wear a beard, and long hair?"
"ولكن ألم تكن بالأمس ترتدي لحية وشعرًا طويلاً؟"

"and was there not dust in your hair?"
"وهل كان في شعرك غبار؟"

"You have observed well, you have seen everything"

"لقد لاحظت جيدا، لقد رأيت كل شيء"

"You have seen Siddhartha, the son of a Brahman"

"لقد رأيت سيدهارتا، ابن البراهمي"

"the Brahman who has left his home to become a Samana"

"البراهمان الذي ترك منزله ليصبح سامانا"

"the Brahman who has been a Samana for three years"

"البراهمان الذي كان سامانا لمدة ثلاث سنوات"

"But now, I have left that path and came into this city"

"لكن الآن تركت هذا الطريق وجئت إلى هذه المدينة"

"and the first one I met, even before I had entered the city, was you"

"وأول شخص قابلته، حتى قبل أن أدخل المدينة، كان أنت"

"To say this, I have come to you, oh Kamala!"

"لأقول هذا، لقد أتيت إليك، يا كامالا!"

"before, Siddhartha addressed all woman with his eyes to the ground"

"قبل ذلك، كان سيدهارتا يخاطب كل النساء بعينيه إلى الأرض"

"You are the first woman whom I address otherwise"

"أنت أول امرأة أخاطبها بطريقة أخرى"

"Never again do I want to turn my eyes to the ground"

"لن أرغب أبدًا في تحويل عيني إلى الأرض مرة أخرى"

"I won't turn when I'm coming across a beautiful woman"

"لن أتحول عندما أقابل امرأة جميلة"

Kamala smiled and played with her fan of peacocks' feathers

ابتسمت كامالا ولعبت بمروحة ريش الطاووس الخاصة بها

"And only to tell me this, Siddhartha has come to me?"

"وفقط ليخبرني بهذا، جاء سيدهارتا إلي؟"

"To tell you this and to thank you for being so beautiful"

"لأخبرك بهذا وأشكرك على كونك جميلاً للغاية"

"I would like to ask you to be my friend and teacher"

"أود أن أطلب منك أن تكون صديقي ومعلمي"

"for I know nothing yet of that art which you have mastered"

"لأني لا أعرف شيئًا بعد عن هذا الفن الذي أتقنته"

At this, Kamala laughed aloud

عند هذا، ضحكت كامالا بصوت عالٍ

"Never before this has happened to me, my friend"

"لم يحدث لي هذا من قبل يا صديقي".

"a Samana from the forest came to me and wanted to learn from me!"

"جاءتني سامانا من الغابة وأرادت أن تتعلم مني!"

"Never before this has happened to me"

"لم يحدث لي هذا من قبل"

"a Samana came to me with long hair and an old, torn loincloth!"

"جاءتني سامانا ذات شعر طويل ومنزر قديم ممزق!"

"Many young men come to me"

"يأتي إليّ العديد من الشباب"

"and there are also sons of Brahmans among them"

"وهناك أيضًا أبناء البراهمة بينهم"

"but they come in beautiful clothes"

"ولكنهم يأتون بملابس جميلة"

"they come in fine shoes"

"إنهم يأتون بأحذية جميلة"

"they have perfume in their hair

"لديهم عطر في شعرهم"

"and they have money in their pouches"

"وعندهم أموال في جيوبهم"

"This is how the young men are like, who come to me"

"هكذا يكون الشباب الذين يأتون إلي"

Spoke Siddhartha, "Already I am starting to learn from you"

قال سيدهارتا "لقد بدأت بالفعل في التعلم منك"

"Even yesterday, I was already learning"

"حتى بالأمس كنت أتعلم بالفعل"

"I have already taken off my beard"

"لقد خلعت لحيتي بالفعل"

"I have combed the hair"

"لقد قمت بتمشيط الشعر"

"and I have oil in my hair"

"و عندي زيت في شعري"

"There is little which is still missing in me"

"هناك القليل الذي لا يزال مفقودًا في داخلي"

"oh excellent one, fine clothes, fine shoes, money in my pouch"

"يا له من أمر رائع، ملابس جميلة، أحذية جميلة، أموال في حقيبتي"

"You shall know Siddhartha has set harder goals for himself"

"يجب أن تعرف أن سيدهارثا قد حدد لنفسه أهدافًا أصعب"

"and he has reached these goals"

"وقد وصل إلى هذه الأهداف"

"How shouldn't I reach that goal?"

"كيف لا أحقق هذا الهدف؟"

"the goal which I have set for myself yesterday"

"الهدف الذي حددته لنفسي بالأمس"

"to be your friend and to learn the joys of love from you"

"أن أكون صديقك وأن أتعلم منك أفراح الحب"

"You'll see that I'll learn quickly, Kamala"

"سترى أنني سأتعلم بسرعة، كامالا"

"I have already learned harder things than what you're supposed to teach me"

"لقد تعلمت بالفعل أشياء أصعب مما يفترض أن تعلميني إياه"

"And now let's get to it"

"والآن دعونا نصل إلى ذلك"

"You aren't satisfied with Siddhartha as he is?"

"أنت لست راضيا عن سيدهارثا كما هو؟"

"with oil in his hair, but without clothes"

"مع الزيت في شعره، ولكن بدون ملابس"

"Siddhartha without shoes, without money"

"سيدهارتا بلا حذاء، بلا مال"

Laughing, Kamala exclaimed, "No, my dear"

ضاحكة، صاحت كامالا، "لا يا عزيزتي"

"he doesn't satisfy me, yet"

"إنه لا يرضيني بعد"

"Clothes are what he must have"

"الملابس هي ما يجب أن يمتلكه"

"pretty clothes, and shoes is what he needs"

"الملابس الجميلة والأحذية هي ما يحتاجه"

"pretty shoes, and lots of money in his pouch"

"حذاء جميل، والكثير من المال في حقيبته"

"and he must have gifts for Kamala"

"ولابد أن يكون لديه هدايا لكامالا"

"Do you know it now, Samana from the forest?"

"هل تعرفين الآن يا سامانا من الغابة؟"

"Did you mark my words?"

هل لاحظت كلماتي؟

"Yes, I have marked your words," Siddhartha exclaimed

"نعم، لقد قمت بتمييز كلماتك"، صاح سيدهارثا

"How should I not mark words which are coming from such a mouth!"

"كيف لا أستطيع تمييز الكلمات التي تأتي من مثل هذا الفم!"

"Your mouth is like a freshly cracked fig, Kamala"

"فمك مثل تينة متشققة حديثًا، كامالا"

"My mouth is red and fresh as well"

"فمي أحمر ومنعش أيضًا"

"it will be a suitable match for yours, you'll see"

"سيكون مناسبًا لك، سترى"

"But tell me, beautiful Kamala"

"ولكن أخبريني يا كامالا الجميلة"

"aren't you at all afraid of the Samana from the forest""

"ألا تخاف على الإطلاق من سامانا من الغابة؟"

"the Samana who has come to learn how to make love"

"سامانا التي جاءت لتتعلم كيفية ممارسة الحب"

"Whatever for should I be afraid of a Samana?"

"لماذا يجب أن أخاف من سامانا؟"

"a stupid Samana from the forest"

"سامانا غبية من الغابة"

"a Samana who is coming from the jackals"

"سامانا قادمة من الذئاب"

"a Samana who doesn't even know yet what women are?"

"سامانا التي لا تعرف بعد ما هي النساء؟"

"Oh, he's strong, the Samana"

"أوه، إنه قوي، سامانا"

"and he isn't afraid of anything"

"وهو لا يخاف من أي شيء"

"He could force you, beautiful girl"

"إنه يستطيع أن يجبرك، يا فتاة جميلة"

"He could kidnap you and hurt you"

"كان بإمكانه اختطافك وإيذائك"

"No, Samana, I am not afraid of this"

"لا، سامانا، أنا لست خائفة من هذا"

"Did any Samana or Brahman ever fear someone might come and grab him?"

"هل خاف أي سامانا أو براهمان من أن يأتي أحد ويخطفه؟"

"could he fear someone steals his learning?

"هل يخاف من أن يسرق أحد تعليمه؟"

"could anyone take his religious devotion"

"هل يمكن لأحد أن يأخذ تفانيه الديني"

"is it possible to take his depth of thought?

"هل من الممكن أن نأخذ عمق تفكيره؟"

"No, because these things are his very own"

"لا، لأن هذه الأشياء تخصه وحده"

"he would only give away the knowledge he is willing to give"

"إنه لن يعطي إلا المعرفة التي يرغب في إعطائها"

"he would only give to those he is willing to give to"

"إنه يعطي فقط لأولئك الذين يرغب في إعطائهم"

"precisely like this it is also with Kamala"

"تمامًا كما هو الحال أيضًا مع كامالا"

"and it is the same way with the pleasures of love"

"وهكذا الحال مع ملذات الحب"

"Beautiful and red is Kamala's mouth," answered Siddhartha

أجاب سيدهارتا: "فم كامالا جميل وأحمر اللون".

"but don't try to kiss it against Kamala's will"

"ولكن لا تحاول تقبيله ضد رغبة كامالا"

"because you will not obtain a single drop of sweetness from it"

"لأنك لن تحصل على قطرة واحدة من الحلاوة منه"

"You are learning easily, Siddhartha"

"أنت تتعلم بسهولة، سيدهارتا"

"you should also learn this"

"يجب عليك أن تتعلم هذا أيضًا"
"love can be obtained by begging, buying"
"يمكن الحصول على الحب بالتسول والشراء"
"you can receive it as a gift"
"يمكنك الحصول عليه كهدية"
"or you can find it in the street"
"أو يمكنك العثور عليه في الشارع"
"but love cannot be stolen"
"ولكن الحب لا يمكن سرقته"
"In this, you have come up with the wrong path"
"لقد أتيت في هذا بالطريق الخطأ"
"it would be a pity if you would want to tackle love in such a wrong manner"
"سيكون من المؤسف أن ترغب في التعامل مع الحب بهذه الطريقة الخاطئة"

Siddhartha bowed with a smile
انحنى سيدهارثا بابتسامة
"It would be a pity, Kamala, you are so right"
"سيكون من المؤسف، كامالا، أنت على حق تمامًا"
"It would be such a great pity"
"سيكون من المؤسف حقًا"
"No, I shall not lose a single drop of sweetness from your mouth"
"لا، لن أفقد قطرة واحدة من الحلاوة من فمك"
"nor shall you lose sweetness from my mouth"
"ولا تزول الحلاوة من فمي"
"So it is agreed. Siddhartha will return"
"لقد اتفقنا على أن سيدهارثا سوف يعود"
"Siddhartha will return once he has what he still lacks"
"سيعود سيدهارثا عندما يحصل على ما ينقصه"
"he will come back with clothes, shoes, and money"
"سوف يعود بالملابس والأحذية والمال"
"But speak, lovely Kamala, couldn't you still give me one small advice?"
"لكن تحدثي يا كامالا الجميلة، هل لا يزال بإمكانك أن تقدمي لي نصيحة صغيرة؟"

"Give you an advice? Why not?"

"أعطيك نصيحة؟ لماذا لا؟"

"Who wouldn't like to give advice to a poor, ignorant Samana?"

"من لا يرغب في تقديم النصيحة لسامانا الفقيرة والجاهلة؟"

"Dear Kamala, where I should go to find these three things most quickly?"

"عزيزتي كامالا، أين يجب أن أذهب للعثور على هذه الأشياء الثلاثة بسرعة؟"

"Friend, many would like to know this"

"صديقي، كثيرون يرغبون في معرفة هذا"

"You must do what you've learned and ask for money"

"يجب عليك أن تفعل ما تعلمته وتطلب المال"

"There is no other way for a poor man to obtain money"

"لا توجد طريقة أخرى للرجل الفقير للحصول على المال"

"What might you be able to do?"

"ماذا قد تكون قادرا على فعله؟"

"I can think. I can wait. I can fast" said Siddhartha

"أستطيع أن أفكر. أستطيع أن أنتظر. أستطيع أن أصوم" قال سيدهارتا

"Nothing else?" asked Kamala

"لا شيء آخر؟" سألت كامالا

"yes, I can also write poetry"

"نعم، أستطيع أيضًا كتابة الشعر"

"Would you like to give me a kiss for a poem?"

"هل ترغب في أن تعطيني قبلة مقابل قصيدة؟"

"I would like to, if I like your poem"

"أود ذلك إذا أعجبتني قصيدتك"

"What would be its title?"

"ما هو عنوانه؟"

Siddhartha spoke, after he had thought about it for a moment

تحدث سيدهارتا، بعد أن فكر في الأمر للحظة

"Into her shady garden stepped the pretty Kamala"

"دخلت كامالا الجميلة إلى حديقتها المظللة"

"At the garden's entrance stood the brown Samana"

"عند مدخل الحديقة وقفت شجرة سامانا البنية"

"Deeply, seeing the lotus's blossom, Bowed that man"
"عندما رأى ذلك الرجل زهرة اللوتس، انحنى بعمق"
"and smiling, Kamala thanked him"
"و ابتسمت كامالا وشكرته"
"More lovely, thought the young man, than offerings for gods"
"أكثر روعة، فكر الشاب، من تقديم القرابين للآلهة"
Kamala clapped her hands so loud that the golden bracelets clanged
صفقت كامالا بيديها بصوتٍ عالٍ حتى رنّت الأساور الذهبية
"Beautiful are your verses, oh brown Samana"
"جميلة هي أبياتك يا سمر سمر"
"and truly, I'm losing nothing when I'm giving you a kiss for them"
"والحقيقة أنني لا أخسر شيئًا عندما أقدم لك قبلة من أجلهم"
She beckoned him with her eyes
أشارت إليه بعينيها
he tilted his head so that his face touched hers
أمال رأسه حتى لامس وجهه وجهها
and he placed his mouth on her mouth
ووضع فمه على فمها
the mouth which was like a freshly cracked fig
الفم الذي كان مثل تينة متشققة حديثًا
For a long time, Kamala kissed him
لفترة طويلة، قبلته كامالا
and with a deep astonishment Siddhartha felt how she taught him
وبدهشة عميقة شعر سيدهارثا كيف علمته
he felt how wise she was
لقد شعر بمدى حكمتها
he felt how she controlled him
لقد شعر كيف أنها تسيطر عليه
he felt how she rejected him
لقد شعر كيف رفضته
he felt how she lured him
لقد شعر كيف أنها أغرته

and he felt how there were to be more kisses
وشعر أنه سيكون هناك المزيد من القبلات
every kiss was different from the others
كل قبلة كانت مختلفة عن الأخرى
he was still, when he received the kisses
كان ساكنًا عندما تلقى القبلات
Breathing deeply, he remained standing where he was
تنفس بعمق وظل واقفا حيث كان
he was astonished like a child about the things worth learning
لقد اندهش مثل الطفل من الأشياء التي تستحق التعلم
the knowledge revealed itself before his eyes
لقد ظهرت المعرفة أمام عينيه
"Very beautiful are your verses" exclaimed Kamala
"إن أبياتك جميلة جدًا" هتفت كامالا
"if I were rich, I would give you pieces of gold for them"
"لو كنت غنيًا، لأعطيتك قطعًا من الذهب مقابلها"
"But it will be difficult for you to earn enough money with verses"
"ولكن سيكون من الصعب عليك أن تكسب ما يكفي من المال بالآيات"
"because you need a lot of money, if you want to be Kamala's friend"
"لأنك تحتاج إلى الكثير من المال، إذا كنت تريد أن تكون صديقًا لكامالا"
"The way you're able to kiss, Kamala!" stammered Siddhartha
"الطريقة التي يمكنك بها التقبيل، كامالا!" تلعثم سيدهارتا
"Yes, this I am able to do"
"نعم، هذا ما أستطيع فعله"
"therefore I do not lack clothes, shoes, bracelets"
"لذلك لا ينقصني الملابس والأحذية والأساور"
"I have all the beautiful things"
"لدي كل الأشياء الجميلة"
"But what will become of you?"
"ولكن ماذا سيحدث لك؟"
"Aren't you able to do anything else?"
"هل أنت غير قادر على فعل أي شيء آخر؟"

"can you do more than think, fast, and make poetry?"
"هل تستطيع أن تفعل أكثر من التفكير، والسرعة، وتأليف الشعر؟"

"I also know the sacrificial songs" said Siddhartha
"أنا أعرف أيضًا أغاني التضحية" قال سيدهارثا

"but I do not want to sing those songs anymore"
"لكنني لا أريد أن أغني هذه الأغاني بعد الآن"

"I also know how to make magic spells"
"أنا أعرف أيضًا كيفية صنع التعاويذ السحرية"

"but I do not want to speak them anymore"
"لكنني لا أريد التحدث بها بعد الآن"

"I have read the scriptures"
"لقد قرأت الكتب المقدسة"

"Stop!" Kamala interrupted him
"توقف!" قاطعته كامالا

"You're able to read and write?"
"هل أنت قادر على القراءة والكتابة؟"

"Certainly, I can do this, many people can"
"بالتأكيد، أستطيع أن أفعل هذا، كثير من الناس يستطيعون ذلك"

"Most people can't," Kamala replied
"معظم الناس لا يستطيعون ذلك" أجابت كامالا

"I am also one of those who can't do it"
"أنا أيضًا من هؤلاء الذين لا يستطيعون فعل ذلك"

"It is very good that you're able to read and write"
"من الجيد جدًا أن تتمكن من القراءة والكتابة"

"you will also find use for the magic spells"
"ستجد أيضًا استخدامًا للتعاويذ السحرية"

In this moment, a maid came running in
في هذه اللحظة، جاءت خادمة راكضة

she whispered a message into her mistress's ear
همست برسالة في أذن سيدتها

"There's a visitor for me" exclaimed Kamala
"هناك زائر لي" هتفت كامالا

"Hurry and get yourself away, Siddhartha"
"أسرع وابتعد عن نفسك يا سيدهارثا"

"nobody may see you in here, remember this!"
"لا يمكن لأحد رؤيتك هنا، تذكر هذا!"

"Tomorrow, I'll see you again"

"غدا سأراك مرة أخرى"

Kamala ordered her maid to give Siddhartha white garments

أمرت كامالا خادمتها بإعطاء سيدهارثا ملابس بيضاء

and then Siddhartha found himself being dragged away by the maid

ثم وجد سيدهارثا نفسه يُجر بعيدًا بواسطة الخادمة

he was brought into a garden-house out of sight of any paths

تم نقله إلى منزل في حديقة بعيدًا عن أنظار أي مسارات

then he was led into the bushes of the garden

ثم تم اقتياده إلى شجيرات الحديقة

he was urged to get himself out of the garden as soon as possible

وحث على الخروج من الحديقة في أقرب وقت ممكن

and he was told he must not be seen

وقيل له أنه لا ينبغي أن يُرى

he did as he had been told

لقد فعل كما قيل له

he was accustomed to the forest

لقد اعتاد على الغابة

so he managed to get out without making a sound

لذلك تمكن من الخروج دون إصدار أي صوت

he returned to the city carrying the rolled up garments under his arm

وعاد إلى المدينة وهو يحمل الثياب الملفوفة تحت إبطه

At the inn, where travellers stay, he positioned himself by the door

في النزل حيث يقيم المسافرون، وضع نفسه عند الباب

without words he asked for food

بدون كلمات طلب الطعام

without a word he accepted a piece of rice-cake

دون أن ينبس ببنت شفة، قبل قطعة من كعكة الأرز.

he thought about how he had always begged

فكر في كيف كان يتوسل دائمًا

"Perhaps as soon as tomorrow I will ask no one for food anymore"

"ربما بحلول الغد لن أطلب الطعام من أحد بعد الآن"

Suddenly, pride flared up in him

فجأة اشتعل الكبرياء بداخله

He was no Samana any more

لم يعد سامانا بعد الآن

it was no longer appropriate for him to beg for food

لم يعد من المناسب له أن يتسوّل الطعام

he gave the rice-cake to a dog

أعطى كعكة الأرز لكلب

and that night he remained without food

وظل تلك الليلة بلا طعام

Siddhartha thought to himself about the city

فكر سيدهارتا في نفسه بشأن المدينة

"Simple is the life which people lead in this world"

"إن الحياة التي يعيشها الناس في هذا العالم بسيطة"

"this life presents no difficulties"

"هذه الحياة لا تقدم أي صعوبات"

"Everything was difficult and toilsome when I was a Samana"

"كان كل شيء صعبًا ومضنيًا عندما كنت سامانا"

"as a Samana everything was hopeless"

"كسامانا كان كل شيء ميؤوسًا منه"

"but now everything is easy"

"ولكن الآن كل شيء أصبح سهلا"

"it is easy like the lesson in kissing from Kamala"

"إنه أمر سهل مثل درس التقبيل من كامالا"

"I need clothes and money, nothing else"

"أحتاج إلى ملابس وأموال، لا شيء آخر"

"these goals are small and achievable"

"هذه الأهداف صغيرة وقابلة للتحقيق"

"such goals won't make a person lose any sleep"

"إن مثل هذه الأهداف لن تجعل الإنسان يفقد أي قدر من النوم"

the next day he returned to Kamala's house

وفي اليوم التالي عاد إلى منزل كامالا

"Things are working out well" she called out to him

"الأمور تسير على ما يرام" صرخت عليه

"They are expecting you at Kamaswami's"

"إنهم ينتظرونك في كاماسوامي"

"he is the richest merchant of the city"

"إنه أغنى تاجر في المدينة"

"If he likes you, he'll accept you into his service"

"إذا كان يحبك، فسوف يقبلك في خدمته"

"but you must be smart, brown Samana"

"لكن يجب أن تكوني ذكية يا سمرا سامانا"

"I had others tell him about you"

"لقد طلبت من الآخرين أن يخبروه عنك"

"Be polite towards him, he is very powerful"

"كن مهذبًا معه، فهو قوي جدًا"

"But I warn you, don't be too modest!"

"ولكنني أحذرك، لا تكن متواضعا للغاية!"

"I do not want you to become his servant"

"لا أريدك أن تصبح خادمه"

"you shall become his equal"

"سوف تصبح مساوياً له"

"or else I won't be satisfied with you"

"وإلا فلن أكون راضيا عنك"

"Kamaswami is starting to get old and lazy"

"بدأ كاماسوامي يتقدم في السن ويصبح كسولًا"

"If he likes you, he'll entrust you with a lot"

"إذا كان يحبك، فسوف يأتمنك على الكثير"

Siddhartha thanked her and laughed

شكرها سيدهارثا وضحك

she found out that he had not eaten

اكتشفت أنه لم يأكل

so she sent him bread and fruits

فأرسلت له الخبز والفواكه

"You've been lucky" she said when they parted

"لقد كنت محظوظًا" قالت عندما افترقا

"I'm opening one door after another for you"

"I'll open one door after another for you"

"أنا أفتح لك بابًا تلو الآخر"

"How come? Do you have a spell?"

"كيف ذلك؟ هل لديك تعويذة؟"

"I told you I knew how to think, to wait, and to fast"

"لقد قلت لك أنني أعرف كيف أفكر، وكيف أنتظر، وكيف أصوم"

"but you thought this was of no use"

"لكنك اعتقدت أن هذا لا فائدة منه"

"But it is useful for many things"

"ولكنه مفيد لأشياء كثيرة"

"Kamala, you'll see that the stupid Samanas are good at learning"

"كامالا، سوف ترين أن السامانا الأغبياء جيدون في التعلم"

"you'll see they are able to do many pretty things in the forest"

"ستجد أنهم قادرون على القيام بالعديد من الأشياء الجميلة في الغابة"

"things which the likes of you aren't capable of"

"الأشياء التي لا يستطيع أمثالك القيام بها"

"The day before yesterday, I was still a shaggy beggar"

"قبل أمس، كنت لا أزال متسولًا أشعثًا"

"as recently as yesterday I have kissed Kamala"

"لقد قمت بتقبيل كامالا مؤخرًا بالأمس"

"and soon I'll be a merchant and have money"

"وسأكون تاجرًا قريبًا وسأحصل على المال"

"and I'll have all those things you insist upon"

"وسوف أحصل على كل تلك الأشياء التي تصر عليها"

"Well yes," she admitted, "but where would you be without me?"

"حسنًا، نعم"، اعترفت، "ولكن أين ستكون بدوني؟"

"What would you be, if Kamala wasn't helping you?"

ماذا كنت لتكون إذا لم تساعدك كامالا؟

"Dear Kamala" said Siddhartha

"عزيزتي كامالا" قال سيدهارثا

and he straightened up to his full height

واستقام إلى كامل طوله

"when I came to you into your garden, I did the first step"

"عندما أتيت إليك إلى حديقتك، قمت بالخطوة الأولى"

"It was my resolution to learn love from this most beautiful woman"

"لقد كان قراري أن أتعلم الحب من هذه المرأة الجميلة"

"that moment I had made this resolution"

"في تلك اللحظة اتخذت هذا القرار"

"and I knew I would carry it out"

"وكنت أعلم أنني سأنفذ ذلك"

"I knew that you would help me"

"كنت أعلم أنك ستساعدني"

"at your first glance at the entrance of the garden I already knew it"

"من أول نظرة لك على مدخل الحديقة كنت أعرف ذلك بالفعل"

"But what if I hadn't been willing?" asked Kamala

"ولكن ماذا لو لم أكن على استعداد؟" سألت كامالا

"You were willing" replied Siddhartha

"لقد كنت على استعداد" أجاب سيدهارثا

"When you throw a rock into water, it takes the fastest course to the bottom"

"عندما ترمي حجرًا في الماء، فإنه يأخذ أسرع مسار إلى القاع"

"This is how it is when Siddhartha has a goal"

"هكذا يكون الأمر عندما يكون لدى سيدهارثا هدف"

"Siddhartha does nothing; he waits, he thinks, he fasts"

"سيدهارتا لا يفعل شيئًا؛ فهو ينتظر، ويفكر، ويصوم"

"but he passes through the things of the world like a rock through water"

"لكنّه يمرّ بأشياء العالم كما يمرّ الصخرة في الماء"

"he passed through the water without doing anything"

"لقد مر عبر الماء دون أن يفعل أي شيء"

"he is drawn to the bottom of the water"

"انه ينجذب إلى قاع الماء"

"he lets himself fall to the bottom of the water"

"يسمح لنفسه بالسقوط في قاع الماء"

"His goal attracts him towards it"

"هدفه يجذبه نحوه"

"he doesn't let anything enter his soul which might oppose the goal"

"لا يسمح لأي شيء أن يدخل روحه مما قد يعارض الهدف"

"This is what Siddhartha has learned among the Samanas"

"هذا ما تعلمه سيدهارثا بين الساماناس"

"This is what fools call magic"

"هذا ما يسميه الحمقى سحرًا"

"they think it is done by daemons"

"يعتقدون أن هذا يتم بواسطة الشياطين"

"but nothing is done by daemons"

"ولكن لا يتم فعل أي شيء بواسطة الشياطين"

"there are no daemons in this world"

"لا يوجد شياطين في هذا العالم"

"Everyone can perform magic, should they choose to"

"يمكن لأي شخص أن يمارس السحر، إذا اختار ذلك"

"everyone can reach his goals if he is able to think"

"كل شخص يستطيع الوصول إلى أهدافه إذا كان قادرًا على التفكير"

"everyone can reach his goals if he is able to wait"

"كل شخص يستطيع الوصول إلى أهدافه إذا كان قادرًا على الانتظار"

"everyone can reach his goals if he is able to fast"

"كل إنسان يستطيع أن يصل إلى أهدافه إذا استطاع أن يصوم"

Kamala listened to him; she loved his voice

استمعت كامالا إليه، لقد أحبت صوته

she loved the look from his eyes

لقد احبت النظرة من عينيه

"Perhaps it is as you say, friend"

"ربما يكون الأمر كما تقول يا صديقي"

"But perhaps there is another explanation"

"ولكن ربما هناك تفسير آخر"

"Siddhartha is a handsome man"

"سيدهارتا رجل وسيم"

"his glance pleases the women"

"نظرته تسعد النساء"

"good fortune comes towards him because of this"

"يأتيه الحظ السعيد بسبب هذا"

With one kiss, Siddhartha bid his farewell

بقبلة واحدة، ودع سيدهارثا

"I wish that it should be this way, my teacher"

"أتمنى أن يكون الأمر هكذا يا معلمي"
"I wish that my glance shall please you"
"أتمنى أن تنال نظراتي إعجابك"
"I wish that that you always bring me good fortune"
"أتمنى أن تجلب لي الحظ السعيد دائمًا"

With the Childlike People
مع الناس الطفوليين

Siddhartha went to Kamaswami the merchant
ذهب سيدهارثا إلى كاماسوامي التاجر

he was directed into a rich house
تم توجيهه إلى منزل غني

servants led him between precious carpets into a chamber
قاده الخدم بين السجاد الثمين إلى غرفة

in the chamber was where he awaited the master of the house
في الغرفة كان ينتظر سيد المنزل

Kamaswami entered swiftly into the room
دخل كاماسوامي بسرعة إلى الغرفة

he was a smoothly moving man
لقد كان رجلاً يتحرك بسلاسة

he had very gray hair and very intelligent, cautious eyes
كان شعره رماديًا جدًا وكان لديه عيون ذكية وحذرة للغاية

and he had a greedy mouth
وكان له فم جشع

Politely, the host and the guest greeted one another
بكل أدب، استقبل المضيف والضيف بعضهما البعض

"I have been told that you were a Brahman" the merchant began
"لقد قيل لي أنك كنت براهمانيًا" بدأ التاجر

"I have been told that you are a learned man"
"لقد قيل لي أنك رجل متعلم"

"and I have also been told something else"
"ولقد قيل لي أيضًا شيئًا آخر"

"you seek to be in the service of a merchant"
"أنت تسعى إلى أن تكون في خدمة التاجر"

"Might you have become destitute, Brahman, so that you seek to serve?"
"هل كان من الممكن أن تصبح معدمًا، يا براهمان، حتى تسعى إلى الخدمة؟"

"No," said Siddhartha, "I have not become destitute"

"لا،" قال سيدهارثا، "لم أصبح معدمًا"
"nor have I ever been destitute" added Siddhartha
"ولم أكن معدمًا أبدًا" أضاف سيدهارتا
"You should know that I'm coming from the Samanas"
"يجب أن تعرف أنني قادم من ساماناس"
"I have lived with them for a long time"
"لقد عشت معهم لفترة طويلة"
"you are coming from the Samanas"
"أنت قادم من ساماناس"
"how could you be anything but destitute?"
"كيف يمكنك أن تكون أي شيء إلا فقيرًا؟"
"Aren't the Samanas entirely without possessions?"
"أليس أهل سامانا خاليين تمامًا من الممتلكات؟"
"I am without possessions, if that is what you mean" said Siddhartha
"أنا بلا ممتلكات، إذا كان هذا ما تقصده" قال سيدهارتا
"But I am without possessions voluntarily"
"لكنني بلا ممتلكات طوعا"
"and therefore I am not destitute"
"ولذلك أنا لست معدمًا"
"But what are you planning to live from, being without possessions?"
"ولكن ما الذي تخطط للعيش منه، وأنت بلا ممتلكات؟"
"I haven't thought of this yet, sir"
"لم أفكر في هذا بعد يا سيدي"
"For more than three years, I have been without possessions"
"منذ أكثر من ثلاث سنوات، كنت بلا ممتلكات"
"and I have never thought about of what I should live"
"ولم أفكر قط في ما ينبغي أن أعيشه"
"So you've lived of the possessions of others"
"لقد عشت من ممتلكات الآخرين"
"Presumable, this is how it is?"
"من المفترض أن هذا هو الحال؟"
"Well, merchants also live of what other people own"
"حسنًا، التجار أيضًا يعيشون على ما يملكه الآخرون"
"Well said," granted the merchant

- 116 -

"حسنًا" قال التاجر

"But he wouldn't take anything from another person for nothing"

"لكن لن يأخذ أي شيء من شخص آخر مجانًا"

"he would give his merchandise in return" said Kamaswami

"سيعطي بضاعته في المقابل" قال كاماسوامي

"So it seems to be indeed"

"يبدو أن الأمر كذلك بالفعل"

"Everyone takes, everyone gives, such is life"

"الجميع يأخذ، والجميع يعطي، هذه هي الحياة"

"But if you don't mind me asking, I have a question"

"ولكن إذا كنت لا تمانع في سؤالي، لدي سؤال"

"being without possessions, what would you like to give?"

"إذا كنت لا تمتلك أي ممتلكات، ماذا تحب أن تعطي؟"

"Everyone gives what he has"

"كل واحد يعطي ما لديه"

"The warrior gives strength"

"المحارب يعطي القوة"

"the merchant gives merchandise"

"التاجر يعطي البضاعة"

"the teacher gives teachings"

"المعلم يعطي تعاليم"

"the farmer gives rice"

"المزارع يعطي الأرز"

"the fisher gives fish"

"الصياد يعطي السمك"

"Yes indeed. And what is it that you've got to give?"

"نعم بالفعل. وما الذي لديك لتقدمه؟"

"What is it that you've learned?"

"ما الذي تعلمته؟"

"what you're able to do?"

"ماذا تستطيع أن تفعل؟"

"I can think. I can wait. I can fast"

"أستطيع التفكير. أستطيع الانتظار. أستطيع الصيام"

"That's everything?" asked Kamaswami

"هذا كل شيء؟" سأل كاماسوامي

"I believe that is everything there is!"

"أعتقد أن هذا كل شيء هناك!"

"And what's the use of that?"

"وما الفائدة من ذلك؟"

"For example; fasting. What is it good for?"

"على سبيل المثال؛ الصيام. ما فائدته؟"

"It is very good, sir"

"إنه جيد جدًا يا سيدي"

"there are times a person has nothing to eat"

"هناك أوقات لا يجد فيها الشخص ما يأكله"

"then fasting is the smartest thing he can do"

"فإن الصيام هو أذكى ما يمكن أن يفعله"

"there was a time where Siddhartha hadn't learned to fast"

"كان هناك وقت حيث لم يتعلم سيدهارثا الصيام"

"in this time he had to accept any kind of service"

"في هذا الوقت كان عليه أن يقبل أي نوع من الخدمة"

"because hunger would force him to accept the service"

"لأن الجوع سيجبره على قبول الخدمة"

"But like this, Siddhartha can wait calmly"

"ولكن هكذا، يمكن لسيدهارتا أن ينتظر بهدوء"

"he knows no impatience, he knows no emergency"

"إنه لا يعرف عدم الصبر، ولا يعرف الطوارئ"

"for a long time he can allow hunger to besiege him"

"لفترة طويلة يمكنه أن يسمح للجوع بمحاصرته"

"and he can laugh about the hunger"

"ويمكنه أن يضحك من الجوع"

"This, sir, is what fasting is good for"

"هذا يا سيدي هو ما يفيده الصيام"

"You're right, Samana" acknowledged Kamaswami

"أنت على حق، سامانا" اعترف كاماسوامي

"Wait for a moment" he asked of his guest

"انتظر لحظة" سأل ضيفه

Kamaswami left the room and returned with a scroll

غادر كاماسوامي الغرفة وعاد ومعه مخطوطة

he handed Siddhartha the scroll and asked him to read it

سلم سيدهارتا المخطوطة وطلب منه أن يقرأها

Siddhartha looked at the scroll handed to him
نظر سيدهارثا إلى المخطوطة التي تم تسليمها له

on the scroll a sales-contract had been written
وقد كتب على المخطوطة عقد بيع

he began to read out the scroll's contents
بدأ بقراءة محتويات المخطوطة

Kamaswami was very pleased with Siddhartha
كان كاماسوامي سعيدًا جدًا بسيدهارتا

"would you write something for me on this piece of paper?"
"هل يمكنك أن تكتب لي شيئا على هذه القطعة من الورق؟"

He handed him a piece of paper and a pen
أعطاه قطعة من الورق وقلمًا

Siddhartha wrote, and returned the paper
كتب سيدهارثا، وأعاد الورقة

Kamaswami read, "Writing is good, thinking is better"
قرأ كاماسوامي: "الكتابة جيدة، والتفكير أفضل"

"Being smart is good, being patient is better"
"أن تكون ذكيا فهذا جيد، وأن تكون صبوراً فهذا أفضل"

"It is excellent how you're able to write" the merchant praised him
"من الرائع أنك قادر على الكتابة" أثنى عليه التاجر

"Many a thing we will still have to discuss with one another"
"هناك الكثير من الأشياء التي لا يزال يتعين علينا مناقشتها مع بعضنا البعض"

"For today, I'm asking you to be my guest"
"اليوم أطلب منك أن تكون ضيفي"

"please come to live in this house"
"من فضلك تعال للعيش في هذا المنزل"

Siddhartha thanked Kamaswami and accepted his offer
شكر سيدهارثا كاماسوامي وقبل عرضه

he lived in the dealer's house from now on
عاش في بيت التاجر منذ ذلك الحين

Clothes were brought to him, and shoes
أحضروا له الملابس والأحذية

and every day, a servant prepared a bath for him
وكان كل يوم خادم يعد له حماما

Twice a day, a plentiful meal was served

مرتين في اليوم، تم تقديم وجبة وفيرة

but Siddhartha only ate once a day

لكن سيدهارثا لم يأكل إلا مرة واحدة في اليوم

and he ate neither meat, nor did he drink wine

ولم يأكل لحماً ولم يشرب خمراً

Kamaswami told him about his trade

أخبره كاماسوامي عن تجارته

he showed him the merchandise and storage-rooms

أظهر له البضاعة والمخازن

he showed him how the calculations were done

أظهر له كيف تتم الحسابات

Siddhartha got to know many new things

تعرف سيدهارثا على العديد من الأشياء الجديدة

he heard a lot and spoke little

سمع الكثير وتكلم قليلا

but he did not forget Kamala's words

ولكنه لم ينسى كلام كامالا

so he was never subservient to the merchant

لذلك لم يكن خاضعًا للتاجر أبدًا

he forced him to treat him as an equal

أجبره على معاملته على قدم المساواة

perhaps he forced him to treat him as even more than an equal

ربما أجبره على معاملته كأنه أكثر من مجرد ند له

Kamaswami conducted his business with care

أدار كاماسوامي أعماله بعناية

and he was very passionate about his business

وكان متحمسًا جدًا لأعماله

but Siddhartha looked upon all of this as if it was a game

لكن سيدهارتا نظر إلى كل هذا كما لو كان لعبة

he tried hard to learn the rules of the game precisely

لقد حاول جاهدا أن يتعلم قواعد اللعبة بدقة

but the contents of the game did not touch his heart

لكن محتوى اللعبة لم يلمس قلبه

He had not been in Kamaswami's house for long
لم يكن في منزل كاماسوامي لفترة طويلة
but soon he took part in his landlord's business
لكن سرعان ما شارك في أعمال مالك العقار

every day he visited beautiful Kamala
كان يزور كامالا الجميلة كل يوم
Kamala had an hour appointed for their meetings
كان لدى كامالا ساعة محددة لاجتماعاتهم
she was wearing pretty clothes and fine shoes
كانت ترتدي ملابس جميلة وأحذية جميلة
and soon he brought her gifts as well
وسرعان ما أحضر لها الهدايا أيضًا
Much he learned from her red, smart mouth
لقد تعلم الكثير من فمها الأحمر الذكي
Much he learned from her tender, supple hand
لقد تعلم الكثير من يدها الرقيقة والمرنة
regarding love, Siddhartha was still a boy
فيما يتعلق بالحب، كان سيدهارتا لا يزال صبيًا
and he had a tendency to plunge into love blindly
وكان لديه ميل للانغماس في الحب بشكل أعمى
he fell into lust like into a bottomless pit
لقد وقع في الشهوة مثل حفرة لا نهاية لها
she taught him thoroughly, starting with the basics
لقد علمته جيدًا، بدءًا من الأساسيات
pleasure cannot be taken without giving pleasure
لا يمكن الحصول على المتعة دون تقديم المتعة
every gesture, every caress, every touch, every look
كل لفتة، كل مداعبة، كل لمسة، كل نظرة
every spot of the body, however small it was, had its secret
كل بقعة من الجسم مهما كانت صغيرة لها سرها
the secrets would bring happiness to those who know them
الأسرار تجلب السعادة لمن يعرفها
lovers must not part from one another after celebrating love
لا يجوز للعاشقين أن يفترقا بعد الاحتفال بالحب
they must not part without one admiring the other

لا ينبغي لهم أن يفترقوا دون أن يعجب أحدهما بالآخر

they must be as defeated as they have been victorious

يجب أن يكونوا مهزومين كما كانوا منتصرين

neither lover should start feeling fed up or bored

لا ينبغي لأي عاشق أن يشعر بالملل أو الملل

they should not get the evil feeling of having been abusive

لا ينبغي لهم أن يشعروا بالسوء بسبب تعرضهم للإساءة

and they should not feel like they have been abused

ولا ينبغي لهم أن يشعروا بأنهم تعرضوا للإساءة

Wonderful hours he spent with the beautiful and smart artist

ساعات رائعة قضاها مع الفنانة الجميلة والذكية

he became her student, her lover, her friend

لقد أصبح تلميذها وحبيبها وصديقها

Here with Kamala was the worth and purpose of his present life

هنا مع كامالا كانت قيمة وهدف حياته الحالية

his purpose was not with the business of Kamaswami

لم يكن هدفه هو العمل مع كاماسوامي

Siddhartha received important letters and contracts

تلقى سيدهارثا رسائل وعقودًا مهمة

Kamaswami began discussing all important affairs with him

بدأ كاماسوامي مناقشة جميع الشؤون المهمة معه

He soon saw that Siddhartha knew little about rice and wool

سرعان ما رأى أن سيدهارثا لا يعرف سوى القليل عن الأرز والصوف

but he saw that he acted in a fortunate manner

ولكنه رأى أنه تصرف بطريقة محظوظة

and Siddhartha surpassed him in calmness and equanimity

وتفوق عليه سيدهارتا في الهدوء والاتزان

he surpassed him in the art of understanding previously unknown people

لقد تفوق عليه في فن فهم الناس الذين لم يعرفهم من قبل

Kamaswami spoke about Siddhartha to a friend

تحدث كاماسوامي عن سيدهارتا لصديق

"This Brahman is no proper merchant"

"هذا البراهمان ليس تاجرًا حقيقيًّا"
"he will never be a merchant"
"لن يكون تاجرا أبدا"
"for business there is never any passion in his soul"
"لا يوجد أي شغف في روحه أبدًا فيما يتعلق بالعمل"
"But he has a mysterious quality about him"
"ولكن لديه صفة غامضة عنه"
"this quality brings success about all by itself"
"هذه الجودة تجلب النجاح في حد ذاتها"
"it could be from a good Star of his birth"
"قد يكون من نجم جيد من ولادته"
"or it could be something he has learned among Samanas"
"أو ربما يكون شيئًا تعلمه بين الساماناس"
"He always seems to be merely playing with our business-affairs"
"يبدو دائمًا أنه يلعب فقط بشؤوننا التجارية"
"his business never fully becomes a part of him"
"لا يصبح عمله جزءًا كاملاً منه أبدًا"
"his business never rules over him"
"عمله لا يسيطر عليه أبدًا"
"he is never afraid of failure"
"إنه لا يخاف من الفشل أبدًا"
"he is never upset by a loss"
"إنه لا ينزعج أبدًا من الخسارة"
The friend advised the merchant
نصح الصديق التاجر
"Give him a third of the profits he makes for you"
"أعطه ثلث الأرباح التي يحققها لك"
"but let him also be liable when there are losses"
"ولكن يجب أن يكون مسؤولاً أيضاً عندما تكون هناك خسائر"
"Then, he'll become more zealous"
"ثم سيصبح أكثر حماسة"
Kamaswami was curious, and followed the advice
كان كاماسوامي فضوليًا، واتبع النصيحة
But Siddhartha cared little about loses or profits
لكن سيدهارثا لم يهتم كثيرًا بالخسائر أو الأرباح

When he made a profit, he accepted it with equanimity
عندما حقق ربحًا، قبله بهدوء
when he made losses, he laughed it off
عندما تكبد خسائر، ضحك عليها
It seemed indeed, as if he did not care about the business
لقد بدا الأمر كما لو أنه لا يهتم بالأعمال التجارية.
At one time, he travelled to a village
في أحد الأوقات، سافر إلى قرية
he went there to buy a large harvest of rice
ذهب هناك لشراء محصول كبير من الأرز
But when he got there, the rice had already been sold
ولكن عندما وصل إلى هناك، كان الأرز قد تم بيعه بالفعل
another merchant had gotten to the village before him
كان تاجر آخر قد وصل إلى القرية قبله
Nevertheless, Siddhartha stayed for several days in that village
ومع ذلك، بقي سيدهارتا لعدة أيام في تلك القرية
he treated the farmers for a drink
لقد عالج المزارعين بالشرب
he gave copper-coins to their children
أعطى عملات نحاسية لأطفالهم
he joined in the celebration of a wedding
انضم إلى الاحتفال بالزفاف
and he returned extremely satisfied from his trip
وعاد راضيا جدا من رحلته
Kamaswami was angry that Siddhartha had wasted time and money
كان كاماسوامي غاضبًا لأن سيدهارتا أهدر الوقت والمال
Siddhartha answered "Stop scolding, dear friend!"
أجاب سيدهارتا "توقف عن التوبيخ يا صديقي العزيز!"
"Nothing was ever achieved by scolding"
"لم يتم تحقيق أي شيء عن طريق التوبيخ"
"If a loss has occurred, let me bear that loss"
"إذا حدثت خسارة، دعني أتحمل تلك الخسارة"
"I am very satisfied with this trip"
"أنا راضٍ جدًا عن هذه الرحلة"

"I have gotten to know many kinds of people"
"لقد تعرفت على العديد من أنواع الناس"
"a Brahman has become my friend"
"لقد أصبح البراهمان صديقي"
"children have sat on my knees"
"لقد جلس الأطفال على ركبتي"
"farmers have shown me their fields"
"لقد أراني المزارعون حقولهم"
"nobody knew that I was a merchant"
"لم يكن أحد يعلم أنني تاجر"
"That's all very nice," exclaimed Kamaswami indignantly
"كل هذا جميل جدًا"، هتف كاماسوامي بغضب
"but in fact, you are a merchant after all"
"لكن في الحقيقة أنت تاجر بعد كل شيء"
"Or did you have only travel for your amusement?"
"أم أن سفرك كان من أجل المتعة فقط؟"
"of course I have travelled for my amusement" Siddhartha laughed
"بالطبع لقد سافرت من أجل تسلية نفسي" ضحك سيدهارثا
"For what else would I have travelled?"
"لماذا كنت سأسافر غير ذلك؟"
"I have gotten to know people and places"
"لقد تعرفت على الناس والأماكن"
"I have received kindness and trust"
"لقد تلقيت اللطف والثقة"
"I have found friendships in this village"
"لقد وجدت صداقات في هذه القرية"
"if I had been Kamaswami, I would have travelled back annoyed"
"لو كنت كاماسوامي، كنت سأعود منزعجًا"
"I would have been in hurry as soon as my purchase failed"
"كنت سأسرع في الشراء بمجرد فشل عملية الشراء"
"and time and money would indeed have been lost"
"وكان من الممكن أن يضيع الوقت والمال بالفعل"
"But like this, I've had a few good days"
"لكن هكذا، لقد أمضيت بضعة أيام جيدة"

"I've learned from my time there"
"لقد تعلمت من وقتي هناك"
"and I have had joy from the experience"
"ولقد استمتعت بهذه التجربة"
"I've neither harmed myself nor others by annoyance and hastiness"
"لم أؤذي نفسي أو الآخرين بالانزعاج والتسرع"
"if I ever return friendly people will welcome me"
"إذا عدت يومًا ما، فسوف يرحب بي الناس الودودون"
"if I return to do business friendly people will welcome me too"
"إذا عدت لممارسة الأعمال التجارية فإن الناس الودودين سوف يرحبون بي أيضًا"
"I praise myself for not showing any hurry or displeasure"
"أشيد بنفسي لأنني لم أظهر أي عجلة أو استياء"
"So, leave it as it is, my friend"
"إذن، اترك الأمر كما هو، يا صديقي"
"and don't harm yourself by scolding"
"ولا تؤذي نفسك بالتوبيخ"
"If you see Siddhartha harming himself, then speak with me"
"إذا رأيت سيدهارتا يؤذي نفسه، فتحدث معي"
"and Siddhartha will go on his own path"
"وسوف يمضي سيدهارتا في طريقه الخاص"
"But until then, let's be satisfied with one another"
"ولكن حتى ذلك الحين، دعونا نكون راضين عن بعضنا البعض"
the merchant's attempts to convince Siddhartha were futile
كانت محاولات التاجر لإقناع سيدهارتا غير مجدية
he could not make Siddhartha eat his bread
لم يستطع أن يجعل سيدهارتا يأكل خبزه
Siddhartha ate his own bread
لقد أكل سيدهارتا خبزه الخاص
or rather, they both ate other people's bread
أو بالأحرى، كلاهما أكل خبز الآخرين
Siddhartha never listened to Kamaswami's worries
لم يستمع سيدهارتا أبدًا إلى مخاوف كاماسوامي

and Kamaswami had many worries he wanted to share
وكان لدى كاماسوامي الكثير من المخاوف التي أراد مشاركتها

there were business-deals going on in danger of failing
كانت هناك صفقات تجارية جارية معرضة لخطر الفشل

shipments of merchandise seemed to have been lost
يبدو أن شحنات البضائع قد ضاعت

debtors seemed to be unable to pay
يبدو أن المدينين غير قادرين على الدفع

Kamaswami could never convince Siddhartha to utter words of worry
لم يتمكن كاماسوامي أبدًا من إقناع سيدارثا بنطق كلمات القلق

Kamaswami could not make Siddhartha feel anger towards business
لم يتمكن كاماسوامي من جعل سيدارثا يشعر بالغضب تجاه الأعمال التجارية

he could not get him to to have wrinkles on the forehead
لم يستطع أن يجعله يظهر التجاعيد على جبهته

he could not make Siddhartha sleep badly
لم يستطع أن يجعل سيدهارثا ينام بشكل سيء

one day, Kamaswami tried to speak with Siddhartha
ذات يوم، حاول كاماسوامي التحدث مع سيدهارثا

"Siddhartha, you have failed to learn anything new"
"سيدهارتا، لقد فشلت في تعلم أي شيء جديد"

but again, Siddhartha laughed at this
ولكن مرة أخرى، ضحك سيدهارثا على هذا

"Would you please not kid me with such jokes"
"أرجوك أن لا تمزح معي بهذه النكات"

"What I've learned from you is how much a basket of fish costs"
"ما تعلمته منك هو كم ثمن سلة السمك"

"and I learned how much interest may be charged on loaned money"
"وتعلمت مقدار الفائدة التي يمكن فرضها على الأموال المقترضة"

"These are your areas of expertise"
"هذه هي مجالات خبرتك"

"I haven't learned to think from you, my dear Kamaswami"
"لم أتعلم التفكير منك يا عزيزي كاماسوامي"
"you ought to be the one seeking to learn from me"
"يجب أن تكون أنت الشخص الذي يسعى للتعلم مني"
Indeed his soul was not with the trade
إن روحه لم تكن مع التجارة
The business was good enough to provide him with money for Kamala
كانت الأعمال جيدة بما يكفي لتزويده بالمال لكامالا
and it earned him much more than he needed
وقد كسب أكثر مما يحتاج إليه
Besides Kamala, Siddhartha's curiosity was with the people
بالإضافة إلى كامالا، كان فضول سيدهارثا مع الناس
their businesses, crafts, worries, and pleasures
أعمالهم، وحرفهم، وهمومهم، ومتعهم
all these things used to be alien to him
كل هذه الأشياء كانت غريبة عليه
their acts of foolishness used to be as distant as the moon
كانت أفعالهم الحمقاء بعيدة مثل القمر
he easily succeeded in talking to all of them
لقد نجح بسهولة في التحدث مع الجميع
he could live with all of them
كان بإمكانه أن يعيش معهم جميعا
and he could continue to learn from all of them
ويمكنه أن يستمر في التعلم منهم جميعًا
but there was something which separated him from them
ولكن كان هناك شيء يفصله عنهم
he could feel a divide between him and the people
كان يشعر بوجود انقسام بينه وبين الناس
this separating factor was him being a Samana
كان هذا العامل الفاصل هو كونه سامانا
He saw mankind going through life in a childlike manner
لقد رأى البشرية تمر بالحياة بطريقة طفولية
in many ways they were living the way animals live
لقد كانوا يعيشون في كثير من النواحي كما تعيش الحيوانات
he loved and also despised their way of life

لقد أحب واحتقر أسلوب حياتهم
He saw them toiling and suffering
لقد رآهم يتعبون ويعانون
they were becoming gray for things unworthy of this price
لقد أصبحوا رماديين بسبب أشياء لا تستحق هذا الثمن
they did things for money and little pleasures
لقد فعلوا أشياء من أجل المال والمتعة الصغيرة
they did things for being slightly honoured
لقد فعلوا أشياء من أجل أن يتم تكريمهم قليلاً
he saw them scolding and insulting each other
لقد رآهم يوبخون ويسبون بعضهم البعض
he saw them complaining about pain
لقد رآهم يشكون من الألم
pains at which a Samana would only smile
آلام لا يمكن لسامانا إلا أن تبتسم لها
and he saw them suffering from deprivations
ورأى أنهم يعانون من الحرمان
deprivations which a Samana would not feel
الحرمان الذي لن يشعر به سامانا
He was open to everything these people brought his way
كان منفتحًا على كل ما جلبه هؤلاء الأشخاص في طريقه
welcome was the merchant who offered him linen for sale
كان مرحبا بالتاجر الذي عرض عليه الكتان للبيع
welcome was the debtor who sought another loan
كان المدين الذي يسعى للحصول على قرض آخر موضع ترحيب
welcome was the beggar who told him the story of his poverty
كان مرحباً بالمتسول الذي أخبره بقصة فقره
the beggar who was not half as poor as any Samana
المتسول الذي لم يكن فقيرًا إلى النصف مثل أي سامانا
He did not treat the rich merchant and his servant different
ولم يعامل التاجر الغني وخادمه بشكل مختلف
he let street-vendor cheat him when buying bananas
سمح لبائع متجول أن يخدعه عند شراء الموز
Kamaswami would often complain to him about his worries
كان كاماسوامي يشكو له كثيرًا من همومه

or he would reproach him about his business
أو يوبخه على عمله
he listened curiously and happily
كان يستمع بفضول وسعادة
but he was puzzled by his friend
ولكنه كان في حيرة من أمر صديقه
he tried to understand him
حاول أن يفهمه
and he admitted he was right, up to a certain point
واعترف بأنه كان على حق، إلى حد معين
there were many who asked for Siddhartha
كان هناك الكثير ممن طلبوا سيدهارتا
many wanted to do business with him
أراد الكثيرون التعامل معه
there were many who wanted to cheat him
كان هناك الكثير ممن أرادوا خداعه
many wanted to draw some secret out of him
أراد الكثيرون أن يستخرجوا منه سرًّا ما
many wanted to appeal to his sympathy
أراد الكثيرون أن يستعينوا بعطفه
many wanted to get his advice
أراد الكثيرون الحصول على نصيحته
He gave advice to those who wanted it
أعطى النصيحة لمن أرادها
he pitied those who needed pity
لقد أشفق على أولئك الذين يحتاجون إلى الشفقة
he made gifts to those who liked presents
لقد قدم هدايا لأولئك الذين أحبوا الهدايا
he let some cheat him a bit
لقد سمح لبعضهم أن يخدعوه قليلا
this game which all people played occupied his thoughts
هذه اللعبة التي لعبها كل الناس كانت تشغل تفكيره
he thought about this game just as much as he had about the Gods
لقد فكر في هذه اللعبة تمامًا كما فكر في الآلهة
deep in his chest he felt a dying voice

في أعماق صدره شعر بصوت يحتضر

this voice admonished him quietly

هذا الصوت وبخه بهدوء

and he hardly perceived the voice inside of himself

ولم يكد يسمع الصوت بداخله

And then, for an hour, he became aware of something

وبعد ذلك، لمدة ساعة، أدرك شيئًا ما

he became aware of the strange life he was leading

لقد أدرك الحياة الغريبة التي كان يعيشها

he realized this life was only a game

أدرك أن هذه الحياة مجرد لعبة

at times he would feel happiness and joy

في بعض الأحيان كان يشعر بالسعادة والفرح

but real life was still passing him by

لكن الحياة الحقيقية كانت لا تزال تمر به

and it was passing by without touching him

وكان يمر دون أن يلمسه

Siddhartha played with his business-deals

لعب سيدهارثا بصفقاته التجارية

Siddhartha found amusement in the people around him

وجد سيدهارثا المتعة في الناس من حوله

but regarding his heart, he was not with them

ولكن من جهة قلبه لم يكن معهم.

The source ran somewhere, far away from him

كان المصدر يركض إلى مكان ما، بعيدًا عنه

it ran and ran invisibly

لقد ركض وركض بشكل غير مرئي

it had nothing to do with his life any more

لم يعد الأمر له علاقة بحياته بعد الآن

at several times he became scared on account of such thoughts

في عدة مرات أصبح خائفًا بسبب مثل هذه الأفكار

he wished he could participate in all of these childlike games

تمنى أن يتمكن من المشاركة في كل هذه الألعاب الطفولية

he wanted to really live

he wanted to really act in their theatre

لقد أراد أن يعيش حقا

he wanted to really enjoy their pleasures

لقد أراد حقًا أن يمثل في مسرحهم

and he wanted to live, instead of just standing by as a spectator

أراد أن يستمتع بمتعهم حقًا

وأراد أن يعيش، بدلاً من مجرد الوقوف متفرجًا

But again and again, he came back to beautiful Kamala

ولكن مرة تلو الأخرى، عاد إلى كامالا الجميلة

he learned the art of love

لقد تعلم فن الحب

and he practised the cult of lust

ومارس عبادة الشهوة

lust, in which giving and taking becomes one

الشهوة، حيث يصبح العطاء والأخذ واحدا

he chatted with her and learned from her

تحدث معها وتعلم منها

he gave her advice, and he received her advice

لقد قدم لها النصيحة وتلقى نصيحتها

She understood him better than Govinda used to understand him

لقد فهمته بشكل أفضل مما كان جوفيندا يفهمه

she was more similar to him than Govinda had been

لقد كانت تشبهه أكثر مما كان عليه جوفيندا

"You are like me," he said to her

"أنت مثلي" قال لها

"you are different from most people"

"أنت مختلف عن معظم الناس"

"You are Kamala, nothing else"

"أنت كامالا، لا شيء آخر"

"and inside of you, there is a peace and refuge"

"وفي داخلك سلام وملجأ"

"a refuge to which you can go at every hour of the day"

"ملجأ يمكنك الذهاب إليه في أي ساعة من اليوم"

"you can be at home with yourself"

"يمكنك أن تكون في منزلك مع نفسك"

"I can do this too"

"أنا أستطيع أن أفعل هذا أيضاً"

"Few people have this place"

"قليل من الناس لديهم هذا المكان"

"and yet all of them could have it"

"ومع ذلك فإنهم جميعا قد يحصلون عليه"

"Not all people are smart" said Kamala

"ليس كل الناس أذكياء" قالت كامالا

"No," said Siddhartha, "that's not the reason why"

"لا،" قال سيدهارثا، "هذا ليس السبب"

"Kamaswami is just as smart as I am"

"كاماسوامي ذكي مثلي تمامًا"

"but he has no refuge in himself"

"ولكن ليس له ملجأ في نفسه"

"Others have it, although they have the minds of children"

"الآخرون لديهم ذلك، رغم أن لديهم عقول أطفال"

"Most people, Kamala, are like a falling leaf"

"معظم الناس، كامالا، مثل ورقة الشجر المتساقطة"

"a leaf which is blown and is turning around through the air"

"ورقة تنفخ في الهواء وتدور حول نفسها"

"a leaf which wavers, and tumbles to the ground"

"ورقة تتأرجح وتسقط على الأرض"

"But others, a few, are like stars"

"لكن الآخرين، قِلة، مثل النجوم"

"they go on a fixed course"

"إنهم يسيرون في مسار ثابت"

"no wind reaches them"

"لا تصل إليهم ريح"

"in themselves they have their law and their course"

"لهم في أنفسهم ناموسهم ومنهجهم"

"Among all the learned men I have met, there was one of this kind"

"من بين جميع الرجال المتعلمين الذين التقيت بهم، كان هناك واحد من هذا النوع"

"he was a truly perfected one"

"لقد كان كاملاً حقًّا"

"I'll never be able to forget him"

"لن أتمكن من نسيانه أبدًا"

"It is that Gotama, the exalted one"

"إنه غوتاما، السامي"

"Thousands of followers are listening to his teachings every day"

"الآلاف من المتابعين يستمعون إلى تعاليمه كل يوم"

"they follow his instructions every hour"

"إنهم يتبعون تعليماته كل ساعة"

"but they are all falling leaves"

"لكنهم جميعا أوراق متساقطة"

"not in themselves they have teachings and a law"

"ليس لهم في أنفسهم تعاليم وناموس"

Kamala looked at him with a smile

نظرت إليه كامالا بابتسامة

"Again, you're talking about him," she said

"مرة أخرى، أنت تتحدث عنه"، قالت

"again, you're having a Samana's thoughts"

"مرة أخرى، لديك أفكار سامانا"

Siddhartha said nothing, and they played the game of love

لم يقل سيدهارثا شيئًا، ولعبوا لعبة الحب

one of the thirty or forty different games Kamala knew

واحدة من الثلاثين أو الأربعين لعبة المختلفة التي عرفتها كامالا

Her body was flexible like that of a jaguar

كان جسدها مرنًا مثل جسد الجاكوار

flexible like the bow of a hunter

مرن مثل قوس الصياد

he who had learned from her how to make love

هو الذي تعلم منها كيفية ممارسة الحب

he was knowledgeable of many forms of lust

وكان عالما بأنواع الشهوات

he that learned from her knew many secrets

من تعلم منها عرف الكثير من الأسرار

For a long time, she played with Siddhartha

لقد لعبت مع سيدهارتا لفترة طويلة

she enticed him and rejected him

أغوته ورفضته

she forced him and embraced him

اجبرته واحتضنته

she enjoyed his masterful skills

لقد استمتعت بمهاراته الرائعة

until he was defeated and rested exhausted by her side

حتى هُزم واستراح منهكًا بجانبها

The courtesan bent over him

انحنت العاهرة عليه

she took a long look at his face

ألقت نظرة طويلة على وجهه

she looked at his eyes, which had grown tired

نظرت إلى عينيه التي أصبحت متعبة

"You are the best lover I have ever seen" she said thoughtfully

"أنت أفضل حبيب رأيته على الإطلاق" قالت بتفكير

"You're stronger than others, more supple, more willing"

"أنت أقوى من الآخرين، وأكثر مرونة، وأكثر استعدادًا"

"You've learned my art well, Siddhartha"

"لقد تعلمت فني جيدًا، سيدهارثا"

"At some time, when I'll be older, I'd want to bear your child"

"في وقت ما، عندما أكبر، أود أن أنجب طفلك"

"And yet, my dear, you've remained a Samana"

"ومع ذلك، يا عزيزتي، لقد بقيتِ سامانا"

"and despite this, you do not love me"

"ورغم هذا فأنت لا تحبني"

"there is nobody that you love"

"لا يوجد أحد تحبه"

"Isn't it so?" asked Kamala

"أليس كذلك؟" سألت كامالا

"It might very well be so," Siddhartha said tiredly

"قد يكون الأمر كذلك حقًّا"، قال سيدهارثا بتعب

"I am like you, because you also do not love"

"أنا مثلكم لأنكم أنتم أيضاً لا تحبون"

"how else could you practise love as a craft?"

"كيف يمكنك أن تمارس الحب كحرفة؟"

"Perhaps, people of our kind can't love"

"ربما لا يستطيع الناس من نوعنا أن يحبوا"

"The childlike people can love, that's their secret"

"الأشخاص الطفوليون قادرون على الحب، هذا هو سرهم"

Sansara
سانسارا

For a long time, Siddhartha had lived in the world and lust
لقد عاش سيدهارثا لفترة طويلة في العالم وكان يشتهي

he lived this way though, without being a part of it
لقد عاش بهذه الطريقة، دون أن يكون جزءًا منها

he had killed this off when he had been a Samana
لقد قتل هذا عندما كان سامانا

but now they had awoken again
ولكن الآن استيقظوا مرة أخرى

he had tasted riches, lust, and power
لقد ذاق الثراء والشهوة والسلطة

for a long time he had remained a Samana in his heart
لقد ظل لفترة طويلة سامانا في قلبه

Kamala, being smart, had realized this quite right
لقد أدركت كامالا هذا الأمر بشكل صحيح لأنها كانت ذكية.

thinking, waiting, and fasting still guided his life
كان التفكير والانتظار والصيام لا يزالان يوجهان حياته

the childlike people remained alien to him
ظل الناس الطفوليون غرباء عنه

and he remained alien to the childlike people
وظل غريبا عن الناس الطفوليين

Years passed by; surrounded by the good life
مرت السنوات، محاطة بالحياة الطيبة

Siddhartha hardly felt the years fading away
لم يشعر سيدهارثا بأن السنوات تتلاشى

He had become rich and possessed a house of his own
لقد أصبح غنيًا ويمتلك منزلًا خاصًا به

he even had his own servants
حتى أنه كان لديه خدمه الخاصين

he had a garden before the city, by the river
كان له حديقة أمام المدينة بجانب النهر

The people liked him and came to him for money or advice
أحبه الناس وجاءوا إليه من أجل المال أو النصيحة

but there was nobody close to him, except Kamala

ولكن لم يكن هناك أحد قريب منه، باستثناء كامالا.

the bright state of being awake

حالة اليقظة المشرقة

the feeling which he had experienced at the height of his youth

الشعور الذي اختبره في ذروة شبابه

in those days after Gotama's sermon

في تلك الأيام بعد خطبة جوتاما

after the separation from Govinda

بعد الانفصال عن جوفيندا

the tense expectation of life

التوقع المتوتر للحياة

the proud state of standing alone

حالة الفخر بالوقوف وحيدًا

being without teachings or teachers

عدم وجود تعاليم أو معلمين

the supple willingness to listen to the divine voice in his own heart

الاستعداد المرن للاستماع إلى الصوت الإلهي في قلبه

all these things had slowly become a memory

كل هذه الأشياء أصبحت مجرد ذكرى ببطء

the memory had been fleeting, distant, and quiet

كانت الذكرى عابرة وبعيدة وهادئة

the holy source, which used to be near, now only murmured

المصدر المقدس الذي كان قريبًا، لم يعد الآن يتردد إلا

the holy source, which used to murmur within himself

المصدر المقدس الذي كان يهمس في داخله

Nevertheless, many things he had learned from the Samanas

ومع ذلك، فقد تعلم الكثير من الأشياء من الساماناس

he had learned from Gotama

لقد تعلم من جوتاما

he had learned from his father the Brahman

لقد تعلم من والده البراهمان

his father had remained within his being for a long time

لقد ظل والده في كيانه لفترة طويلة

moderate living, the joy of thinking, hours of meditation

العيش المعتدل، متعة التفكير، ساعات من التأمل

the secret knowledge of the self; his eternal entity
المعرفة السرية للذات، كيانها الأبدي

the self which is neither body nor consciousness
الذات التي ليست جسداً ولا وعياً

Many a part of this he still had
لا يزال لديه الكثير من هذا

but one part after another had been submerged
ولكن جزء تلو الآخر كان مغموراً

and eventually each part gathered dust
وفي النهاية جمع كل جزء الغبار

a potter's wheel, once in motion, will turn for a long time
عجلة الخزاف، بمجرد أن تبدأ في الحركة، سوف تدور لفترة طويلة

it loses its vigour only slowly
إنه يفقد قوته ببطء فقط

and it comes to a stop only after time
ولا يتوقف إلا بعد مرور الوقت

Siddhartha's soul had kept on turning the wheel of asceticism
ظلت روح سيدهارتا تدور عجلة الزهد

the wheel of thinking had kept turning for a long time
ظلت عجلة التفكير تدور لفترة طويلة

the wheel of differentiation had still turned for a long time
ظلت عجلة التمايز تدور لفترة طويلة

but it turned slowly and hesitantly
لكنها تحولت ببطء وتردد

and it was close to coming to a standstill
وكان على وشك التوقف

Slowly, like humidity entering the dying stem of a tree
ببطء، مثل الرطوبة التي تدخل جذع الشجرة المحتضرة

filling the stem slowly and making it rot
ملء الجذع ببطء مما يجعله يتعفن

the world and sloth had entered Siddhartha's soul
لقد دخل العالم والكسل إلى روح سيدهارتا

slowly it filled his soul and made it heavy
لقد امتلأت روحه ببطء وجعلتها ثقيلة

it made his soul tired and put it to sleep

لقد أتعب روحه وجعلها تنام

On the other hand, his senses had become alive

ومن ناحية أخرى، أصبحت حواسه حية.

there was much his senses had learned

لقد تعلمت حواسه الكثير

there was much his senses had experienced

لقد كان هناك الكثير مما شهدته حواسه

Siddhartha had learned to trade

لقد تعلم سيدهارثا التجارة

he had learned how to use his power over people

لقد تعلم كيفية استخدام سلطته على الناس

he had learned how to enjoy himself with a woman

لقد تعلم كيف يستمتع مع امرأة

he had learned how to wear beautiful clothes

لقد تعلم كيفية ارتداء الملابس الجميلة

he had learned how to give orders to servants

لقد تعلم كيفية إعطاء الأوامر للخدم

he had learned how to bathe in perfumed waters

لقد تعلم كيفية الاستحمام في المياه المعطرة

He had learned how to eat tenderly and carefully prepared food

لقد تعلم كيفية تناول الطعام المعد بعناية ولطف

he even ate fish, meat, and poultry

حتى أنه أكل السمك واللحوم والدواجن

spices and sweets and wine, which causes sloth and forgetfulness

التوابل والحلويات والنبيذ، مما يسبب الكسل والنسيان

He had learned to play with dice and on a chess-board

لقد تعلم اللعب بالنرد وعلى رقعة الشطرنج

he had learned to watch dancing girls

لقد تعلم مشاهدة الفتيات الراقصات

he learned to have himself carried about in a sedan-chair

لقد تعلم أن يحمل نفسه على كرسي متحرك

he learned to sleep on a soft bed

لقد تعلم النوم على سرير ناعم

But still he felt different from others
لكنه لا يزال يشعر بأنه مختلف عن الآخرين
he still felt superior to the others
لا يزال يشعر بأنه متفوق على الآخرين
he always watched them with some mockery
كان يراقبهم دائمًا ببعض السخرية
there was always some mocking disdain to how he felt about them
كان هناك دائمًا بعض الازدراء الساخر لكيفية شعوره تجاههم
the same disdain a Samana feels for the people of the world
نفس الازدراء الذي يشعر به سامانا تجاه شعوب العالم

Kamaswami was ailing and felt annoyed
كان كاماسوامي مريضًا وشعر بالانزعاج
he felt insulted by Siddhartha
لقد شعر بالإهانة من قبل سيدهارتا
and he was vexed by his worries as a merchant
وكان منزعجًا من همومه كتاجر
Siddhartha had always watched these things with mockery
لقد كان سيدهارتا يراقب هذه الأشياء دائمًا بسخرية
but his mockery had become more tired
لكن سخريته أصبحت أكثر إرهاقا
his superiority had become more quiet
لقد أصبح تفوقه أكثر هدوءا
as slowly imperceptible as the rainy season passing by
ببطء غير محسوس مثل موسم الأمطار الذي يمر
slowly, Siddhartha had assumed something of the childlike people's ways
ببطء، افترض سيدهارتا شيئًا من طرق الأطفال
he had gained some of their childishness
لقد اكتسب بعضًا من طفولتهم
and he had gained some of their fearfulness
وقد اكتسب بعضًا من خوفهم
And yet, the more be become like them the more he envied them
ومع ذلك، كلما أصبح مثلهم، زاد حسده لهم.

He envied them for the one thing that was missing from him
لقد حسدهم على الشيء الوحيد الذي كان مفقودًا منه
the importance they were able to attach to their lives
الأهمية التي تمكنوا من منحها لحياتهم
the amount of passion in their joys and fears
كمية العاطفة في أفراحهم ومخاوفهم
the fearful but sweet happiness of being constantly in love
السعادة المخيفة ولكن الحلوة التي تنجم عن الوقوع في الحب باستمرار
These people were in love with themselves all of the time
كان هؤلاء الناس يحبون أنفسهم طوال الوقت
women loved their children, with honours or money
أحبت النساء أطفالهن، بالشرف أو المال
the men loved themselves with plans or hopes
أحب الرجال أنفسهم بالخطط أو الآمال
But he did not learn this from them
ولكنه لم يتعلم هذا منهم
he did not learn the joy of children
لم يتعلم فرحة الاطفال
and he did not learn their foolishness
ولم يتعلم حمقهم
what he mostly learned were their unpleasant things
ما تعلمه في الغالب هو الأشياء غير السارة
and he despised these things
وكان يحتقر هذه الأشياء
in the morning, after having had company
في الصباح، بعد أن كان لديك شركة
more and more he stayed in bed for a long time
ظل في السرير لفترة أطول فأكثر
he felt unable to think, and was tired
شعر بعدم القدرة على التفكير وكان متعبًا
he became angry and impatient when Kamaswami bored him with his worries
لقد أصبح غاضبًا وغير صبور عندما أزعجه كاماسوامي بقلقه
he laughed just too loud when he lost a game of dice
لقد ضحك بصوت مرتفع للغاية عندما خسر لعبة النرد
His face was still smarter and more spiritual than others

كان وجهه لا يزال أكثر ذكاءً وروحانية من الآخرين

but his face rarely laughed anymore

لكن وجهه لم يعد يضحك إلا نادرا

slowly, his face assumed other features

ببطء، بدأ وجهه يأخذ ملامح أخرى

the features often found in the faces of rich people

السمات التي نجدها عادة في وجوه الأثرياء

features of discontent, of sickliness, of ill-humour

سمات السخط والمرض وسوء المزاج

features of sloth, and of a lack of love

سمات الكسل وقلة الحب

the disease of the soul which rich people have

مرض الروح الذي يعاني منه الأغنياء

Slowly, this disease grabbed hold of him

ببطء، استولى عليه هذا المرض

like a thin mist, tiredness came over Siddhartha

مثل ضباب رقيق، سيطر التعب على سيدهارتا

slowly, this mist got a bit denser every day

ببطء، أصبح هذا الضباب أكثر كثافة كل يوم

it got a bit murkier every month

لقد أصبح الأمر أكثر غموضًا كل شهر

and every year it got a bit heavier

وفي كل عام أصبح الأمر أثقل قليلاً

dresses become old with time

الفساتين تصبح قديمة مع مرور الوقت

clothes lose their beautiful colour over time

تفقد الملابس لونها الجميل مع مرور الوقت

they get stains, wrinkles, worn off at the seams

تظهر عليها البقع والتجاعيد وتتآكل عند اللحامات

they start to show threadbare spots here and there

يبدأون في إظهار بقع رثة هنا وهناك

this is how Siddhartha's new life was

هكذا كانت حياة سيدهارتا الجديدة

the life which he had started after his separation from Govinda

الحياة التي بدأها بعد انفصاله عن جوفيندا

his life had grown old and lost colour
لقد أصبحت حياته قديمة وفقدت لونها
there was less splendour to it as the years passed by
لقد أصبح أقل روعة مع مرور السنين
his life was gathering wrinkles and stains
كانت حياته مليئة بالتجاعيد والبقع
and hidden at bottom, disappointment and disgust were waiting
وفي الأسفل كان هناك خيبة أمل واشمئزاز في انتظارنا
they were showing their ugliness
لقد أظهروا قبحهم
Siddhartha did not notice these things
لم يلاحظ سيدهارتا هذه الأشياء
he remembered the bright and reliable voice inside of him
تذكر الصوت المشرق والموثوق بداخله
he noticed the voice had become silent
لاحظ أن الصوت أصبح صامتا
the voice which had awoken in him at that time
الصوت الذي استيقظ فيه في ذلك الوقت
the voice that had guided him in his best times
الصوت الذي كان يرشده في أفضل أوقاته
he had been captured by the world
لقد تم القبض عليه من قبل العالم
he had been captured by lust, covetousness, sloth
لقد وقع في قبضة الشهوة والطمع والكسل
and finally he had been captured by his most despised vice
وأخيرا وقع في قبضة رذيلته الأكثر احتقارا
the vice which he mocked the most
الرذيلة التي سخر منها أكثر من غيرها
the most foolish one of all vices
أكثر الرذائل حمقا على الإطلاق
he had let greed into his heart
لقد سمح للجشع بالدخول إلى قلبه
Property, possessions, and riches also had finally captured him
كما استولى عليه في النهاية الممتلكات والممتلكات والثروات

having things was no longer a game to him
لم يعد امتلاك الأشياء لعبة بالنسبة له

his possessions had become a shackle and a burden
أصبحت ممتلكاته قيداً وعبئاً

It had happened in a strange and devious way
لقد حدث ذلك بطريقة غريبة ومخادعة

Siddhartha had gotten this vice from the game of dice
لقد حصل سيدهارثا على هذه الرذيلة من لعبة النرد

he had stopped being a Samana in his heart
لقد توقف عن كونه سامانا في قلبه

and then he began to play the game for money
وبعد ذلك بدأ يلعب اللعبة مقابل المال

first he joined the game with a smile
أولا انضم إلى اللعبة بابتسامة

at this time he only played casually
في هذا الوقت كان يلعب بشكل عرضي فقط

he wanted to join the customs of the childlike people
أراد الانضمام إلى عادات الناس الطفولية

but now he played with an increasing rage and passion
لكن الآن لعب بغضب وشغف متزايدين

He was a feared gambler among the other merchants
كان مقامرًا مخيفًا بين التجار الآخرين

his stakes were so audacious that few dared to take him on
كانت رهاناته جريئة للغاية لدرجة أن القليل من الناس تجرأوا على مواجهته

He played the game due to a pain of his heart
لقد لعب اللعبة بسبب ألم في قلبه

losing and wasting his wretched money brought him an angry joy
لقد أدى فقدان وإهدار أمواله البائسة إلى جلب له فرحة غاضبة

he could demonstrate his disdain for wealth in no other way
لم يكن بوسعه أن يُظهر ازدرائه للثروة بأي طريقة أخرى

he could not mock the merchants' false god in a better way
لم يكن بوسعه أن يسخر من إله التجار الزائف بطريقة أفضل

so he gambled with high stakes
لذلك قام بالمقامرة بمخاطر عالية

he mercilessly hated himself and mocked himself
لقد كره نفسه بلا رحمة وسخر من نفسه
he won thousands, threw away thousands
لقد ربح الآلاف، وألقى الآلاف
he lost money, jewellery, a house in the country
لقد خسر أموالاً ومجوهرات ومنزلاً في الريف
he won it again, and then he lost again
فاز بها مرة أخرى، ثم خسر مرة أخرى
he loved the fear he felt while he was rolling the dice
لقد أحب الخوف الذي شعر به أثناء رمي النرد
he loved feeling worried about losing what he gambled
كان يحب الشعور بالقلق بشأن خسارة ما راهن عليه
he always wanted to get this fear to a slightly higher level
لقد أراد دائمًا رفع هذا الخوف إلى مستوى أعلى قليلاً
he only felt something like happiness when he felt this fear
لم يشعر إلا بشيء من السعادة عندما شعر بهذا الخوف
it was something like an intoxication
كان الأمر أشبه بالتسمم
something like an elevated form of life
شيء مثل شكل رفيع من أشكال الحياة
something brighter in the midst of his dull life
شيء أكثر إشراقا في وسط حياته المملة
And after each big loss, his mind was set on new riches
وبعد كل خسارة كبيرة، كان يفكر في ثروات جديدة
he pursued the trade more zealously
لقد مارس التجارة بحماسة أكبر
he forced his debtors more strictly to pay
لقد أجبر مدينيه على الدفع بشكل أكثر صرامة
because he wanted to continue gambling
لأنه أراد الاستمرار في المقامرة
he wanted to continue squandering
أراد أن يستمر في التبذير
he wanted to continue demonstrating his disdain of wealth
أراد أن يستمر في إظهار ازدرائه للثروة
Siddhartha lost his calmness when losses occurred
لقد فقد سيدهارتا هدوءه عندما حدثت الخسائر

he lost his patience when he was not paid on time
لقد فقد صبره عندما لم يتم دفع راتبه في الوقت المحدد
he lost his kindness towards beggars
لقد فقد لطفه تجاه المتسولين
He gambled away tens of thousands at one roll of the dice
لقد قام بالمقامرة بعشرات الآلاف في رمية واحدة للنرد
he became more strict and more petty in his business
لقد أصبح أكثر صرامة وأكثر تافهة في عمله
occasionally, he was dreaming at night about money!
في بعض الأحيان كان يحلم في الليل بالمال!
whenever he woke up from this ugly spell, he continued fleeing
كلما استيقظ من هذه التعويذة القبيحة، استمر في الفرار
whenever he found his face in the mirror to have aged, he found a new game
كلما وجد وجهه في المرآة قد تقدم في السن، وجد لعبة جديدة
whenever embarrassment and disgust came over him, he numbed his mind
كلما أصابه الحرج والاشمئزاز، كان يخدر عقله
he numbed his mind with sex and wine
لقد خدر عقله بالجنس والنبيذ
and from there he fled back into the urge to pile up and obtain possessions
ومن هناك فر مرة أخرى إلى الرغبة في التكديس والحصول على الممتلكات

In this pointless cycle he ran
في هذه الدورة التي لا معنى لها ركض
from his life he grow tired, old, and ill
من حياته أصبح متعبًا، وشيخًا، ومريضًا

Then the time came when a dream warned him
ثم جاء الوقت الذي حذره فيه حلم
He had spent the hours of the evening with Kamala
لقد أمضى ساعات المساء مع كامالا
he had been in her beautiful pleasure-garden
لقد كان في حديقتها الجميلة

They had been sitting under the trees, talking
لقد كانوا يجلسون تحت الأشجار ويتحدثون
and Kamala had said thoughtful words
وقالت كامالا كلمات مدروسة
words behind which a sadness and tiredness lay hidden
كلمات يختبئ خلفها الحزن والتعب
She had asked him to tell her about Gotama
لقد طلبت منه أن يخبرها عن جوتاما
she could not hear enough of him
لم تستطع سماع ما يكفي منه
she loved how clear his eyes were
لقد أحبت مدى وضوح عينيه
she loved how still and beautiful his mouth was
لقد أحبت فمه الهادئ والجميل
she loved the kindness of his smile
لقد احبت لطف ابتسامته
she loved how peaceful his walk had been
لقد أحبت مدى هدوء مشيته
For a long time, he had to tell her about the exalted Buddha
لفترة طويلة، كان عليه أن يخبرها عن بوذا العظيم
and Kamala had sighed, and spoke
وتنهدت كامالا وتحدثت
"One day, perhaps soon, I'll also follow that Buddha"
"في يوم من الأيام، ربما قريبًا، سأتبع هذا بوذا أيضًا"
"I'll give him my pleasure-garden for a gift"
"سأعطيه حديقتي الترفيهية كهدية"
"and I will take my refuge in his teachings"
"وسألجأ إلى تعاليمه"
But after this, she had aroused him
ولكن بعد هذا، أثارته
she had tied him to her in the act of making love
لقد ربطته بها أثناء ممارسة الحب
with painful fervour, biting and in tears
بحماسة مؤلمة، وعض ودموع
it was as if she wanted to squeeze the last sweet drop out of this wine

- 148 -

كان الأمر وكأنها تريد عصر آخر قطرة حلوة من هذا النبيذ

Never before had it become so strangely clear to Siddhartha

لم يسبق من قبل أن أصبح الأمر واضحًا بشكل غريب لسيدهارتا

he felt how close lust was akin to death

لقد شعر بمدى قرب الشهوة من الموت

he laid by her side, and Kamala's face was close to him

استلقى بجانبها، وكان وجه كامالا قريبًا منه.

under her eyes and next to the corners of her mouth

تحت عينيها وبجانب زوايا فمها

it was as clear as never before

لقد كان واضحا كما لم يكن من قبل

there read a fearful inscription

هناك قرأت نقشًا مخيفًا

an inscription of small lines and slight grooves

نقش من خطوط صغيرة وأخاديد طفيفة

an inscription reminiscent of autumn and old age

نقش يذكرنا بالخريف والشيخوخة

here and there, gray hairs among his black ones

هنا وهناك، شعر رمادي بين شعره الأسود

Siddhartha himself, who was only in his forties, noticed the same thing

لقد لاحظ سيدهارثا نفسه، الذي كان في الأربعينيات من عمره فقط، نفس الشيء

Tiredness was written on Kamala's beautiful face

كان التعب مكتوبا على وجه كامالا الجميل

tiredness from walking a long path

التعب من المشي في طريق طويل

a path which has no happy destination

طريق ليس له وجهة سعيدة

tiredness and the beginning of withering

التعب وبداية الذبول

fear of old age, autumn, and having to die

الخوف من الشيخوخة والخريف والموت

With a sigh, he had bid his farewell to her

مع تنهد، ودعها

the soul full of reluctance, and full of concealed anxiety

الروح المملوءة بالتردد، والمليئة بالقلق الخفي

Siddhartha had spent the night in his house with dancing girls
كان سيدهارثا قد أمضى الليل في منزله مع الفتيات الراقصات

he acted as if he was superior to them
لقد تصرف وكأنه متفوق عليهم

he acted superior towards the fellow-members of his caste
لقد تصرف بتفوق تجاه زملائه من أفراد طبقته

but this was no longer true
ولكن هذا لم يعد صحيحا

he had drunk much wine that night
لقد شرب الكثير من النبيذ تلك الليلة

and he went to bed a long time after midnight
وذهب إلى الفراش لفترة طويلة بعد منتصف الليل

tired and yet excited, close to weeping and despair
متعب ولكن متحمس، على وشك البكاء واليأس

for a long time he sought to sleep, but it was in vain
لفترة طويلة حاول النوم، لكن دون جدوى

his heart was full of misery
كان قلبه مليئا بالبؤس

he thought he could not bear any longer
اعتقد أنه لم يعد يستطيع التحمل

he was full of a disgust, which he felt penetrating his entire body
كان مليئا بالاشمئزاز، الذي شعر به يخترق جسده بالكامل

like the lukewarm repulsive taste of the wine
مثل طعم النبيذ الفاتر المثير للاشمئزاز

the dull music was a little too happy
كانت الموسيقى المملة سعيدة بعض الشيء

the smile of the dancing girls was a little too soft
كانت ابتسامة الفتيات الراقصات ناعمة بعض الشيء

the scent of their hair and breasts was a little too sweet
كانت رائحة شعرهم وثدييهم حلوة بعض الشيء

But more than by anything else, he was disgusted by himself

ولكن أكثر من أي شيء آخر، كان يشعر بالاشمئزاز من نفسه
he was disgusted by his perfumed hair
كان يشمئز من شعره المعطر
he was disgusted by the smell of wine from his mouth
كان يشمئز من رائحة الخمر التي تخرج من فمه
he was disgusted by the listlessness of his skin
كان يشعر بالاشمئزاز من خمول جلده
Like when someone who has eaten and drunk far too much
مثل عندما يأكل شخص ويشرب كثيرًا
they vomit it back up again with agonising pain
يتقيؤونها مرة أخرى بألم مبرح
but they feel relieved by the vomiting
لكنهم يشعرون بالارتياح بسبب القيء
this sleepless man wished to free himself of these pleasures
كان هذا الرجل الذي لا ينام يرغب في تحرير نفسه من هذه الملذات
he wanted to be rid of these habits
أراد التخلص من هذه العادات
he wanted to escape all of this pointless life
لقد أراد الهروب من كل هذه الحياة التي لا معنى لها
and he wanted to escape from himself
وأراد أن يهرب من نفسه
it wasn't until the light of the morning when he had slightly fallen sleep

لم يكن قد نام إلا مع ضوء الصباح
the first activities in the street were already beginning
كانت الأنشطة الأولى في الشارع قد بدأت بالفعل
for a few moments he had found a hint of sleep
لقد وجد في لحظات إشارة إلى النوم
In those moments, he had a dream
في تلك اللحظات كان لديه حلم
Kamala owned a small, rare singing bird in a golden cage
كانت كامالا تمتلك طائرًا صغيرًا نادرًا يغني في قفص ذهبي
it always sung to him in the morning
كانت تغني له دائما في الصباح
but then he dreamt this bird had become mute
ولكن بعد ذلك حلم أن هذا الطائر أصبح أخرس

since this arose his attention, he stepped in front of the cage
منذ أن لفت هذا انتباهه، خطى أمام القفص
he looked at the bird inside the cage
نظر إلى الطائر داخل القفص
the small bird was dead, and lay stiff on the ground
كان الطائر الصغير ميتًا، وملقى جامدًا على الأرض
He took the dead bird out of its cage
أخرج الطائر الميت من قفصه
he took a moment to weigh the dead bird in his hand
أخذ لحظة ليزن الطائر الميت في يده
and then threw it away, out in the street
ثم ألقيته في الشارع
in the same moment he felt terribly shocked
في نفس اللحظة شعر بصدمة شديدة
his heart hurt as if he had thrown away all value
كان قلبه يؤلمه وكأنه تخلص من كل القيم
everything good had been inside of this dead bird
كل شيء جيد كان موجودا داخل هذا الطائر الميت
Starting up from this dream, he felt encompassed by a deep sadness
انطلاقا من هذا الحلم، شعر بأنه محاط بحزن عميق
everything seemed worthless to him
كل شيء بدا له بلا قيمة
worthless and pointless was the way he had been going through life
كانت حياته بلا قيمة ولا معنى.
nothing which was alive was left in his hands
لم يبق في يديه شيء حي
nothing which was in some way delicious could be kept
لا يمكن الاحتفاظ بأي شيء لذيذ بطريقة ما
nothing worth keeping would stay
لن يبقى شيء يستحق الاحتفاظ به
alone he stood there, empty like a castaway on the shore
كان واقفا هناك وحيدًا، فارغًا مثل شخص تائه على الشاطئ

- 152 -

With a gloomy mind, Siddhartha went to his pleasure-garden

بعقل كئيب، ذهب سيدهارتا إلى حديقة المتعة الخاصة به

he locked the gate and sat down under a mango-tree

أغلق الباب وجلس تحت شجرة المانجو

he felt death in his heart and horror in his chest

شعر بالموت في قلبه والرعب في صدره

he sensed how everything died and withered in him

أحس كيف مات كل شيء وذبل بداخله

By and by, he gathered his thoughts in his mind

وبمرور الوقت، جمع أفكاره في ذهنه

once again, he went through the entire path of his life

مرة أخرى، مر بنفس المسار الذي سلكه طوال حياته

he started with the first days he could remember

بدأ بالأيام الأولى التي يتذكرها

When was there ever a time when he had felt a true bliss?

متى كانت هناك لحظة شعر فيها بالسعادة الحقيقية؟

Oh yes, several times he had experienced such a thing

أوه نعم، لقد مر بمثل هذا الشيء عدة مرات

In his years as a boy he had had a taste of bliss

في سنوات طفولته كان يتذوق طعم النعيم

he had felt happiness in his heart when he obtained praise from the Brahmans

لقد شعر بالسعادة في قلبه عندما حصل على الثناء من البراهمة

"There is a path in front of the one who has distinguished himself"

"هناك طريق أمام من تميز"

he had felt bliss reciting the holy verses

لقد شعر بالبهجة وهو يتلو الآيات الكريمة

he had felt bliss disputing with the learned ones

لقد شعر بالنعيم وهو يجادل العلماء

he had felt bliss when he was an assistant in the offerings

لقد شعر بالسعادة عندما كان مساعدًا في تقديم القرابين

Then, he had felt it in his heart

ثم شعر بذلك في قلبه

"There is a path in front of you"

"هناك طريق أمامك"
"you are destined for this path"

"لقد قدر لك هذا الطريق"
"the gods are awaiting you"

"الآلهة في انتظارك"
And again, as a young man, he had felt bliss

ومرة أخرى، عندما كان شابًا، شعر بالنعيم
when his thoughts separated him from those thinking on the same things

عندما انفصلت أفكاره عن أولئك الذين يفكرون في نفس الأشياء
when he wrestled in pain for the purpose of Brahman

عندما كان يتصارع في الألم من أجل البراهمان
when every obtained knowledge only kindled new thirst in him

عندما كان كل ما اكتسبه من معرفة لا يزيده إلا عطشًا جديدًا
in the midst of the pain he felt this very same thing

في وسط الألم شعر بنفس الشيء
"Go on! You are called upon!"

"استمر! لقد تم استدعاؤك!"
He had heard this voice when he had left his home

لقد سمع هذا الصوت عندما غادر منزله
he heard heard this voice when he had chosen the life of a Samana

لقد سمع هذا الصوت عندما اختار حياة سامانا
and again he heard this voice when left the Samanas

وسمع هذا الصوت مرة أخرى عندما غادر ساماناس
he had heard the voice when he went to see the perfected one

لقد سمع الصوت عندما ذهب لرؤية الشخص الكامل
and when he had gone away from the perfected one, he had heard the voice

ولما ابتعد عن الكامل سمع الصوت
he had heard the voice when he went into the uncertain

لقد سمع الصوت عندما ذهب إلى المكان غير المؤكد
For how long had he not heard this voice anymore?

منذ متى لم يسمع هذا الصوت بعد؟

for how long had he reached no height anymore?
منذ متى لم يصل إلى ارتفاع بعد؟

how even and dull was the manner in which he went through life?
كم كانت حياته مملة ومتوازنة؟

for many long years without a high goal
لسنوات طويلة دون هدف كبير

he had been without thirst or elevation
لقد كان بلا عطش أو ارتفاع

he had been content with small lustful pleasures
لقد كان راضيا بالمتع الشهوانية الصغيرة

and yet he was never satisfied!
ومع ذلك لم يكن راضيا أبدا!

For all of these years he had tried hard to become like the others
طوال هذه السنوات كان يحاول جاهدا أن يصبح مثل الآخرين

he longed to be one of the childlike people
كان يتوق إلى أن يكون من الناس الطفوليين

but he didn't know that that was what he really wanted
ولكنه لم يكن يعلم أن هذا هو ما يريده حقًا

his life had been much more miserable and poorer than theirs
لقد كانت حياته أكثر بؤسًا وفقرًا من حياتهم

because their goals and worries were not his
لأن أهدافهم ومخاوفهم لم تكن في صالحه.

the entire world of the Kamaswami-people had only been a game to him
كان عالم شعب كاماسوامي بأكمله مجرد لعبة بالنسبة له

their lives were a dance he would watch
كانت حياتهم عبارة عن رقصة كان يشاهدها

they performed a comedy he could amuse himself with
لقد قاموا بتقديم كوميديا كان بإمكانه أن يسلي نفسه بها

Only Kamala had been dear and valuable to him
فقط كامالا كانت عزيزة وقيمة بالنسبة له

but was she still valuable to him?
ولكن هل كانت لا تزال ذات قيمة بالنسبة له؟

Did he still need her?

هل مازال يحتاجها؟

Or did she still need him?

أم أنها لا زالت بحاجة إليه؟

Did they not play a game without an ending?

ألم يلعبوا لعبة بلا نهاية؟

Was it necessary to live for this?

هل كان من الضروري أن نعيش من أجل هذا؟

No, it was not necessary!

لا لم يكن ذلك ضروريا!

The name of this game was Sansara

اسم هذه اللعبة هو سانسارا

a game for children which was perhaps enjoyable to play once

لعبة للأطفال ربما كان من الممتع لعبها ذات يوم

maybe it could be played twice

ربما يمكن لعبها مرتين

perhaps you could play it ten times

ربما يمكنك تشغيله عشر مرات

but should you play it for ever and ever?

ولكن هل ينبغي عليك أن تلعبها إلى الأبد؟

Then, Siddhartha knew that the game was over

ثم عرف سيدهارثا أن اللعبة انتهت

he knew that he could not play it any more

كان يعلم أنه لم يعد يستطيع اللعب بعد الآن

Shivers ran over his body and inside of him

سرت قشعريرة في جسده وداخله

he felt that something had died

شعر أن شيئا ما قد مات

That entire day, he sat under the mango-tree

جلس طوال ذلك اليوم تحت شجرة المانجو

he was thinking of his father

كان يفكر في والده

he was thinking of Govinda

كان يفكر في جوفيندا

- 156 -

and he was thinking of Gotama
وكان يفكر في جوتاما

Did he have to leave them to become a Kamaswami?
هل كان عليه أن يتركهم ليصبح كاماسوامي؟

He was still sitting there when the night had fallen
كان لا يزال جالسا هناك عندما حل الليل

he caught sight of the stars, and thought to himself
لقد رأى النجوم، وفكر في نفسه

"Here I'm sitting under my mango-tree in my pleasure-garden"
"أنا هنا جالس تحت شجرة المانجو في حديقتي الترفيهية".

He smiled a little to himself
ابتسم قليلا لنفسه

was it really necessary to own a garden?
هل كان من الضروري حقا امتلاك حديقة؟

was it not a foolish game?
ألم تكن لعبة حمقاء؟

did he need to own a mango-tree?
هل كان يحتاج إلى امتلاك شجرة مانجو؟

He also put an end to this
كما وضع حدا لهذا

this also died in him
وهذا مات فيه أيضا

He rose and bid his farewell to the mango-tree
قام وودع شجرة المانجو

he bid his farewell to the pleasure-garden
ودع حديقة المتعة

Since he had been without food this day, he felt strong hunger
وبما أنه لم يأكل هذا اليوم فقد شعر بجوع شديد

and he thought of his house in the city
وفكر في بيته في المدينة

he thought of his chamber and bed
كان يفكر في غرفته وسريره

he thought of the table with the meals on it
كان يفكر في الطاولة التي عليها الوجبات

He smiled tiredly, shook himself, and bid his farewell to these things

ابتسم بتعب، وهز نفسه، وودع هذه الأشياء

In the same hour of the night, Siddhartha left his garden

في نفس الساعة من الليل، غادر سيدهارثا حديقته

he left the city and never came back

غادر المدينة ولم يعد أبدًا

For a long time, Kamaswami had people look for him

لفترة طويلة، كان كاماسوامي يطلب من الناس البحث عنه

they thought he had fallen into the hands of robbers

ظنوا أنه وقع في أيدي اللصوص

Kamala had no one look for him

لم يكن لدى كامالا أحد يبحث عنه

she was not astonished by his disappearance

لم تكن مندهشة من اختفائه

Did she not always expect it?

ألم تكن تتوقع ذلك دائمًا؟

Was he not a Samana?

ألم يكن سامانا؟

a man who was at home nowhere, a pilgrim

رجل لم يكن في بيته في أي مكان، حاج

she had felt this the last time they had been together

لقد شعرت بهذا في المرة الأخيرة التي كانا فيها معًا

she was happy despite all the pain of the loss

كانت سعيدة رغم كل الألم الذي شعرت به بسبب الخسارة

she was happy she had been with him one last time

كانت سعيدة لأنها كانت معه للمرة الأخيرة

she was happy she had pulled him so affectionately to her heart

كانت سعيدة لأنها جذبته إلى قلبها بمودة

she was happy she had felt completely possessed and penetrated by him

كانت سعيدة لأنها شعرت بأنها مسكونة ومخترقة بالكامل من قبله

When she received the news, she went to the window

عندما تلقت الخبر ذهبت إلى النافذة

at the window she held a rare singing bird
عند النافذة كانت تحمل طائرًا مغردًا نادرًا

the bird was held captive in a golden cage
تم احتجاز الطائر في قفص ذهبي

She opened the door of the cage
فتحت باب القفص

she took the bird out and let it fly
أخذت الطائر وتركته يطير

For a long time, she gazed after it
لفترة طويلة، نظرت إليه

From this day on, she received no more visitors
منذ هذا اليوم، لم تعد تستقبل أي زوار.

and she kept her house locked
وأبقت بيتها مغلقا

But after some time, she became aware that she was pregnant
لكن بعد مرور بعض الوقت أدركت أنها حامل.

she was pregnant from the last time she was with Siddhartha
كانت حاملاً منذ آخر مرة كانت فيها مع سيدهارتا

By the River
بجانب النهر

Siddhartha walked through the forest
سار سيدهارثا عبر الغابة

he was already far from the city
لقد كان بعيدًا بالفعل عن المدينة

and he knew nothing but one thing
ولم يكن يعرف إلا شيئا واحدا

there was no going back for him
لم يكن هناك عودة له

the life that he had lived for many years was over
لقد انتهت الحياة التي عاشها لسنوات عديدة

he had tasted all of this life
لقد ذاق كل هذه الحياة

he had sucked everything out of this life
لقد امتص كل شيء من هذه الحياة

until he was disgusted with it
حتى اشمئز منه

the singing bird he had dreamt of was dead
لقد مات الطائر المغرد الذي حلم به

and the bird in his heart was dead too
والطائر في قلبه مات أيضا

he had been deeply entangled in Sansara
لقد كان متورطًا بشدة في سانسارا

he had sucked up disgust and death into his body
لقد امتص الاشمئزاز والموت في جسده

like a sponge sucks up water until it is full
مثل الاسفنجة التي تمتص الماء حتى تمتلئ

he was full of misery and death
كان مليئا بالبؤس والموت

there was nothing left in this world which could have attracted him
لم يبق شيء في هذا العالم يمكن أن يجذبه

nothing could have given him joy or comfort
لا شيء يمكن أن يمنحه الفرح أو الراحة

he passionately wished to know nothing about himself anymore

كان يتمنى بشدة ألا يعرف أي شيء عن نفسه بعد الآن

he wanted to have rest and be dead

أراد أن يحصل على الراحة ويموت

he wished there was a lightning-bolt to strike him dead!

تمنى أن تضربه صاعقة فتقتله!

If there only was a tiger to devour him!

لو كان هناك نمر يلتهمه!

If there only was a poisonous wine which would numb his senses

لو كان هناك نبيذ سام يخدر حواسه

a wine which brought him forgetfulness and sleep

نبيذ يجلب له النسيان والنوم

a wine from which he wouldn't awake from

نبيذ لا يستيقظ منه

Was there still any kind of filth he had not soiled himself with?

هل كان هناك أي نوع من القذارة لم يلوث نفسه بها؟

was there a sin or foolish act he had not committed?

هل كان هناك خطيئة أو فعل أحمق لم يرتكبه؟

was there a dreariness of the soul he didn't know?

هل كان هناك كآبة في الروح لم يعرفها؟

was there anything he had not brought upon himself?

هل كان هناك أي شيء لم يجلبه على نفسه؟

Was it still at all possible to be alive?

هل كان من الممكن أن أبقى على قيد الحياة على الإطلاق؟

Was it possible to breathe in again and again?

هل كان من الممكن أن أتنفس مرارا وتكرارا؟

Could he still breathe out?

هل مازال بإمكانه التنفس؟

was he able to bear hunger?

هل كان قادرا على تحمل الجوع؟

was there any way to eat again?

هل كانت هناك أي طريقة لتناول الطعام مرة أخرى؟

was it possible to sleep again?

هل كان من الممكن النوم مرة أخرى؟
could he sleep with a woman again?
هل يستطيع أن ينام مع امرأة مرة أخرى؟
had this cycle not exhausted itself?
ألم تستنفد هذه الدورة نفسها؟
were things not brought to their conclusion?
ولم تصل الأمور إلى نهايتها؟

Siddhartha reached the large river in the forest
وصل سيدهارتا إلى النهر الكبير في الغابة
it was the same river he crossed when he had still been a young man
كان نفس النهر الذي عبره عندما كان لا يزال شابًا
it was the same river he crossed from the town of Gotama
كان نفس النهر الذي عبره من بلدة غوتاما
he remembered a ferryman who had taken him over the river
تذكر رجل العبارة الذي أخذه عبر النهر
By this river he stopped, and hesitantly he stood at the bank
توقف عند هذا النهر، ووقف على ضفته مترددا
Tiredness and hunger had weakened him
لقد أضعفه التعب والجوع
"what should I walk on for?"
"لماذا يجب أن أمشي؟"
"to what goal was there left to go?"
"إلى أي هدف بقي أن نذهب؟"
No, there were no more goals
لا، لم يكن هناك المزيد من الأهداف
there was nothing left but a painful yearning to shake off this dream
لم يبق شيء سوى الشوق المؤلم للتخلص من هذا الحلم
he yearned to spit out this stale wine
كان يتوق إلى بصق هذا النبيذ الفاسد
he wanted to put an end to this miserable and shameful life
أراد أن يضع حداً لهذه الحياة البائسة والمخزية
a coconut-tree bent over the bank of the river

شجرة جوز الهند تتحني على ضفة النهر

Siddhartha leaned against its trunk with his shoulder

استند سيدهارثا على جذعها بكتفه

he embraced the trunk with one arm

احتضن الجذع بذراعه الواحدة

and he looked down into the green water

ونظر إلى أسفل إلى المياه الخضراء

the water ran under him

كان الماء يجري تحته

he looked down and found himself to be entirely filled with the wish to let go

نظر إلى أسفل فوجد نفسه ممتلئًا تمامًا بالرغبة في التخلي

he wanted to drown in these waters

أراد أن يغرق في هذه المياه

the water reflected a frightening emptiness back at him

انعكست على الماء فراغًا مخيفًا

the water answered to the terrible emptiness in his soul

أجاب الماء على الفراغ الرهيب في روحه

Yes, he had reached the end

نعم لقد وصل إلى النهاية

There was nothing left for him, except to annihilate himself

لم يبق له شيء إلا أن يهلك نفسه

he wanted to smash the failure into which he had shaped his life

أراد أن يحطم الفشل الذي شكل حياته فيه

he wanted to throw his life before the feet of mockingly laughing gods

أراد أن يلقي بحياته أمام أقدام الآلهة الساخرة

This was the great vomiting he had longed for; death

كان هذا هو القيء العظيم الذي كان يتوق إليه؛ الموت

the smashing to bits of the form he hated

تحطيم إلى أجزاء من الشكل الذي يكرهه

Let him be food for fishes and crocodiles

فليكن طعاما للأسماك والتماسيح

Siddhartha the dog, a lunatic

سيدهارتا الكلب، مجنون

a depraved and rotten body; a weakened and abused soul!

جسد فاسد ومتعفن، روح ضعيفة ومُساء معاملتها!

let him be chopped to bits by the daemons

دعه يقطع إلى أشلاء بواسطة الشياطين

With a distorted face, he stared into the water

بوجه مشوه، حدق في الماء

he saw the reflection of his face and spat at it

رأى انعكاس وجهه فبصق عليه

In deep tiredness, he took his arm away from the trunk of the tree

في تعب شديد، أزال ذراعه عن جذع الشجرة

he turned a bit, in order to let himself fall straight down

استدار قليلا ليسمح لنفسه بالسقوط مباشرة إلى الأسفل

in order to finally drown in the river

من أجل الغرق في النهر في النهاية

With his eyes closed, he slipped towards death

مع عينيه مغلقتين، انزلق نحو الموت

Then, out of remote areas of his soul, a sound stirred up

ثم خرج من مناطق نائية من روحه صوت

a sound stirred up out of past times of his now weary life

صوت ينشأ من أوقات ماضية من حياته المتعبة الآن

It was a singular word, a single syllable

كانت كلمة مفردة، مقطع لفظي واحد

without thinking he spoke the voice to himself

دون تفكير تحدث بصوته إلى نفسه

he slurred the beginning and the end of all prayers of the Brahmans

لقد نطق ببداية ونهاية كل صلوات البراهمة

he spoke the holy Om

لقد تحدث بالأووم المقدس

"that what is perfect" or "the completion"

"ذلك ما هو كامل" أو "الاكتمال"

And in the moment he realized the foolishness of his actions

وفي تلك اللحظة أدرك حماقة أفعاله

the sound of Om touched Siddhartha's ear

صوت أوم لامس أذن سيدهارتا

his dormant spirit suddenly woke up

استيقظت روحه النائمة فجأة

Siddhartha was deeply shocked

لقد أصيب سيدهارثا بصدمة عميقة

he saw this was how things were with him

لقد رأى أن هذه هي الطريقة التي كانت بها الأمور معه

he was so doomed that he had been able to seek death

لقد كان محكوما عليه بالهلاك لدرجة أنه كان قادرا على طلب الموت

he had lost his way so much that he wished the end

لقد فقد طريقه كثيرًا لدرجة أنه تمنى النهاية

the wish of a child had been able to grow in him

كانت رغبة الطفل قادرة على النمو بداخله

he had wished to find rest by annihilating his body!

لقد كان يرغب في إيجاد الراحة عن طريق تدمير جسده!

all the agony of recent times

كل آلام الأوقات الأخيرة

all sobering realizations that his life had created

كل الإدراكات المذهلة التي خلقتها حياته

all the desperation that he had felt

كل اليأس الذي شعر به

these things did not bring about this moment

هذه الأشياء لم تؤدي إلى هذه اللحظة

when the Om entered his consciousness he became aware of himself

عندما دخل أوم إلى وعيه أصبح مدركًا لنفسه

he realized his misery and his error

أدرك بؤسه وخطئه

Om! he spoke to himself

أوم! تحدث إلى نفسه

Om! and again he knew about Brahman

أوم! ومرة أخرى عرف عن براهمان

Om! he knew about the indestructibility of life

أوه! لقد عرف أن الحياة لا يمكن تدميرها

Om! he knew about all that is divine, which he had forgotten

أوه! لقد عرف كل ما هو إلهي، والذي نسيه.

But this was only a moment that flashed before him
ولكن هذه كانت مجرد لحظة مرت أمامه
By the foot of the coconut-tree, Siddhartha collapsed
عند سفح شجرة جوز الهند، انهار سيدهارثا
he was struck down by tiredness
لقد أصابه التعب
mumbling "Om", he placed his head on the root of the tree
تمتم "أوم" ووضع رأسه على جذر الشجرة
and he fell into a deep sleep
وسقط في نوم عميق
Deep was his sleep, and without dreams
كان نومه عميقا، وبدون أحلام
for a long time he had not known such a sleep any more
لم يعرف مثل هذا النوم لفترة طويلة

When he woke up after many hours, he felt as if ten years had passed
عندما استيقظ بعد ساعات طويلة شعر وكأن عشر سنوات مرت
he heard the water quietly flowing
سمع الماء يتدفق بهدوء
he did not know where he was
لم يكن يعرف أين هو
and he did not know who had brought him here
ولم يكن يعلم من الذي أتى به إلى هنا
he opened his eyes and looked with astonishment
فتح عينيه ونظر بدهشة
there were trees and the sky above him
وكانت هناك أشجار والسماء فوقه
he remembered where he was and how he got here
تذكر أين كان وكيف وصل إلى هنا
But it took him a long while for this
لكن الأمر استغرق منه وقتا طويلا حتى فعل هذا
the past seemed to him as if it had been covered by a veil
لقد بدا له الماضي وكأنه كان مغطى بحجاب
infinitely distant, infinitely far away, infinitely meaningless
بعيد بلا حدود، بعيد بلا حدود، بلا معنى بلا حدود

He only knew that his previous life had been abandoned

كل ما عرفه هو أن حياته السابقة قد تم التخلي عنها

this past life seemed to him like a very old, previous incarnation

بدت له هذه الحياة الماضية وكأنها تجسد سابق قديم جدًا

this past life felt like a pre-birth of his present self

لقد شعر أن هذه الحياة الماضية كانت بمثابة ولادة مبكرة لذاته الحالية

full of disgust and wretchedness, he had intended to throw his life away

كان مليئًا بالاشمئزاز والبؤس، وكان ينوي التخلص من حياته

he had come to his senses by a river, under a coconut-tree

لقد عاد إلى رشده عند النهر، تحت شجرة جوز الهند

the holy word "Om" was on his lips

كانت الكلمة المقدسة "أوم" على شفتيه

he had fallen asleep and had now woken up

لقد نام واستيقظ الآن

he was looking at the world as a new man

كان ينظر إلى العالم كرجل جديد

Quietly, he spoke the word "Om" to himself

بهدوء، قال كلمة "أوم" لنفسه

the "Om" he was speaking when he had fallen asleep

"أوم" كان يقولها عندما نام

his sleep felt like nothing more than a long meditative recitation of "Om"

بدا نومه وكأنه مجرد تلاوة تأملية طويلة لـ "أوم"

all his sleep had been a thinking of "Om"

كان كل نومه يفكر في "أوم"

a submergence and complete entering into "Om"

الانغماس والدخول الكامل في "أوم"

a going into the perfected and completed

الذهاب إلى الكمال والاكتمال

What a wonderful sleep this had been!

لقد كان هذا نومًا رائعًا!

he had never before been so refreshed by sleep

لم يكن منتعشا من النوم من قبل

Perhaps, he really had died

ربما كان قد مات حقا

maybe he had drowned and was reborn in a new body?

ربما غرق وولد في جسد جديد؟

But no, he knew himself and who he was

لكن لا، لقد عرف نفسه ومن هو

he knew his hands and his feet

كان يعرف يديه وقدميه

he knew the place where he lay

كان يعرف المكان الذي يرقد فيه

he knew this self in his chest

لقد عرف هذا الذات في صدره

Siddhartha the eccentric, the weird one

سيدهارتا الغريب الأطوار

but this Siddhartha was nevertheless transformed

لكن هذا سيدهارتا تحول مع ذلك

he was strangely well rested and awake

لقد كان مرتاحًا ومستيقظًا بشكل غريب

and he was joyful and curious

وكان سعيدًا وفضوليًا

Siddhartha straightened up and looked around

استقام سيدهارتا ونظر حوله

then he saw a person sitting opposite to him

ثم رأى شخصاً جالساً أمامه

a monk in a yellow robe with a shaven head

راهب يرتدي ثوبًا أصفر ورأس محلوق

he was sitting in the position of pondering

كان جالسا في وضع التأمل

He observed the man, who had neither hair on his head nor a beard

فلاحظ الرجل الذي لم يكن له شعر على رأسه ولا لحية

he had not observed him for long when he recognised this monk

لم يكن قد لاحظه لفترة طويلة عندما تعرف على هذا الراهب

it was Govinda, the friend of his youth

كان جوفيندا صديق شبابه

Govinda, who had taken his refuge with the exalted Buddha
جوفيندا، الذي لجأ إلى بوذا العظيم

Like Siddhartha, Govinda had also aged
مثل سيدهارتا، كان جوفيندا قد تقدم في السن أيضًا

but his face still bore the same features
لكن وجهه لا يزال يحمل نفس الملامح

his face still expressed zeal and faithfulness
لا يزال وجهه يعبر عن الحماس والإخلاص

you could see he was still searching, but timidly
يمكنك أن ترى أنه كان لا يزال يبحث، ولكن بخجل

Govinda sensed his gaze, opened his eyes, and looked at him
أحس جوفيندا بنظراته، ففتح عينيه ونظر إليه

Siddhartha saw that Govinda did not recognise him
رأى سيدهارتا أن جوفيندا لم يتعرف عليه

Govinda was happy to find him awake
كان جوفيندا سعيدًا عندما وجده مستيقظًا

apparently, he had been sitting here for a long time
على ما يبدو أنه كان يجلس هنا لفترة طويلة

he had been waiting for him to wake up
لقد كان ينتظره حتى يستيقظ

he waited, although he did not know him
انتظر رغم أنه لم يعرفه

"I have been sleeping" said Siddhartha
"لقد كنت نائمًا" قال سيدهارتا

"How did you get here?"
"كيف وصلت إلى هنا؟"

"You have been sleeping" answered Govinda
"لقد كنت نائما" أجاب جوفيندا

"It is not good to be sleeping in such places"
"ليس من الجيد النوم في مثل هذه الأماكن"

"snakes and the animals of the forest have their paths here"
"الثعابين وحيوانات الغابة لها مساراتها هنا"

"I, oh sir, am a follower of the exalted Gotama"
"أنا يا سيدي، من أتباع غوتاما الرفيع"

"I was on a pilgrimage on this path"

"I saw you lying and sleeping in a place where it is dangerous to sleep"

"كنت في رحلة حج على هذا الطريق"

"رأيتك مستلقيًا نائمًا في مكان خطير النوم فيه"

"Therefore, I sought to wake you up"

"لذلك، سعيت لإيقاظك"

"but I saw that your sleep was very deep"

"ولكن رأيت أن نومك كان عميقًا جدًا"

"so I stayed behind from my group"

"لذلك بقيت خلف مجموعتي"

"and I sat with you until you woke up"

"وجلست معك حتى استيقظت"

"And then, so it seems, I have fallen asleep myself"

"وبعد ذلك، يبدو أنني نمت بنفسي"

"I, who wanted to guard your sleep, fell asleep"

"أنا الذي أردت أن أحرس نومك، نمت"

"Badly, I have served you"

"لقد خدمتك بشكل سيء"

"tiredness had overwhelmed me"

"لقد أصابني التعب"

"But since you're awake, let me go to catch up with my brothers"

"ولكن بما أنك مستيقظ، دعني أذهب لألتقي بإخوتي"

"I thank you, Samana, for watching out over my sleep" spoke Siddhartha

"أشكرك يا سامانا على مراقبتك لنومي" قال سيدهارتا

"You're friendly, you followers of the exalted one"

"أنتم ودودون يا أتباع العالي"

"Now you may go to them"

"الآن يمكنك الذهاب إليهم"

"I'm going, sir. May you always be in good health"

"أنا ذاهب سيدي، أتمنى لك الصحة والعافية دائمًا"

"I thank you, Samana"

"شكرا لك، سامانا"

Govinda made the gesture of a salutation and said "Farewell"

قام جوفيندا بإيماءة التحية وقال "وداعًا"

"Farewell, Govinda" said Siddhartha

"وداعًا، جوفيندا" قال سيدهارثا

The monk stopped as if struck by lightning

توقف الراهب كأنه أصيب ببرق

"Permit me to ask, sir, from where do you know my name?"

"اسمح لي أن أسأل، سيدي، من أين تعرف اسمي؟"

Siddhartha smiled, "I know you, oh Govinda, from your father's hut"

ابتسم سيدهارتا، "أنا أعرفك، يا جوفيندا، من كوخ والدك"

"and I know you from the school of the Brahmans"

"وأنا أعرفك من مدرسة البراهمة"

"and I know you from the offerings"

"وأنا أعرفك من القرابين"

"and I know you from our walk to the Samanas"

"وأنا أعرفك من خلال نزهتنا إلى ساماناس"

"and I know you from when you took refuge with the exalted one"

"وأنا أعرفك حين أويت إلى الأعلى"

"You're Siddhartha," Govinda exclaimed loudly, "Now, I recognise you"

"أنت سيدهارتا" صاح جوفيندا بصوت عالٍ، "الآن، تعرفت عليك"

"I don't comprehend how I couldn't recognise you right away"

"لا أفهم كيف لم أتمكن من التعرف عليك على الفور"

"Siddhartha, my joy is great to see you again"

"سيدهارتا، سعادتي كبيرة لرؤيتك مرة أخرى"

"It also gives me joy, to see you again" spoke Siddhartha

"إنه لمن دواعي سروري أيضًا أن أراك مرة أخرى" تحدث سيدهارتا

"You've been the guard of my sleep"

"لقد كنت حارس نومي"

"again, I thank you for this"

"مرة أخرى، أشكرك على هذا"

"but I wouldn't have required any guard"

"لكنني لم أكن بحاجة إلى أي حارس"

"Where are you going to, oh friend?"

"إلى أين أنت ذاهب يا صديقي؟"
"I'm going nowhere," answered Govinda
"أنا لن أذهب إلى أي مكان" أجاب جوفيندا
"We monks are always travelling"
"نحن الرهبان نسافر دائمًا"
"whenever it is not the rainy season, we move from one place to another"
"عندما لا يكون موسم الأمطار، ننتقل من مكان إلى آخر"
"we live according to the rules of the teachings passed on to us"
"نحن نعيش وفقًا لقواعد التعاليم التي تم نقلها إلينا"
"we accept alms, and then we move on"
"نحن نقبل الصدقات، ثم ننتقل"
"It is always like this"
"إنه دائمًا مثل هذا"
"But you, Siddhartha, where are you going to?"
"ولكن أنت يا سيدهارثا، إلى أين أنت ذاهب؟"
"for me it is as it is with you"
"بالنسبة لي الأمر كما هو الحال معك"
"I'm going nowhere; I'm just travelling"
"أنا لا أذهب إلى أي مكان؛ أنا فقط أسافر"
"I'm also on a pilgrimage"
"أنا أيضا في الحج"
Govinda spoke "You say you're on a pilgrimage, and I believe you"
قال جوفيندا "أنت تقول أنك في رحلة حج وأنا أصدقك"
"But, forgive me, oh Siddhartha, you do not look like a pilgrim"
"ولكن سامحني يا سيدهارثا، أنت لا تبدو كحاج"
"You're wearing a rich man's garments"
"أنت ترتدي ملابس رجل غني"
"you're wearing the shoes of a distinguished gentleman"
"أنت ترتدي حذاء رجل محترم"
"and your hair, with the fragrance of perfume, is not a pilgrim's hair"
"وشعرك برائحة العطر ليس شعر حاج"

"you do not have the hair of a Samana"

"ليس لديك شعر سامانا"

"you are right, my dear"

"أنت على حق يا عزيزتي"

"you have observed things well"

"لقد لاحظت الأمور جيدا"

"your keen eyes see everything"

"عيناك الثاقبتان ترى كل شيء"

"But I haven't said to you that I was a Samana"

"ولكن لم أقل لك أنني سامانا"

"I said I'm on a pilgrimage"

"قلت أنني في رحلة حج"

"And so it is, I'm on a pilgrimage"

"وهكذا هو الحال، أنا في رحلة حج"

"You're on a pilgrimage" said Govinda

"أنت في رحلة حج" قال جوفيندا

"But few would go on a pilgrimage in such clothes"

"ولكن قليلون هم الذين يذهبون للحج بهذه الملابس"

"few would pilger in such shoes"

"قليلون هم الذين قد يرتكبون مثل هذه الأخطاء"

"and few pilgrims have such hair"

"وقليل من الحجاج لديهم مثل هذا الشعر"

"I have never met such a pilgrim"

"لم أقابل مثل هذا الحاج من قبل"

"and I have been a pilgrim for many years"

"ولقد كنت حاجًا لسنوات عديدة"

"I believe you, my dear Govinda"

"أنا أصدقك يا عزيزي جوفيندا"

"But now, today, you've met a pilgrim just like this"

"لكن الآن، اليوم، التقيت بحاج مثل هذا تمامًا"

"a pilgrim wearing these kinds of shoes and garment"

"حاج يرتدي هذا النوع من الأحذية والملابس"

"Remember, my dear, the world of appearances is not eternal"

"تذكري يا عزيزتي أن عالم المظاهر ليس أبديًا"

"our shoes and garments are anything but eternal"

"أحذيتنا وملابسنا ليست أبدية على الإطلاق"
"our hair and bodies are not eternal either"
"شعرنا وأجسادنا ليست أبدية أيضًا"
"I'm wearing a rich man's clothes"
"أنا أرتدي ملابس رجل غني"
"you've seen this quite right"
"لقد رأيت هذا بشكل صحيح"
"I'm wearing them, because I have been a rich man"
"أنا أرتديها لأنني كنت رجلاً ثريًا"
"and I'm wearing my hair like the worldly and lustful people"
"وأنا أرتدي شعري مثل الناس الدنيويين والشهوانيين"
"because I have been one of them"
"لأنني كنت واحدا منهم"
"And what are you now, Siddhartha?" Govinda asked
"وماذا أنت الآن يا سيدهارثا؟" سأل جوفيندا
"I don't know it, just like you"
"لا أعرف ذلك، مثلك تمامًا"
"I was a rich man, and now I am not a rich man anymore"
"كنت رجلاً غنياً، والآن لم أعد رجلاً غنياً"
"and what I'll be tomorrow, I don't know"
"وما سأكون عليه غدًا، لا أعلم"
"You've lost your riches?" asked Govinda
"لقد فقدت ثروتك؟" سأل جوفيندا
"I've lost my riches, or they have lost me"
"لقد فقدت ثروتي، أو فقدوني"
"My riches somehow happened to slip away from me"
"لقد اختفت ثروتي من بين يدي بطريقة ما"
"The wheel of physical manifestations is turning quickly, Govinda"
"عجلة المظاهر الجسدية تدور بسرعة، جوفيندا"
"Where is Siddhartha the Brahman?"
"أين سيدهارتا البراهمان؟"
"Where is Siddhartha the Samana?"
"أين سيدهارتا السامانا؟"
"Where is Siddhartha the rich man?"

"أين سيدهارتا الرجل الغني؟"
"Non-eternal things change quickly, Govinda, you know it"
"الأشياء غير الأبدية تتغير بسرعة، جوفيندا، أنت تعلم ذلك"
Govinda looked at the friend of his youth for a long time
نظر جوفيندا إلى صديق شبابه لفترة طويلة
he looked at him with doubt in his eyes
نظر إليه بشك في عينيه
After that, he gave him the salutation which one would use on a gentleman
وبعد ذلك أعطاه التحية التي يستخدمها الرجل مع الرجل المحترم.
and he went on his way, and continued his pilgrimage
ومضى في طريقه، وأكمل حجه.
With a smiling face, Siddhartha watched him leave
وبوجه مبتسم، شاهده سيدهارثا وهو يغادر
he loved him still, this faithful, fearful man
لقد أحبه حتى الآن، هذا الرجل المخلص الخائف
how could he not have loved everybody and everything in this moment?
كيف لم يكن يحب الجميع وكل شيء في هذه اللحظة؟
in the glorious hour after his wonderful sleep, filled with Om!
في الساعة المجيدة بعد نومه الرائع، المليئة بـ "أوم"!
The enchantment, which had happened inside of him in his sleep
السحر الذي حدث بداخله أثناء نومه
this enchantment was everything that he loved
كان هذا السحر هو كل ما أحبه
he was full of joyful love for everything he saw
كان مليئا بالحب السعيد لكل ما رآه
exactly this had been his sickness before
بالضبط هذا كان مرضه من قبل
he had not been able to love anybody or anything
لم يكن قادرا على حب أي شخص أو أي شيء
With a smiling face, Siddhartha watched the leaving monk
وبوجه مبتسم، شاهد سيدهارثا الراهب وهو يغادر

The sleep had strengthened him a lot

لقد كان النوم قد عزز قوته كثيرا

but hunger gave him great pain

لكن الجوع سبب له ألما شديدا

by now he had not eaten for two days

بحلول هذا الوقت لم يأكل لمدة يومين

the times were long past when he could resist such hunger

لقد مضى وقت طويل عندما كان بإمكانه مقاومة مثل هذا الجوع

With sadness, and yet also with a smile, he thought of that time

بحزن، ومع ذلك بابتسامة أيضًا، فكر في ذلك الوقت

In those days, so he remembered, he had boasted of three things to Kamala

في تلك الأيام، كما يتذكر، كان يتفاخر بثلاثة أشياء أمام كامالا

he had been able to do three noble and undefeatable feats

لقد كان قادرًا على القيام بثلاثة أعمال نبيلة لا يمكن هزيمتها

he was able to fast, wait, and think

كان قادرا على الصيام والانتظار والتفكير

These had been his possessions; his power and strength

كانت هذه ممتلكاته وقوته وسلطانه

in the busy, laborious years of his youth, he had learned these three feats

في سنوات شبابه المزدحمة والمتعبة، تعلم هذه المهارات الثلاث

And now, his feats had abandoned him

والآن، تخلت عنه مآثره

none of his feats were his any more

لم يعد أي من إنجازاته ملكًا له

neither fasting, nor waiting, nor thinking

لا صيام ولا انتظار ولا تفكير

he had given them up for the most wretched things

لقد تخلى عنهم من أجل أشياء بائسة

what is it that fades most quickly?

ما هو الشيء الذي يتلاشى بسرعة؟

sensual lust, the good life, and riches!

الشهوة الحسية، والحياة الطيبة، والثروات!

His life had indeed been strange

لقد كانت حياته غريبة بالفعل

And now, so it seemed, he had really become a childlike person

والآن، كما بدا، أصبح حقًا شخصًا طفوليًا

Siddhartha thought about his situation

فكر سيدهارثا في وضعه

Thinking was hard for him now

كان التفكير صعبا بالنسبة له الآن

he did not really feel like thinking

لم يكن يشعر حقا بالرغبة في التفكير

but he forced himself to think

لكنه أجبر نفسه على التفكير

"all these most easily perishing things have slipped from me"

"لقد فقدت كل هذه الأشياء التي تفسد بسهولة"

"again, now I'm standing here under the sun"

"مرة أخرى، الآن أنا واقف هنا تحت الشمس"

"I am standing here just like a little child"

"أنا واقف هنا مثل طفل صغير"

"nothing is mine, I have no abilities"

"لا شيء لي، ليس لدي أي قدرات"

"there is nothing I could bring about"

"لا يوجد شيء يمكنني تحقيقه"

"I have learned nothing from my life"

"لم أتعلم شيئا من حياتي"

"How wondrous all of this is!"

"كم هو رائع كل هذا!"

"it's wondrous that I'm no longer young"

"من العجيب أنني لم أعد شابًا"

"my hair is already half gray and my strength is fading"

"شعري أصبح نصفه رماديًا وقوتي تتلاشى"

"and now I'm starting again at the beginning, as a child!"

"والآن أبدأ من جديد من البداية، كطفل!"

Again, he had to smile to himself

مرة أخرى، كان عليه أن يبتسم لنفسه

Yes, his fate had been strange!

نعم لقد كان مصيره غريبًا!
Things were going downhill with him
كانت الأمور تسير نحو الأسوأ معه
and now he was again facing the world naked and stupid
والآن كان يواجه العالم مرة أخرى عاريًا وغبيًا
But he could not feel sad about this
ولكنه لم يستطع أن يشعر بالحزن بشأن هذا
no, he even felt a great urge to laugh
لا، حتى أنه شعر برغبة كبيرة في الضحك
he felt an urge to laugh about himself
شعر برغبة في الضحك على نفسه
he felt an urge to laugh about this strange, foolish world
لقد شعر برغبة في الضحك على هذا العالم الغريب السخيف
"Things are going downhill with you!" he said to himself
"الأمور تسير نحو الأسوأ معك!" قال لنفسه
and he laughed about his situation
وضحك على حالته
as he was saying it he happened to glance at the river
بينما كان يقول ذلك، صادف أن ألقى نظرة على النهر
and he also saw the river going downhill
ورأى أيضًا النهر ينحدر إلى أسفل
it was singing and being happy about everything
كان يغني ويسعد بكل شيء
He liked this, and kindly he smiled at the river
لقد أعجبه هذا، وابتسم بلطف للنهر
Was this not the river in which he had intended to drown himself?
أليس هذا هو النهر الذي كان ينوي أن يغرق نفسه فيه؟
in past times, a hundred years ago
في الماضي، منذ مائة عام
or had he dreamed this?
أم أنه حلم بهذا؟
"Wondrous indeed was my life" he thought
"كانت حياتي رائعة حقًا" فكر
"my life has taken wondrous detours"
"لقد اتخذت حياتي طرقًا ملتوية رائعة"

"As a boy, I only dealt with gods and offerings"
"عندما كنت صبيًا، كنت أتعامل فقط مع الآلهة والقرابين"
"As a youth, I only dealt with asceticism"
"في شبابي، كنت أتعامل فقط مع الزهد"
"I spent my time in thinking and meditation"
"لقد قضيت وقتي في التفكير والتأمل"
"I was searching for Brahman
"كنت أبحث عن براهمان"
"and I worshipped the eternal in the Atman"
"وكنت أعبد الأبدي في الأتمان"
"But as a young man, I followed the penitents"
"ولكن عندما كنت شابًا، كنت أتبع التائبين"
"I lived in the forest and suffered heat and frost"
"لقد عشت في الغابة وعانيت من الحر والصقيع"
"there I learned how to overcome hunger"
"هناك تعلمت كيفية التغلب على الجوع"
"and I taught my body to become dead"
"وعلمت جسدي أن يصبح ميتًا"
"Wonderfully, soon afterwards, insight came towards me"
"من الرائع أنه بعد فترة وجيزة، جاءتني البصيرة"
"insight in the form of the great Buddha's teachings"
"البصيرة في شكل تعاليم بوذا العظيم"
"I felt the knowledge of the oneness of the world"
"لقد شعرت بمعرفة وحدة العالم"
"I felt it circling in me like my own blood"
"شعرت به يدور في داخلي مثل دمي"
"But I also had to leave Buddha and the great knowledge"
"لكن كان عليّ أيضًا أن أترك بوذا والمعرفة العظيمة"
"I went and learned the art of love with Kamala"
"ذهبت وتعلمت فن الحب مع كامالا"
"I learned trading and business with Kamaswami"
"لقد تعلمت التجارة والأعمال مع كاماسوامي"
"I piled up money, and wasted it again"
"لقد جمعت المال وأهدرته مرة أخرى"
"I learned to love my stomach and please my senses"
"لقد تعلمت أن أحب معدتي وأرضي حواسي"

"I had to spend many years losing my spirit"
"لقد أمضيت سنوات عديدة وأنا أفقد روحي"
"and I had to unlearn thinking again"
"وكان علي أن أتعلم كيف أتخلص من التفكير مرة أخرى"
"there I had forgotten the oneness"
"هناك نسيت الوحدة"
"Isn't it just as if I had turned slowly from a man into a child"?
"أليس الأمر كما لو أنني تحولت ببطء من رجل إلى طفل؟"
"from a thinker into a childlike person"
"من مفكر إلى شخص طفولي"
"And yet, this path has been very good"
"ومع ذلك، كان هذا المسار جيدًا جدًا"
"and yet, the bird in my chest has not died"
"ومع ذلك، فإن الطائر في صدري لم يمت"
"what a path has this been!"
"يا له من طريق!"
"I had to pass through so much stupidity"
"لقد كان علي أن أمر بكل هذا الغباء"
"I had to pass through so much vice"
"لقد كان علي أن أمر بالكثير من الرذيلة"
"I had to make so many errors"
"لقد كان علي أن أرتكب العديد من الأخطاء"
"I had to feel so much disgust and disappointment"
"لقد شعرت بالكثير من الاشمئزاز وخيبة الأمل"
"I had to do all this to become a child again"
"لقد كان علي أن أفعل كل هذا لأصبح طفلاً مرة أخرى"
"and then I could start over again"
"وبعد ذلك يمكنني أن أبدأ من جديد"
"But it was the right way to do it"
"ولكن كانت هذه هي الطريقة الصحيحة للقيام بذلك"
"my heart says yes to it and my eyes smile to it"
"قلبي يقول نعم لها وعيني تبتسم لها"
"I've had to experience despair"
"لقد اضطررت إلى تجربة اليأس"
"I've had to sink down to the most foolish of all thoughts"

"لقد اضطررت إلى الانغماس في أكثر الأفكار حمقًا"
"I've had to think to the thoughts of suicide"
"لقد اضطررت إلى التفكير في الانتحار"
"only then would I be able to experience divine grace"
"فقط حينها سأكون قادرًا على تجربة النعمة الإلهية"
"only then could I hear Om again"
"فقط حينها أستطيع أن أسمع أوم مرة أخرى"
"only then would I be able to sleep properly and awake again"
"فقط حينها سأكون قادرًا على النوم بشكل صحيح والاستيقاظ مرة أخرى"
"I had to become a fool, to find Atman in me again"
"كان علي أن أصبح أحمقًا حتى أجد الأتمان في داخلي مرة أخرى"
"I had to sin, to be able to live again"
"كان علي أن أرتكب الخطيئة حتى أتمكن من العيش مرة أخرى"
"Where else might my path lead me to?"
"إلى أين قد يقودني طريقي؟"
"It is foolish, this path, it moves in loops"
"إن هذا المسار أحمق، فهو يتحرك في حلقات"
"perhaps it is going around in a circle"
"ربما يكون الأمر يدور في دائرة"
"Let this path go where it likes"
"دع هذا الطريق يذهب إلى حيث يحلو له"
"where ever this path goes, I want to follow it"
"أينما يذهب هذا الطريق، أريد أن أتبعه"
he felt joy rolling like waves in his chest
شعر بالفرح يتدفق مثل الأمواج في صدره
he asked his heart, "from where did you get this happiness?"
فسأل قلبه: من أين لك هذه السعادة؟
"does it perhaps come from that long, good sleep?"
"هل يأتي هذا ربما من هذا النوم الطويل الجيد؟"
"the sleep which has done me so much good"
"النوم الذي أفادني كثيرًا"
"or does it come from the word Om, which I said?"
"أم أنها جاءت من كلمة "أوم" التي قلتها؟"
"Or does it come from the fact that I have escaped?"
"أم أن هذا يأتي من حقيقة هروبي؟"

"does this happiness come from standing like a child under the sky?"

"هل تأتي هذه السعادة من الوقوف مثل طفل تحت السماء؟"

"Oh how good is it to have fled"

"أوه كم هو جيد أن نهرب"

"it is great to have become free!"

"من الرائع أن أصبح حرا!"

"How clean and beautiful the air here is"

"كم هو نظيف وجميل الهواء هنا"

"the air is good to breath"

"الهواء جيد للتنفس"

"where I ran away from everything smelled of ointments"

"حيث هربت من كل شيء كان رائحته مثل المراهم"

"spices, wine, excess, sloth"

"التوابل، النبيذ، الإفراط، الكسل"

"How I hated this world of the rich"

"كم كنت أكره عالم الأغنياء هذا"

"I hated those who revel in fine food and the gamblers!"

"كنت أكره أولئك الذين يتلذذون بالطعام الجيد والمقامرين!"

"I hated myself for staying in this terrible world for so long!

"لقد كرهت نفسي لأنني بقيت في هذا العالم الرهيب لفترة طويلة!

"I have deprived, poisoned, and tortured myself"

"لقد حرمت نفسي، وسممت، وعذبت نفسي"

"I have made myself old and evil!"

"لقد جعلت نفسي عجوزًا وشريرًا!"

"No, I will never again do the things I liked doing so much"

"لا، لن أفعل مرة أخرى الأشياء التي أحببت القيام بها كثيرًا"

"I won't delude myself into thinking that Siddhartha was wise!"

"لن أخدع نفسي بالاعتقاد أن سيدهارثا كان حكيمًا!"

"But this one thing I have done well"

"ولكن هذا الشيء الوحيد الذي قمت به بشكل جيد"

"this I like, this I must praise"

"هذا ما أحبه، وهذا ما يجب أن أثني عليه"

"I like that there is now an end to that hatred against myself"

"أنا أحب أن هناك الآن نهاية لتلك الكراهية ضد نفسي"

"there is an end to that foolish and dreary life!"
"هناك نهاية لتلك الحياة الحمقاء والكئيبة!"
"I praise you, Siddhartha, after so many years of foolishness"
"أثني عليك يا سيدهارثا بعد كل هذه السنوات من الحماقة"
"you have once again had an idea"
"لقد كانت لديك فكرة مرة أخرى"
"you have heard the bird in your chest singing"
"لقد سمعت الطائر في صدرك يغني"
"and you followed the song of the bird!"
"وتبعت أغنية الطائر!"

with these thoughts he praised himself
وبهذه الأفكار أشاد بنفسه

he had found joy in himself again
لقد وجد الفرح في نفسه مرة أخرى

he listened curiously to his stomach rumbling with hunger
كان يستمع بفضول إلى معدته وهي تقرقر من الجوع

he had tasted and spat out a piece of suffering and misery
لقد ذاق وبصق قطعة من المعاناة والبؤس

in these recent times and days, this is how he felt
في هذه الأوقات والأيام الأخيرة، هكذا كان يشعر

he had devoured it up to the point of desperation and death
لقد التهمها حتى اليأس والموت

how everything had happened was good
كيف حدث كل شيء كان جيدا

he could have stayed with Kamaswami for much longer
كان بإمكانه البقاء مع كاماسوامي لفترة أطول

he could have made more money, and then wasted it
كان بإمكانه أن يجني المزيد من المال، ثم يهدره

he could have filled his stomach and let his soul die of thirst
كان بإمكانه أن يملأ معدته ويترك روحه تموت من العطش

he could have lived in this soft upholstered hell much longer
كان بإمكانه أن يعيش في هذا الجحيم المنجد الناعم لفترة أطول بكثير

if this had not happened, he would have continued this life
لو لم يحدث هذا لاستمر في هذه الحياة

the moment of complete hopelessness and despair

لحظة اليأس والقنوط الكامل

the most extreme moment when he hung over the rushing waters

اللحظة الأكثر تطرفًا عندما كان معلقًا فوق المياه المتدفقة

the moment he was ready to destroy himself

اللحظة التي كان مستعدًا فيها لتدمير نفسه

the moment he had felt this despair and deep disgust

في اللحظة التي شعر فيها بهذا اليأس والاشمئزاز العميق

he had not succumbed to it

لم يستسلم لها

the bird was still alive after all

كان الطائر لا يزال على قيد الحياة بعد كل شيء

this was why he felt joy and laughed

لهذا السبب شعر بالفرح وضحك

this was why his face was smiling brightly under his hair

لهذا السبب كان وجهه يبتسم بشكل مشرق تحت شعره

his hair which had now turned gray

شعره الذي تحول الآن إلى اللون الرمادي

"It is good," he thought, "to get a taste of everything for oneself"

"من الجيد"، كما فكر، "أن يتذوق المرء كل شيء بنفسه"

"everything which one needs to know"

"كل ما يحتاج المرء إلى معرفته"

"lust for the world and riches do not belong to the good things"

"إن شهوة الدنيا والغنى لا تنتمي إلى الخيرات"

"I have already learned this as a child"

"لقد تعلمت هذا بالفعل عندما كنت طفلاً"

"I have known it for a long time"

"لقد عرفت ذلك منذ زمن طويل"

"but I hadn't experienced it until now"

"لكنني لم أشعر بذلك حتى الآن"

"And now that I I've experienced it I know it"

"والآن بعد أن عشت ذلك أعلم ذلك"

"I don't just know it in my memory, but in my eyes, heart, and stomach"

"لا أعرف ذلك في ذاكرتي فحسب، بل في عيني وقلبي ومعدتي"
"it is good for me to know this!"
"من الجيد بالنسبة لي أن أعرف هذا!"

For a long time, he pondered his transformation
لفترة طويلة، كان يفكر في تحوله
he listened to the bird, as it sang for joy
كان يستمع إلى الطائر وهو يغني فرحًا
Had this bird not died in him?
ألم يمت هذا الطائر فيه؟
had he not felt this bird's death?
ألم يشعر بموت هذا الطائر؟
No, something else from within him had died
لا، لقد مات شيء آخر بداخله
something which yearned to die had died
لقد مات شيء كان يتوق للموت
Was it not this that he used to intend to kill?
أليس هذا ما كان ينوي قتله؟
Was it not his his small, frightened, and proud self that had died?
ألم يكن هو ذاته الصغيرة، الخائفة، والفخورة التي ماتت؟
he had wrestled with his self for so many years
لقد كان يتصارع مع نفسه لسنوات عديدة
the self which had defeated him again and again
الذات التي هزمته مرارا وتكرارا
the self which was back again after every killing
الذات التي عادت مرة أخرى بعد كل قتل
the self which prohibited joy and felt fear?
الذات التي تحرم الفرح وتشعر بالخوف؟
Was it not this self which today had finally come to its death?
أليس هذا هو الذات التي وصلت اليوم إلى موتها النهائي؟
here in the forest, by this lovely river
هنا في الغابة، بجانب هذا النهر الجميل
Was it not due to this death, that he was now like a child?
ألم يكن بسبب هذا الموت أنه أصبح الآن مثل الطفل؟

so full of trust and joy, without fear

مليئة بالثقة والفرح، بلا خوف

Now Siddhartha also got some idea of why he had fought this self in vain

الآن أصبح لدى سيدهارثا أيضًا فكرة عن سبب محاربته لذاته دون جدوى

he knew why he couldn't fight his self as a Brahman

لقد عرف لماذا لم يستطع محاربة نفسه باعتباره براهمانًا

Too much knowledge had held him back

لقد أعاقته المعرفة الزائدة

too many holy verses, sacrificial rules, and self-castigation

الكثير من الآيات المقدسة، والقواعد التضحية، والتوبيخ الذاتي

all these things held him back

كل هذه الأشياء أعاقته

so much doing and striving for that goal!

لقد بذلنا الكثير من الجهد والعمل لتحقيق هذا الهدف!

he had been full of arrogance

لقد كان مليئا بالغطرسة

he was always the smartest

لقد كان دائمًا الأذكى

he was always working the most

لقد كان يعمل دائمًا أكثر من أي شيء آخر

he had always been one step ahead of all others

لقد كان دائمًا متقدمًا بخطوة واحدة عن الآخرين

he was always the knowing and spiritual one

لقد كان دائمًا عالمًا وروحانيًا

he was always considered the priest or wise one

كان يعتبر دائمًا الكاهن أو الحكيم

his self had retreated into being a priest, arrogance, and spirituality

لقد تراجعت ذاته إلى كونه كاهنًا وغطرسة وروحانية

there it sat firmly and grew all this time

لقد جلست هناك بقوة ونمت طوال هذا الوقت

and he had thought he could kill it by fasting

وكان يعتقد أنه يستطيع قتله بالصيام

Now he saw his life as it had become

والآن رأى حياته كما أصبحت

- 186 -

he saw that the secret voice had been right

لقد رأى أن الصوت السري كان على حق

no teacher would ever have been able to bring about his salvation

لن يتمكن أي معلم أبدًا من تحقيق خلاصه

Therefore, he had to go out into the world

لذلك كان عليه أن يخرج إلى العالم

he had to lose himself to lust and power

كان عليه أن يفقد نفسه للشهوة والسلطة

he had to lose himself to women and money

كان عليه أن يخسر نفسه من أجل النساء والمال

he had to become a merchant, a dice-gambler, a drinker

كان عليه أن يصبح تاجرًا، ومقامرًا بالنرد، وشاربًا

and he had to become a greedy person

وكان عليه أن يصبح شخصًا جشعًا

he had to do this until the priest and Samana in him was dead

كان عليه أن يفعل هذا حتى مات الكاهن وسامانا بداخله

Therefore, he had to continue bearing these ugly years

لذلك كان عليه أن يستمر في تحمل هذه السنوات القبيحة

he had to bear the disgust and the teachings

كان عليه أن يتحمل الاشمئزاز والتعاليم

he had to bear the pointlessness of a dreary and wasted life

كان عليه أن يتحمل عبثية الحياة الكئيبة والمهدرة

he had to conclude it up to its bitter end

كان عليه أن يختتم الأمر حتى نهايته المريرة

he had to do this until Siddhartha the lustful could also die

كان عليه أن يفعل هذا حتى يتمكن سيدهارتا الشهواني أيضًا من الموت

He had died and a new Siddhartha had woken up from the sleep

لقد مات واستيقظ سيدهارتا جديد من النوم

this new Siddhartha would also grow old

هذا السيدهارتا الجديد سوف يكبر أيضًا

he would also have to die eventually

وسوف يضطر إلى الموت في نهاية المطاف أيضًا

Siddhartha was still mortal, as is every physical form

كان سيدهارتا لا يزال بشريًا، كما هو الحال مع كل شكل مادي

But today he was young and a child and full of joy

لكن اليوم كان صغيرا وطفلا ومليئا بالفرح

He thought these thoughts to himself

لقد فكر في هذه الأفكار لنفسه

he listened with a smile to his stomach

كان يستمع بابتسامة على معدته

he listened gratefully to a buzzing bee

كان يستمع بامتنان إلى صوت النحلة الطنانة

Cheerfully, he looked into the rushing river

نظر إلى النهر المتدفق بمرح

he had never before liked a water as much as this one

لم يحب الماء من قبل بقدر ما أحبه هذا

he had never before perceived the voice so stronger

لم يسبق له أن رأى الصوت أقوى من ذلك

he had never understood the parable of the moving water so strongly

لم يكن قد فهم قط مثل الماء المتحرك بهذه القوة

he had never before noticed how beautifully the river moved

لم يلاحظ من قبل مدى جمال حركة النهر

It seemed to him, as if the river had something special to tell him

بدا له وكأن النهر لديه شيء خاص ليخبره به

something he did not know yet, which was still awaiting him

شيء لم يكن يعرفه بعد، والذي ما زال ينتظره

In this river, Siddhartha had intended to drown himself

في هذا النهر، كان سيدهارتا ينوي أن يغرق نفسه

in this river the old, tired, desperate Siddhartha had drowned today

في هذا النهر غرق سيدهارتا العجوز المتعب اليائس اليوم

But the new Siddhartha felt a deep love for this rushing water

لكن سيدهارتا الجديد شعر بحب عميق لهذه المياه المتدفقة

and he decided for himself, not to leave it very soon

وقرر بنفسه ألا يتركها سريعا

The Ferryman
المراكبي

"By this river I want to stay," thought Siddhartha
"بجانب هذا النهر أريد أن أبقى" فكر سيدهارتا

"it is the same river which I have crossed a long time ago"
"إنه نفس النهر الذي عبرته منذ زمن طويل"

"I was on my way to the childlike people"
"كنت في طريقي إلى الناس الطفوليين"

"a friendly ferryman had guided me across the river"
"كان هناك سائق قارب ودود يرشدني عبر النهر"

"he is the one I want to go to"
"هو الشخص الذي أريد أن أذهب إليه"

"starting out from his hut, my path led me to a new life"
"بدءًا من كوخه، قادني طريقي إلى حياة جديدة"

"a path which had grown old and is now dead"
"مسار أصبح قديمًا ومات الآن"

"my present path shall also take its start there!"
"سوف يبدأ طريقي الحالي أيضًا من هناك!"

Tenderly, he looked into the rushing water
نظر بحنان إلى المياه المتدفقة

he looked into the transparent green lines the water drew
نظر إلى الخطوط الخضراء الشفافة التي رسمها الماء

the crystal lines of water were rich in secrets
كانت خطوط المياه البلورية غنية بالأسرار

he saw bright pearls rising from the deep
رأى لآلئ لامعة ترتفع من الأعماق

quiet bubbles of air floating on the reflecting surface
فقاعات هواء هادئة تطفو على السطح العاكس

the blue of the sky depicted in the bubbles
اللون الأزرق للسماء كما هو موضح في الفقاعات

the river looked at him with a thousand eyes

- 189 -

نظر إليه النهر بألف عين

the river had green eyes and white eyes

كان للنهر عيون خضراء وعيون بيضاء

the river had crystal eyes and sky-blue eyes

كان للنهر عيون بلورية وعيون زرقاء سماوية

he loved this water very much, it delighted him

لقد أحب هذا الماء كثيرًا، لقد أسعده

he was grateful to the water

كان ممتنًا للماء

In his heart he heard the voice talking

سمع في قلبه صوتا يتكلم

"Love this water! Stay near it!"

"أحب هذه المياه! ابق بالقرب منها!"

"Learn from the water!" his voice commanded him

"تعلم من الماء!" أمره صوته

Oh yes, he wanted to learn from it

أوه نعم، أراد أن يتعلم منه

he wanted to listen to the water

أراد أن يستمع إلى صوت الماء

He who would understand this water's secrets

من أراد أن يفهم أسرار هذه المياه

he would also understand many other things

وسوف يفهم أيضًا أشياء أخرى كثيرة

this is how it seemed to him

هكذا بدا له

But out of all secrets of the river, today he only saw one

ولكن من بين كل أسرار النهر، لم ير اليوم سوى سر واحد

this secret touched his soul

هذا السر لامس روحه

this water ran and ran, incessantly

كان هذا الماء يجري ويجري بلا انقطاع

the water ran, but nevertheless it was always there

كان الماء يجري، ولكن مع ذلك كان هناك دائمًا

the water always, at all times, was the same

كان الماء دائمًا، في جميع الأوقات، هو نفسه

and at the same time it was new in every moment

وفي نفس الوقت كان جديدا في كل لحظة

he who could grasp this would be great

من يستطيع فهم هذا سيكون عظيما

but he didn't understand or grasp it

ولكنه لم يفهمه أو يستوعبه

he only felt some idea of it stirring

لم يشعر إلا بفكرة ما عن تحريكها

it was like a distant memory, a divine voices

لقد كان الأمر أشبه بذكريات بعيدة، أصوات إلهية

Siddhartha rose as the workings of hunger in his body became unbearable

نهض سيدهارتا عندما أصبح الجوع في جسده لا يطاق

In a daze he walked further away from the city

في حالة ذهول سار بعيدًا عن المدينة

he walked up the river along the path by the bank

كان يسير على طول النهر على طول الطريق بجوار الضفة

he listened to the current of the water

كان يستمع إلى تيار الماء

he listened to the rumbling hunger in his body

كان يستمع إلى الجوع الهادر في جسده

When he reached the ferry, the boat was just arriving

عندما وصل إلى العبارة، كان القارب قد وصل للتو

the same ferryman who had once transported the young Samana across the river

نفس القارب الذي نقل سامانا الصغيرة عبر النهر ذات يوم

he stood in the boat and Siddhartha recognised him

كان واقفا في القارب وتعرف عليه سيدهارتا

he had also aged very much

لقد تقدم في السن كثيرا

the ferryman was astonished to see such an elegant man walking on foot

لقد اندهش صاحب العبارة عندما رأى مثل هذا الرجل الأنيق يمشي على قدميه

"Would you like to ferry me over?" he asked

"هل ترغب في نقلي؟" سأل

he took him into his boat and pushed it off the bank
أخذه إلى قاربه ودفعه بعيدًا عن الشاطئ
"It's a beautiful life you have chosen for yourself" the passenger spoke
"إنها حياة جميلة اخترتها لنفسك" تحدث الراكب
"It must be beautiful to live by this water every day"
"لا بد أن يكون من الجميل أن نعيش بجانب هذه المياه كل يوم"
"and it must be beautiful to cruise on it on the river"
"ولا بد أن يكون جميلاً أن نبحر عليه في النهر"
With a smile, the man at the oar moved from side to side
وبابتسامة، تحرك الرجل الموجود عند المجداف من جانب إلى آخر
"It is as beautiful as you say, sir"
"إنه جميل كما تقول يا سيدي"
"But isn't every life and all work beautiful?"
"ولكن أليست كل حياة وكل عمل جميلاً؟"
"This may be true" replied Siddhartha
"قد يكون هذا صحيحًا" أجاب سيدهارتا
"But I envy you for your life"
"لكنني أحسدك على حياتك"
"Ah, you would soon stop enjoying it"
"آه، سوف تتوقف قريبًا عن الاستمتاع بها"
"This is no work for people wearing fine clothes"
"هذا ليس عملاً للأشخاص الذين يرتدون ملابس فاخرة"
Siddhartha laughed at the observation
ضحك سيدهارتا على الملاحظة
"Once before, I have been looked upon today because of my clothes"
"لقد تم النظر إليّ من قبل اليوم بسبب ملابسي"
"I have been looked upon with distrust"
"لقد تم النظر إليّ بعدم ثقة"
"they are a nuisance to me"
"إنهم مصدر إزعاج بالنسبة لي"
"Wouldn't you, ferryman, like to accept these clothes"
"ألا ترغب، أيها القارب، في قبول هذه الملابس؟"
"because you must know, I have no money to pay your fare"
"لأنك يجب أن تعرف أنني لا أملك المال لدفع أجرة سفرك"

"You're joking, sir," the ferryman laughed
"أنت تمزح يا سيدي" ضحك سائق العبارة
"I'm not joking, friend"
"أنا لا أمزح يا صديقي"
"once before you have ferried me across this water in your boat"
"لقد نقلتني مرة واحدة عبر هذه المياه في قاربك"
"you did it for the immaterial reward of a good deed"
"لقد فعلت ذلك من أجل المكافأة المعنوية للعمل الصالح"
"ferry me across the river and accept my clothes for it"
"أرسلني عبر النهر واقبل ملابسي مقابل ذلك"
"And do you, sir, intent to continue travelling without clothes?"
"وأنت يا سيدي، هل تنوي الاستمرار في السفر بدون ملابس؟"
"Ah, most of all I wouldn't want to continue travelling at all"
"أوه، الأهم من ذلك كله أنني لا أرغب في مواصلة السفر على الإطلاق"
"I would rather you gave me an old loincloth"
"أفضّل أن تعطيني مئزرًا قديمًا"
"I would like it if you kept me with you as your assistant"
"أود لو أبقيتني معك كمساعد لك"
"or rather, I would like if you accepted me as your trainee"
"أو بالأحرى، أود لو قبلتني كمتدرب لديك"
"because first I'll have to learn how to handle the boat"
"لأنني أولاً سأضطر إلى تعلم كيفية التعامل مع القارب"
For a long time, the ferryman looked at the stranger
لفترة طويلة، نظر القارب إلى الغريب
he was searching in his memory for this strange man
كان يبحث في ذاكرته عن هذا الرجل الغريب
"Now I recognise you," he finally said
"الآن أعرفك" قال أخيرا
"At one time, you've slept in my hut"
"في أحد الأوقات، كنت تنام في كوخي"
"this was a long time ago, possibly more than twenty years"
"لقد حدث هذا منذ زمن طويل، ربما منذ أكثر من عشرين عامًا"
"and you've been ferried across the river by me"
"ولقد تم نقلك عبر النهر عن طريقي"

"that day we parted like good friends"
"في ذلك اليوم افترقنا مثل الأصدقاء الجيدين"
"Haven't you been a Samana?"
"ألم تكن سامانا؟"
"I can't think of your name anymore"
"لا أستطيع أن أفكر في اسمك بعد الآن"
"My name is Siddhartha, and I was a Samana"
"اسمي سيدهارثا، وكنت سامانا"
"I had still been a Samana when you last saw me"
"كنت لا أزال سامانا عندما رأيتني آخر مرة"
"So be welcome, Siddhartha. My name is Vasudeva"
"مرحبًا بك، سيدهارثا. اسمي فاسوديفا"
"You will, so I hope, be my guest today as well"
"آمل أن تكون ضيفي اليوم أيضًا"
"and you may sleep in my hut"
"ويمكنك النوم في كوخي"
"and you may tell me, where you're coming from"
"ويمكنك أن تخبرني من أين أتيت"
"and you may tell me why these beautiful clothes are such a nuisance to you"
"ويمكنك أن تخبرني لماذا هذه الملابس الجميلة تسبب لك الإزعاج"
They had reached the middle of the river
لقد وصلوا إلى منتصف النهر
Vasudeva pushed the oar with more strength
دفع فاسوديفا المجداف بقوة أكبر
in order to overcome the current
من أجل التغلب على الوضع الحالي
He worked calmly, with brawny arms
لقد عمل بهدوء، وبأذرع قوية
his eyes were fixed in on the front of the boat
كانت عيناه مثبتتين على مقدمة القارب
Siddhartha sat and watched him
جلس سيدهارثا وراقبه
he remembered his time as a Samana
لقد تذكر وقته كسامانا

he remembered how love for this man had stirred in his heart

تذكر كيف كان حب هذا الرجل يشتعل في قلبه

Gratefully, he accepted Vasudeva's invitation

وبكل امتنان، قبل دعوة فاسوديفا

When they had reached the bank, he helped him to tie the boat to the stakes

عندما وصلوا إلى الضفة، ساعده في ربط القارب بالأوتاد

after this, the ferryman asked him to enter the hut

بعد ذلك طلب منه صاحب العبارة الدخول إلى الكوخ

he offered him bread and water, and Siddhartha ate with eager pleasure

قدم له الخبز والماء، فأكل سيدهارتا بلهفة.

and he also ate with eager pleasure of the mango fruits Vasudeva offered him

وأكل أيضًا بلهفة شديدة من ثمار المانجو التي قدمها له فاسوديفا

Afterwards, it was almost the time of the sunset

وبعد ذلك، كان الوقت قد اقترب من غروب الشمس

they sat on a log by the bank

جلسوا على جذع شجرة بجانب البنك

Siddhartha told the ferryman about where he originally came from

أخبر سيدهارتا صاحب العبارة عن المكان الذي أتى منه في الأصل

he told him about his life as he had seen it today

أخبره عن حياته كما رآها اليوم

the way he had seen it in that hour of despair

الطريقة التي رآها بها في تلك الساعة من اليأس

the tale of his life lasted late into the night

استمرت قصة حياته حتى وقت متأخر من الليل

Vasudeva listened with great attention

استمع فاسوديفا باهتمام كبير

Listening carefully, he let everything enter his mind

بعد الاستماع بعناية، سمح لكل شيء بالدخول إلى ذهنه

birthplace and childhood, all that learning

مكان الميلاد والطفولة وكل هذا التعلم

all that searching, all joy, all distress

كل هذا البحث، كل الفرح، كل الضيق

This was one of the greatest virtues of the ferryman

كانت هذه واحدة من أعظم فضائل العبّارة

like only a few, he knew how to listen

مثل القليل فقط، كان يعرف كيف يستمع

he did not have to speak a word

لم يكن عليه أن يتكلم بكلمة واحدة

but the speaker sensed how Vasudeva let his words enter his mind

لكن المتحدث شعر كيف سمح فاسوديفا لكلماته بالدخول إلى ذهنه

his mind was quiet, open, and waiting

كان عقله هادئًا ومنفتحًا ومنتظرًا

he did not lose a single word

لم يفقد كلمة واحدة

he did not await a single word with impatience

لم ينتظر كلمة واحدة بفارغ الصبر

he did not add his praise or rebuke

ولم يزد على مدحه أو توبيخه

he was just listening, and nothing else

لقد كان يستمع فقط، ولا شيء آخر

Siddhartha felt what a happy fortune it is to confess to such a listener

شعر سيدهارتا بمدى سعادته بالاعتراف لمثل هذا المستمع

he felt fortunate to bury in his heart his own life

لقد شعر بأنه محظوظ لأنه دفن حياته في قلبه

he buried his own search and suffering

لقد دفن بحثه ومعاناته

he told the tale of Siddhartha's life

لقد روى قصة حياة سيدهارتا

when he spoke of the tree by the river

عندما تحدث عن الشجرة بجانب النهر

when he spoke of his deep fall

عندما تحدث عن سقوطه العميق

when he spoke of the holy Om

عندما تحدث عن أوم المقدس

when he spoke of how he had felt such a love for the river
عندما تحدث عن مدى حبه للنهر

the ferryman listened to these things with twice as much attention
استمع القارب إلى هذه الأشياء بقدر مضاعف من الاهتمام

he was entirely and completely absorbed by it
لقد كان منغمسًا فيها تمامًا وكاملًا

he was listening with his eyes closed
كان يستمع وعيناه مغلقتين

when Siddhartha fell silent a long silence occurred
عندما صمت سيدهارتا حدث صمت طويل

then Vasudeva spoke "It is as I thought"
ثم تحدث فاسوديفا "إنه كما اعتقدت"

"The river has spoken to you"
"لقد تحدث إليك النهر"

"the river is your friend as well"
"النهر صديقك أيضًا"

"the river speaks to you as well"
"النهر يتحدث إليك أيضًا"

"That is good, that is very good"
"هذا جيد، هذا جيد جدًا"

"Stay with me, Siddhartha, my friend"
"ابق معي يا سيدهارتا يا صديقي"

"I used to have a wife"
"لقد كانت لي زوجة"

"her bed was next to mine"
"سريرها كان بجوار سريري"

"but she has died a long time ago"
"لكنها ماتت منذ زمن طويل"

"for a long time, I have lived alone"
"لقد عشت بمفردي لفترة طويلة"

"Now, you shall live with me"
"الآن سوف تعيش معي"

"there is enough space and food for both of us"
"هناك مساحة كافية وطعام لكلا منا"

"I thank you," said Siddhartha

"أشكرك" قال سيدهارثا
"I thank you and accept"

"أشكرك وأقبل"
"And I also thank you for this, Vasudeva"

"وأنا أيضًا أشكرك على هذا، فاسوديفا"
"I thank you for listening to me so well"

"أشكركم على الاستماع لي بشكل جيد"
"people who know how to listen are rare"

"الناس الذين يعرفون كيفية الاستماع نادرون"
"I have not met a single person who knew it as well as you do"

"لم أقابل شخصًا واحدًا يعرف ذلك جيدًا كما تفعل"
"I will also learn in this respect from you"

"وسوف أتعلم منك أيضا في هذا الصدد"
"You will learn it," spoke Vasudeva

"سوف تتعلم ذلك"، تحدث فاسوديفا
"but you will not learn it from me"

"ولكنك لن تتعلم ذلك مني"
"The river has taught me to listen"

"لقد علمني النهر الاستماع"
"you will learn to listen from the river as well"

"سوف تتعلم الاستماع من النهر أيضًا"
"It knows everything, the river"

"إنه يعرف كل شيء، النهر"
"everything can be learned from the river"

"كل شيء يمكن تعلمه من النهر"
"See, you've already learned this from the water too"

"انظر، لقد تعلمت هذا بالفعل من الماء أيضًا"
"you have learned that it is good to strive downwards"

"لقد تعلمت أنه من الجيد أن تسعى نحو الأسفل"
"you have learned to sink and to seek depth"

"لقد تعلمت كيف تغرق وتبحث عن العمق"
"The rich and elegant Siddhartha is becoming an oarsman's servant"

"سيدارثا الغني والأنيق يصبح خادمًا للمجدف"
"the learned Brahman Siddhartha becomes a ferryman"

"البراهمان المتعلم سيدهارتا يصبح قاربًا"
"this has also been told to you by the river"
"لقد قيل لك هذا أيضًا عن طريق النهر"
"You'll learn the other thing from it as well"
"سوف تتعلم الشيء الآخر منه أيضًا"
Siddhartha spoke after a long pause
تحدث سيدهارتا بعد فترة توقف طويلة
"What other things will I learn, Vasudeva?"
"ما هي الأشياء الأخرى التي سأتعلمها، فاسوديفا؟"
Vasudeva rose. "It is late," he said
نهض فاسوديفا وقال: "لقد تأخر الوقت".
and Vasudeva proposed going to sleep
واقترح فاسوديفا الذهاب إلى النوم
"I can't tell you that other thing, oh friend"
"لا أستطيع أن أخبرك بهذا الشيء الآخر، يا صديقي"
"You'll learn the other thing, or perhaps you know it already"
"سوف تتعلم الشيء الآخر، أو ربما تعرفه بالفعل"
"See, I'm no learned man"
"انظر، أنا لست رجلاً متعلمًا"
"I have no special skill in speaking"
"ليس لدي مهارة خاصة في التحدث"
"I also have no special skill in thinking"
"ليس لدي أيضًا مهارة خاصة في التفكير"
"All I'm able to do is to listen and to be godly"
"كل ما أستطيع فعله هو الاستماع وأن أكون تقيًّا"
"I have learned nothing else"
"لم أتعلم أي شيء آخر"
"If I was able to say and teach it, I might be a wise man"
"لو كنت قادراً على قول ذلك وتعليمه، لكنت رجلاً حكيماً"
"but like this I am only a ferryman"
"لكن هكذا أنا مجرد قارب"
"and it is my task to ferry people across the river"
"ومن مهمتي نقل الناس عبر النهر"
"I have transported many thousands of people"
"لقد نقلت آلافًا عديدة من الناس"

"and to all of them, my river has been nothing but an obstacle"

"ولهم جميعًا، لم يكن نهري سوى عقبة"

"it was something that got in the way of their travels"

"لقد كان شيئًا ما أعاق سفرهم"

"they travelled to seek money and business"

"لقد سافروا بحثًا عن المال والأعمال"

"they travelled for weddings and pilgrimages"

"لقد سافروا لحضور حفلات الزفاف والحج"

"and the river was obstructing their path"

"وكان النهر يعترض طريقهم"

"the ferryman's job was to get them quickly across that obstacle"

"كانت مهمة العبّارة هي نقلهم بسرعة عبر تلك العقبة"

"But for some among thousands, a few, the river has stopped being an obstacle"

"ولكن بالنسبة لبعض من بين الآلاف، قِلة، لم يعد النهر يشكل عائقًا"

"they have heard its voice and they have listened to it"

"لقد سمعوا صوته وأصغوا إليه"

"and the river has become sacred to them"

"وأصبح النهر مقدسا لهم"

"it become sacred to them as it has become sacred to me"

"لقد أصبح الأمر مقدسًا بالنسبة لهم كما أصبح مقدسًا بالنسبة لي"

"for now, let us rest, Siddhartha"

"في الوقت الحالي، دعنا نرتاح، سيدهارثا"

Siddhartha stayed with the ferryman and learned to operate the boat

بقي سيدهارتا مع صاحب العبارة وتعلم كيفية تشغيل القارب

when there was nothing to do at the ferry, he worked with Vasudeva in the rice-field

عندما لم يكن هناك ما يمكن فعله في العبارة، عمل مع فاسوديفا في حقل الأرز

he gathered wood and plucked the fruit off the banana-trees

كان يجمع الحطب ويقطف الثمار من أشجار الموز

He learned to build an oar and how to mend the boat

تعلم كيفية بناء المجذاف وكيفية إصلاح القارب

he learned how to weave baskets and repaid the hut

تعلم كيفية نسج السلال وسدد الكوخ

and he was joyful because of everything he learned

وكان سعيدًا بكل ما تعلمه

the days and months passed quickly

مرت الأيام والأشهر بسرعة

But more than Vasudeva could teach him, he was taught by the river

ولكن أكثر مما كان فاسوديفا قادرًا على تعليمه، كان النهر هو الذي علمه.

Incessantly, he learned from the river

لقد تعلم من النهر بلا انقطاع

Most of all, he learned to listen

الأهم من ذلك كله، أنه تعلم الاستماع

he learned to pay close attention with a quiet heart

لقد تعلم أن ينتبه جيدًا بقلب هادئ

he learned to keep a waiting, open soul

لقد تعلم أن يحافظ على روح منتظرة ومنفتحة

he learned to listen without passion

لقد تعلم الاستماع دون شغف

he learned to listen without a wish

لقد تعلم الاستماع دون رغبة

he learned to listen without judgement

لقد تعلم الاستماع دون إصدار أحكام

he learned to listen without an opinion

لقد تعلم الاستماع دون رأي

In a friendly manner, he lived side by side with Vasudeva

لقد عاش جنبًا إلى جنب مع فاسوديفا بطريقة ودية

occasionally they exchanged some words

في بعض الأحيان كانوا يتبادلون بعض الكلمات

then, at length, they thought about the words

ثم فكروا أخيرًا في الكلمات

Vasudeva was no friend of words

لم يكن فاسوديفا صديقًا للكلمات

Siddhartha rarely succeeded in persuading him to speak

نادرًا ما نجح سيدهارثا في إقناعه بالتحدث

"did you too learn that secret from the river?"

"هل تعلمت أنت أيضًا هذا السر من النهر؟"

"the secret that there is no time?"

"السر في عدم وجود الوقت؟"

Vasudeva's face was filled with a bright smile

كان وجه فاسوديفا مليئًا بابتسامة مشرقة

"Yes, Siddhartha," he spoke

"نعم، سيدهارتا،" قال

"I learned that the river is everywhere at once"

"لقد تعلمت أن النهر موجود في كل مكان في نفس الوقت"

"it is at the source and at the mouth of the river"

"إنه عند منبع النهر وعند مصب النهر"

"it is at the waterfall and at the ferry"

"إنه عند الشلال وعند العبارة"

"it is at the rapids and in the sea"

"إنه عند المنحدرات وفي البحر"

"it is in the mountains and everywhere at once"

"إنه في الجبال وفي كل مكان في آن واحد"

"and I learned that there is only the present time for the river"

"وتعلمت أنه لا يوجد سوى الوقت الحاضر للنهر"

"it does not have the shadow of the past"

"لا يوجد فيه ظل الماضي"

"and it does not have the shadow of the future"

"ولا يوجد فيه ظل المستقبل"

"is this what you mean?" he asked

"هل هذا ما تقصده؟" سأل

"This is what I meant," said Siddhartha

"هذا ما قصدته" قال سيدهارثا

"And when I had learned it, I looked at my life"

"وعندما علمت ذلك، نظرت إلى حياتي"

"and my life was also a river"

"وكانت حياتي نهرًا أيضًا"

"the boy Siddhartha was only separated from the man Siddhartha by a shadow"

"كان الصبي سيدهارتا منفصلاً عن الرجل سيدهارتا فقط بظل"
"and a shadow separated the man Siddhartha from the old man Siddhartha"
"وفصل ظل الرجل سيدهارتا عن الرجل العجوز سيدهارتا"
"things are separated by a shadow, not by something real"
"الأشياء مفصولة بظل، وليس بشيء حقيقي"
"Also, Siddhartha's previous births were not in the past"
"أيضًا، لم تكن ولادات سيدهارتا السابقة في الماضي"
"and his death and his return to Brahma is not in the future"
"وموته وعودته إلى براهما لن يكون في المستقبل"
"nothing was, nothing will be, but everything is"
"لم يكن هناك شيء، ولن يكون هناك شيء، ولكن كل شيء موجود"
"everything has existence and is present"
"كل شيء له وجود وحاضر"

Siddhartha spoke with ecstasy

تحدث سيدهارتا ببهجة

this enlightenment had delighted him deeply

لقد أسعده هذا التنوير بشدة

"was not all suffering time?"
"ألم يكن كل هذا الوقت معاناة؟"
"were not all forms of tormenting oneself a form of time?"
"ألم تكن كل أشكال تعذيب النفس شكلاً من أشكال الزمن؟"
"was not everything hard and hostile because of time?"
"ألم يكن كل شيء صعبًا وعدائيًا بسبب الوقت؟"
"is not everything evil overcome when one overcomes time?"
"أليس كل الشرور تُهزم عندما يتغلب الإنسان على الزمن؟"
"as soon as time leaves the mind, does suffering leave too?"
"بمجرد أن يغادر الوقت العقل، هل يغادره المعاناة أيضًا؟"

Siddhartha had spoken in ecstatic delight

لقد تحدث سيدهارتا في سعادة غامرة

but Vasudeva smiled at him brightly and nodded in confirmation

لكن فاسوديفا ابتسم له بمرح وأومأ برأسه في تأكيد.

silently he nodded and brushed his hand over Siddhartha's shoulder

أومأ برأسه بصمت ثم وضع يده على كتف سيدهارتا

and then he turned back to his work

ثم عاد إلى عمله

And Siddhartha asked Vasudeva again another time

وسأل سيدهارثا فاسوديفا مرة أخرى

the river had just increased its flow in the rainy season

لقد زاد تدفق النهر للتو في موسم الأمطار

and it made a powerful noise

وأحدثت ضجة قوية

"Isn't it so, oh friend, the river has many voices?"

"أليس كذلك يا صديقي، النهر له أصوات كثيرة؟"

"Hasn't it the voice of a king and of a warrior?"

"أليس هذا صوت ملك ومحارب؟"

"Hasn't it the voice of of a bull and of a bird of the night?"

"أليس هذا صوت ثور وطائر الليل؟"

"Hasn't it the voice of a woman giving birth and of a sighing man?"

"أليس هذا صوت امرأة تلد وصوت رجل يتأوه؟"

"and does it not also have a thousand other voices?"

"وهل ليس له أيضًا ألف صوت آخر؟"

"it is as you say it is," Vasudeva nodded

"إنه كما تقول،" أومأ فاسوديفا برأسه

"all voices of the creatures are in its voice"

"كل أصوات المخلوقات في صوته"

"And do you know..." Siddhartha continued

"و هل تعلم..." تابع سيدهارثا

"what word does it speak when you succeed in hearing all of voices at once?"

"ما هي الكلمة التي تتحدث بها عندما تنجح في سماع جميع الأصوات في وقت واحد؟"

Happily, Vasudeva's face was smiling

لحسن الحظ، كان وجه فاسوديفا مبتسما

he bent over to Siddhartha and spoke the holy Om into his ear

انحنى نحو سيدهارتا وتحدث بالأوم المقدس في أذنه

And this had been the very thing which Siddhartha had also been hearing
وكان هذا هو نفس الشيء الذي كان سيدهارثا يسمعه أيضًا

time after time, his smile became more similar to the ferryman's
مرة بعد مرة، أصبحت ابتسامته أكثر تشابهًا بابتسامة القارب.

his smile became almost just as bright as the ferryman's
أصبحت ابتسامته مشرقة تقريبًا مثل ابتسامة القارب.

it was almost just as thoroughly glowing with bliss
لقد كان متوهجًا بالنعيم تقريبًا تمامًا

shining out of thousand small wrinkles
تتألق من بين آلاف التجاعيد الصغيرة

just like the smile of a child
مثل ابتسامة الطفل

just like the smile of an old man
مثل ابتسامة رجل عجوز

Many travellers, seeing the two ferrymen, thought they were brothers
اعتقد العديد من المسافرين، عند رؤية العبّارتين، أنهما شقيقان

Often, they sat in the evening together by the bank
في كثير من الأحيان، كانوا يجلسون معًا في المساء بجوار البنك

they said nothing and both listened to the water
لم يقولا شيئًا واستمع كلاهما إلى الماء

the water, which was not water to them
الماء الذي لم يكن ماءً بالنسبة لهم

it wasn't water, but the voice of life
لم يكن ماءً، بل كان صوت الحياة

the voice of what exists and what is eternally taking shape
صوت ما هو موجود وما هو في طور التشكل إلى الأبد

it happened from time to time that both thought of the same thing
لقد حدث من وقت لآخر أن كلاهما يفكران في نفس الشيء

they thought of a conversation from the day before
لقد فكروا في محادثة من اليوم السابق

they thought of one of their travellers

لقد فكروا في أحد مسافريهم

they thought of death and their childhood

لقد فكروا في الموت وفي طفولتهم

they heard the river tell them the same thing

سمعوا النهر يقول لهم نفس الشيء

both delighted about the same answer to the same question

كلاهما مسرور بنفس الإجابة على نفس السؤال

There was something about the two ferrymen which was transmitted to others

كان هناك شيء ما عن العبّارتين الذي انتقل إلى الآخرين

it was something which many of the travellers felt

لقد كان شيئًا شعر به العديد من المسافرين

travellers would occasionally look at the faces of the ferrymen

كان المسافرون ينظرون أحيانًا إلى وجوه عمال العبّارة

and then they told the story of their life

ثم أخبروا قصة حياتهم

they confessed all sorts of evil things

اعترفوا بكل أنواع الشرور

and they asked for comfort and advice

وطلبوا الراحة والنصيحة

occasionally someone asked for permission to stay for a night

في بعض الأحيان يطلب شخص ما الإذن بالبقاء لليلة واحدة

they also wanted to listen to the river

أرادوا أيضًا الاستماع إلى النهر

It also happened that curious people came

وقد حدث أيضًا أن جاء أشخاص فضوليون

they had been told that there were two wise men

لقد قيل لهم أن هناك رجلين حكيمين

or they had been told there were two sorcerers

أو قيل لهم أن هناك ساحرين

The curious people asked many questions

لقد طرح الفضوليون العديد من الأسئلة

but they got no answers to their questions

ولكن لم يحصلوا على إجابات لأسئلتهم

they found neither sorcerers nor wise men
فلم يجدوا سحرة ولا حكماء
they only found two friendly little old men, who seemed to be mute
لم يجدوا سوى رجلين عجوزين صغيرين ودودين، بدا عليهما الصمم.
they seemed to have become a bit strange in the forest by themselves
يبدو أنهم أصبحوا غريبين بعض الشيء في الغابة من تلقاء أنفسهم
And the curious people laughed about what they had heard
وضحك الفضوليون مما سمعوا
they said common people were foolishly spreading empty rumours
قالوا إن عامة الناس ينشرون الشائعات الفارغة بغباء

The years passed by, and nobody counted them
مرت السنوات ولم يحسبها أحد
Then, at one time, monks came by on a pilgrimage
ثم في أحد الأوقات، جاء الرهبان في رحلة حج
they were followers of Gotama, the Buddha
كانوا من أتباع غوتاما، بوذا
they asked to be ferried across the river
لقد طلبوا أن يتم نقلهم عبر النهر
they told them they were in a hurry to get back to their wise teacher
فأخبروهم أنهم في عجلة من أمرهم للعودة إلى معلمهم الحكيم
news had spread the exalted one was deadly sick
انتشرت أخبار تفيد بأن الشخص الرفيع كان مريضًا بشكل مميت
he would soon die his last human death
سوف يموت قريبا موتته البشرية الأخيرة
in order to become one with the salvation
لكي نصبح واحدا مع الخلاص
It was not long until a new flock of monks came
ولم يمض وقت طويل حتى جاء قطيع جديد من الرهبان
they were also on their pilgrimage
وكانوا في الحج أيضا
most of the travellers spoke of nothing other than Gotama

تحدث معظم المسافرين عن شيء آخر غير غوتاما
his impending death was all they thought about
كان موته الوشيك هو كل ما فكروا فيه
if there had been war, just as many would travel
لو كانت هناك حرب، لكان الكثيرون سيسافرون
just as many would come to the coronation of a king
كما سيأتي الكثيرون إلى تتويج الملك
they gathered like ants in droves
لقد تجمعوا مثل النمل في قطعان
they flocked, like being drawn onwards by a magic spell
لقد توافدوا، وكأنهم يتجهون نحو الأمام بفعل تعويذة سحرية
they went to where the great Buddha was awaiting his death
ذهبوا إلى حيث كان بوذا العظيم ينتظر موته
the perfected one of an era was to become one with the glory
كان من المقرر أن يصبح الشخص الكامل في عصر ما واحدًا مع المجد
Often, Siddhartha thought in those days of the dying wise man
في كثير من الأحيان، كان سيدهارتا يفكر في تلك الأيام في الرجل الحكيم المحتضر
the great teacher whose voice had admonished nations
المعلم العظيم الذي كان صوته ينبه الأمم
the one who had awoken hundreds of thousands
الذي أيقظ مئات الآلاف
a man whose voice he had also once heard
رجل سمع صوته أيضًا ذات مرة
a teacher whose holy face he had also once seen with respect
معلم كان قد رأى وجهه المقدس ذات يوم باحترام
Kindly, he thought of him
من فضلك، فكر فيه
he saw his path to perfection before his eyes
لقد رأى طريقه إلى الكمال أمام عينيه
and he remembered with a smile those words he had said to him
وتذكر بابتسامة تلك الكلمات التي قالها له
when he was a young man and spoke to the exalted one
حين كان شاباً وتحدث إلى الأعلى

They had been, so it seemed to him, proud and precious words
لقد كانت، كما بدا له، كلمات فخورة وثمينة
with a smile, he remembered the the words
مع ابتسامة، تذكر الكلمات
he knew that there was nothing standing between Gotama and him any more
لقد علم أنه لم يعد هناك شيء يقف بينه وبين جوتاما
he had known this for a long time already
لقد كان يعرف هذا منذ فترة طويلة بالفعل
though he was still unable to accept his teachings
على الرغم من أنه لا يزال غير قادر على قبول تعاليمه
there was no teaching a truly searching person
لم يكن هناك تعليم لشخص باحث حقًا
someone who truly wanted to find, could accept
من أراد حقًا أن يجد، يمكنه أن يقبل
But he who had found the answer could approve of any teaching
ولكن من وجد الإجابة يمكنه الموافقة على أي تعليم
every path, every goal, they were all the same
كل طريق، كل هدف، كانا متشابهين
there was nothing standing between him and all the other thousands any more
لم يعد هناك شيء يقف بينه وبين كل الآلاف الآخرين
the thousands who lived in that what is eternal
الآلاف الذين عاشوا في ذلك الذي هو أبدي
the thousands who breathed what is divine
الآلاف الذين تنفسوا ما هو إلهي

On one of these days, Kamala also went to him
وفي أحد هذه الأيام ذهبت إليه كامالا أيضًا
she used to be the most beautiful of the courtesans
كانت أجمل العاهرات
A long time ago, she had retired from her previous life
منذ فترة طويلة، تقاعدت من حياتها السابقة
she had given her garden to the monks of Gotama as a gift

لقد أعطت حديقتها لرهبان جوتاما كهدية
she had taken her refuge in the teachings
لقد لجأت إلى التعاليم
she was among the friends and benefactors of the pilgrims
كانت من بين أصدقاء الحجاج ومحسنيهم
she was together with Siddhartha, the boy
كانت مع سيدهارتاء الصبي
Siddhartha the boy was her son
كان سيدهارتا الصبي ابنها
she had gone on her way due to the news of the near death of Gotama
لقد ذهبت في طريقها بسبب الأخبار التي تفيد بموت جوتاما الوشيك
she was in simple clothes and on foot
كانت ترتدي ملابس بسيطة وتمشي على الأقدام
and she was With her little son
وكانت مع ابنها الصغير
she was travelling by the river
كانت مسافرة على ضفة النهر
but the boy had soon grown tired
لكن الصبي سرعان ما سئم
he desired to go back home
كان يرغب في العودة إلى المنزل
he desired to rest and eat
كان يرغب في الراحة والأكل
he became disobedient and started whining
لقد عصى وبدأ في التذمر
Kamala often had to take a rest with him
كان على كامالا في كثير من الأحيان أن تأخذ قسطًا من الراحة معه
he was accustomed to getting what he wanted
لقد اعتاد على الحصول على ما يريد
she had to feed him and comfort him
كان عليها أن تطعمه وتواسيه
she had to scold him for his behaviour
كان عليها أن توبخه على سلوكه
He did not comprehend why he had to go on this exhausting pilgrimage

he did not know why he had to go to an unknown place

لم يكن يعلم لماذا كان عليه أن يذهب إلى مكان غير معروف

he did know why he had to see a holy dying stranger

لقد كان يعلم لماذا كان عليه أن يرى شخصًا مقدسًا غريبًا يحتضر

"So what if he died?" he complained

"فماذا لو مات؟" اشتكى

why should this concern him?

لماذا يجب أن يشغله هذا الأمر؟

The pilgrims were getting close to Vasudeva's ferry

كان الحجاج يقتربون من عبارة فاسوديفا

little Siddhartha once again forced his mother to rest

أجبر سيدهارتا الصغير والدته مرة أخرى على الراحة

Kamala had also become tired

كما أصبحت كامالا متعبة أيضًا

while the boy was chewing a banana, she crouched down on the ground

بينما كان الصبي يمضغ الموز، جلست القرفصاء على الأرض

she closed her eyes a bit and rested

أغمضت عينيها قليلا واستراحت

But suddenly, she uttered a wailing scream

ولكن فجأة أطلقت صرخة عويل

the boy looked at her in fear

نظر إليها الصبي بخوف

he saw her face had grown pale from horror

رأى وجهها أصبح شاحبًا من الرعب

and from under her dress, a small, black snake fled

ومن تحت فستانها هربت ثعبان صغير أسود اللون.

a snake by which Kamala had been bitten

الثعبان الذي عضه كامالا

Hurriedly, they both ran along the path, to reach people

ركضا بسرعة على طول الطريق ليصلا إلى الناس

they got near to the ferry and Kamala collapsed

لقد اقتربوا من العبارة وانهارت كامالا

she was not able to go any further

لم تكن قادرة على الذهاب إلى أبعد من ذلك

the boy started crying miserably

بدأ الصبي يبكي بشدة

his cries were only interrupted when he kissed his mother

لم يتوقف صراخه إلا عندما قبل أمه

she also joined his loud screams for help

كما انضمت إلى صراخه العالي طلبا للمساعدة

she screamed until the sound reached Vasudeva's ears

صرخت حتى وصل الصوت إلى آذان فاسوديفا

Vasudeva quickly came and took the woman on his arms

جاء فاسوديفا بسرعة وأخذ المرأة بين ذراعيه

he carried her into the boat and the boy ran along

حملها إلى القارب وركض الصبي معه

soon they reached the hut, where Siddhartha stood by the stove

وسرعان ما وصلوا إلى الكوخ، حيث وقف سيدهارثا بجانب الموقد.

he was just lighting the fire

لقد كان يشعل النار فقط

He looked up and first saw the boy's face

نظر إلى الأعلى ورأى وجه الصبي أولاً

it wondrously reminded him of something

لقد ذكّرته بشيء عجيب

like a warning to remember something he had forgotten

مثل تحذير لتذكر شيء نسيه

Then he saw Kamala, whom he instantly recognised

ثم رأى كامالا، التي تعرف عليها على الفور

she lay unconscious in the ferryman's arms

كانت فاقدة للوعي بين ذراعي القارب

now he knew that it was his own son

الآن عرف أنه كان ابنه

his son whose face had been such a warning reminder to him

ابنه الذي كان وجهه بمثابة تذكير تحذيري له

and the heart stirred in his chest

وتحرك القلب في صدره

Kamala's wound was washed, but had already turned black

تم غسل جرح كامالا، لكنه تحول بالفعل إلى اللون الأسود

and her body was swollen
وكان جسدها منتفخا

she was made to drink a healing potion
لقد تم إجبارها على شرب جرعة شفاء

Her consciousness returned and she lay on Siddhartha's bed
لقد عاد وعيها واستلقت على سرير سيدهارثا

Siddhartha stood over Kamala, who he used to love so much
وقف سيدهارثا فوق كامالا، التي كان يحبها كثيرًا

It seemed like a dream to her
لقد بدا لها وكأنه حلم

with a smile, she looked at her friend's face
بابتسامة نظرت إلى وجه صديقتها

slowly she realized her situation
أدركت وضعها ببطء

she remembered she had been bitten
تذكرت أنها تعرضت للعض

and she timidly called for her son
ودعت ابنها بخجل

"He's with you, don't worry," said Siddhartha
"إنه معك، لا تقلق"، قال سيدهارثا

Kamala looked into his eyes
نظرت كامالا في عينيه

She spoke with a heavy tongue, paralysed by the poison
تحدثت بلسان ثقيل، مشلولة بالسم

"You've become old, my dear," she said
"لقد أصبحت عجوزًا يا عزيزتي" قالت

"you've become gray," she added
"لقد أصبحت رماديًا"، أضافت

"But you are like the young Samana, who came without clothes"
"لكنك مثل الشابة سامانا التي جاءت بدون ملابس"

"you're like the Samana who came into my garden with dusty feet"
"أنت مثل سامانا التي دخلت حديقتي بأقدام متربة"

"You are much more like him than you were when you left me"

"أنت تشبهه أكثر بكثير مما كنت عليه عندما تركتني"
"In the eyes, you're like him, Siddhartha"
"في العيون، أنت مثله، سيدهارثا"
"Alas, I have also grown old"
"آه، لقد كبرت أيضًا"
"could you still recognise me?"
هل لا زال بإمكانك التعرف علي؟
Siddhartha smiled, "Instantly, I recognised you, Kamala, my dear"
ابتسم سيدهارثا، "على الفور، تعرفت عليك، كامالا، عزيزتي"
Kamala pointed to her boy
أشارت كامالا إلى ولدها
"Did you recognise him as well?"
"هل تعرفت عليه أيضًا؟"
"He is your son," she confirmed
"إنه ابنك" أكدت
Her eyes became confused and fell shut
أصبحت عيناها مشوشة وأغلقت
The boy wept and Siddhartha took him on his knees
بكى الصبي وأخذه سيدهارثا على ركبتيه
he let him weep and petted his hair
تركه يبكي ومسح على شعره
at the sight of the child's face, a Brahman prayer came to his mind
عند رؤية وجه الطفل، جاءت صلاة براهمانية إلى ذهنه
a prayer which he had learned a long time ago
صلاة تعلمها منذ زمن طويل
a time when he had been a little boy himself
الوقت الذي فيه كان طفلاً صغيراً
Slowly, with a singing voice, he started to speak
ببطء، وبصوت غنائي، بدأ يتحدث
from his past and childhood, the words came flowing to him
من ماضيه وطفولته، كانت الكلمات تتدفق إليه
And with that song, the boy became calm
ومع تلك الأغنية أصبح الصبي هادئا
he was only now and then uttering a sob

كان يبكي فقط من حين لآخر

and finally he fell asleep

وأخيرا نام

Siddhartha placed him on Vasudeva's bed

وضعه سيدهارثا على سرير فاسوديفا

Vasudeva stood by the stove and cooked rice

وقف فاسوديفا بجانب الموقد وطهى الأرز

Siddhartha gave him a look, which he returned with a smile

ألقى عليه سيدهارثا نظرة، فعاد إليها بابتسامة.

"She'll die," Siddhartha said quietly

"سوف تموت" قال سيدهارثا بهدوء

Vasudeva knew it was true, and nodded

عرف فاسوديفا أن هذا صحيح، وأومأ برأسه

over his friendly face ran the light of the stove's fire

كان ضوء نار الموقد ينير وجهه الودود

once again, Kamala returned to consciousness

مرة أخرى، عادت كامالا إلى وعيها

the pain of the poison distorted her face

ألم السم شوه وجهها

Siddhartha's eyes read the suffering on her mouth

تقرأ عيون سيدهارتا المعاناة على فمها

from her pale cheeks he could see that she was suffering

من خديها الشاحبين استطاع أن يرى أنها كانت تعاني

Quietly, he read the pain in her eyes

بهدوء قرأ الألم في عينيها

attentively, waiting, his mind become one with her suffering

باهتمام، منتظرًا، يصبح عقله واحدًا مع معاناتها

Kamala felt it and her gaze sought his eyes

شعرت كامالا بذلك ونظرت إلى عينيه

Looking at him, she spoke

نظرت إليه وتحدثت

"Now I see that your eyes have changed as well"

"الآن أرى أن عينيك تغيرت أيضًا"

"They've become completely different"

"لقد أصبحوا مختلفين تماما"

"what do I still recognise in you that is Siddhartha?

"ما الذي لا أزال أتعرف عليه فيك وهو سيدهارتا؟"

"It's you, and it's not you"

"إنه أنت، وليس أنت"

Siddhartha said nothing, quietly his eyes looked at hers

لم يقل سيدهارثا شيئًا، ونظر بهدوء إلى عينيها.

"You have achieved it?" she asked

"لقد حققت ذلك؟" سألت

"You have found peace?"

"هل وجدت السلام؟"

He smiled and placed his hand on hers

ابتسم ووضع يده على يدها

"I'm seeing it" she said

"أنا أرى ذلك" قالت

"I too will find peace"

"أنا أيضا سأجد السلام"

"You have found it," Siddhartha spoke in a whisper

"لقد وجدته" تحدث سيدهارثا بصوت هامس

Kamala never stopped looking into his eyes

لم تتوقف كامالا أبدًا عن النظر في عينيه

She thought about her pilgrimage to Gotama

فكرت في رحلتها إلى غوتاما

the pilgrimage which she wanted to take

الحج الذي أرادت أن تقوم به

in order to see the face of the perfected one

لكي نرى وجه الكامل

in order to breathe his peace

من أجل أن يتنفس سلامه

but she had now found it in another place

لكنها وجدته الآن في مكان آخر

and this she thought that was good too

وهذا ما اعتقدته أنه جيد أيضًا

it was just as good as if she had seen the other one

لقد كان الأمر جيدًا تمامًا كما لو كانت قد رأت الآخر

She wanted to tell this to him

أرادت أن تخبره بهذا

but her tongue no longer obeyed her will

- 216 -

لكن لسانها لم يعد يطيع إرادتها

Without speaking, she looked at him

نظرت إليه دون أن تتكلم

he saw the life fading from her eyes

رأى الحياة تتلاشى من عينيها

the final pain filled her eyes and made them grow dim

ملأ الألم النهائي عينيها وجعلها تصبح باهتة

the final shiver ran through her limbs

سرت القشعريرة الأخيرة في أطرافها

his finger closed her eyelids

أغمض إصبعه جفونها

For a long time, he sat and looked at her peacefully dead face

جلس لفترة طويلة ينظر إلى وجهها الميت بسلام

For a long time, he observed her mouth

لفترة طويلة، لاحظ فمها

her old, tired mouth, with those lips, which had become thin

فمها القديم المتعب، مع تلك الشفاه التي أصبحت رقيقة

he remembered he used to compare this mouth with a freshly cracked fig

تذكر أنه اعتاد أن يقارن هذا الفم بثمرة تين متشققة حديثًا

this was in the spring of his years

كان هذا في ربيع عمره

For a long time, he sat and read the pale face

جلس لفترة طويلة يقرأ الوجه الشاحب

he read the tired wrinkles

قرأ التجاعيد المتعبة

he filled himself with this sight

لقد امتلأ نفسه بهذا المنظر

he saw his own face in the same manner

لقد رأى وجهه بنفس الطريقة

he saw his face was just as white

لقد رأى وجهه كان أبيض تماما

he saw his face was just as quenched out

لقد رأى وجهه مطفأ تماما

at the same time he saw his face and hers being young

في نفس الوقت رأى وجهه ووجهها شابين

their faces with red lips and fiery eyes

وجوههم بشفاه حمراء وعيون نارية

the feeling of both being real at the same time

الشعور بأن كلاهما حقيقي في نفس الوقت

the feeling of eternity completely filled every aspect of his being

كان الشعور بالخلود يملأ كل جانب من جوانب كيانه

in this hour he felt more deeply than than he had ever felt before

في هذه الساعة شعر بعمق أكبر مما شعر به من قبل

he felt the indestructibility of every life

لقد شعر بأن كل حياة لا يمكن تدميرها

he felt the eternity of every moment

لقد شعر بأبدية كل لحظة

When he rose, Vasudeva had prepared rice for him

عندما نهض، كان فاسوديفا قد أعد له الأرز.

But Siddhartha did not eat that night

ولكن سيدهارتا لم يأكل تلك الليلة

In the stable their goat stood

في الإسطبل وقفت عنزتهم

the two old men prepared beds of straw for themselves

قام الرجلان العجوزان بإعداد أسرة من القش لأنفسهما

Vasudeva laid himself down to sleep

وضع فاسوديفا نفسه للنوم

But Siddhartha went outside and sat before the hut

لكن سيدهارتا خرج وجلس أمام الكوخ

he listened to the river, surrounded by the past

كان يستمع إلى النهر، محاطًا بالماضي

he was touched and encircled by all times of his life at the same time

لقد تأثر وتأثر بكل مراحل حياته في نفس الوقت

occasionally he rose and he stepped to the door of the hut

في بعض الأحيان كان ينهض ويخطو نحو باب الكوخ

he listened whether the boy was sleeping

كان يستمع إذا كان الصبي نائما

before the sun could be seen, Vasudeva came out of the stable

قبل أن تتمكن الشمس من الرؤية، خرج فاسوديفا من الإسطبل

he walked over to his friend

لقد ذهب إلى صديقه

"You haven't slept," he said

"لم تنم" قال

"No, Vasudeva. I sat here"

"لا، فاسوديفا. جلست هنا"

"I was listening to the river"

"كنت أستمع إلى النهر"

"the river has told me a lot"

"لقد اخبرني النهر كثيرًا"

"it has deeply filled me with the healing thought of oneness"

"لقد ملأتني بعمق فكرة الشفاء المتمثلة في الوحدة"

"You've experienced suffering, Siddhartha"

"لقد عانيت من المعاناة، سيدهارثا"

"but I see no sadness has entered your heart"

"لكنني لا أرى أي حزن دخل قلبك"

"No, my dear, how should I be sad?"

"لا يا عزيزتي كيف أحزن؟"

"I, who have been rich and happy"

"أنا الذي كنت غنيًا وسعيدًا"

"I have become even richer and happier now"

"لقد أصبحت أكثر ثراءً وسعادة الآن"

"My son has been given to me"

"لقد أعطيت لي ابني"

"Your son shall be welcome to me as well"

"سوف يكون ابنك مرحباً به عندي أيضاً"

"But now, Siddhartha, let's get to work"

"ولكن الآن، سيدهارثا، دعنا نبدأ العمل"

"there is much to be done"

"هناك الكثير الذي يتعين القيام به"

"Kamala has died on the same bed on which my wife had died"

"توفيت كامالا على نفس السرير الذي ماتت عليه زوجتي"

"Let us build Kamala's funeral pile on the hill"

"دعونا نبني كومة جنازة كامالا على التل"

"the hill on which I my wife's funeral pile is"

"التل الذي دفنت عليه جنازة زوجتي"

While the boy was still asleep, they built the funeral pile

بينما كان الصبي لا يزال نائما، قاموا ببناء كومة الجنازة

The Son
الابن

Timid and weeping, the boy had attended his mother's funeral

حضر الصبي جنازة والدته خجولًا وباكيًا.

gloomy and shy, he had listened to Siddhartha

كان كئيبًا وخجولًا، وكان يستمع إلى سيدهارتا

Siddhartha greeted him as his son

استقبله سيدهارتا كابنه

he welcomed him at his place in Vasudeva's hut

رحب به في مكانه في كوخ فاسوديفا

Pale, he sat for many days by the hill of the dead

شاحبًا، جلس لأيام عديدة عند تلة الموتى

he did not want to eat

لم يكن يريد أن يأكل

he did not look at anyone

لم ينظر إلى أحد

he did not open his heart

لم يفتح قلبه

he met his fate with resistance and denial

لقد لقي مصيره بالمقاومة والإنكار

Siddhartha spared giving him lessons

لقد وفّر سيدهارتا عليه الدروس

and he let him do as he pleased

وتركه يفعل ما يشاء

Siddhartha honoured his son's mourning

كرّم سيدهارتا حزن ابنه

he understood that his son did not know him

لقد فهم أن ابنه لا يعرفه

he understood that he could not love him like a father

لقد فهم أنه لا يستطيع أن يحبه كأب

Slowly, he also understood that the eleven-year-old was a pampered boy

ببطء، أدرك أيضًا أن الطفل البالغ من العمر أحد عشر عامًا كان صبيًا مدللًا

he saw that he was a mother's boy

رأى أنه ابن أمه

he saw that he had grown up in the habits of rich people

رأى أنه نشأ في عادات الأغنياء

he was accustomed to finer food and a soft bed

كان معتاذًا على الطعام الفاخر والفراش الناعم

he was accustomed to giving orders to servants

كان معتاذًا على إعطاء الأوامر للخدم

the mourning child could not suddenly be content with a life among strangers

لم يعد الطفل الحزين قادرًا على أن يرضى فجأة بحياة بين الغرباء

Siddhartha understood the pampered child would not willingly be in poverty

لقد فهم سيدهارثا أن الطفل المدلل لن يكون طوعًا فقيرًا

He did not force him to do these these things

ولم يجبره على فعل هذه الأشياء

Siddhartha did many chores for the boy

لقد قام سيدهارثا بالعديد من الأعمال المنزلية للصبي

he always saved the best piece of the meal for him

لقد احتفظ دائمًا بأفضل قطعة من الوجبة له

Slowly, he hoped to win him over, by friendly patience

ببطء، كان يأمل في كسبه، من خلال الصبر الودي

Rich and happy, he had called himself, when the boy had come to him

كان يطلق على نفسه لقب الغني والسعيد عندما جاء إليه الصبي.

Since then some time had passed

لقد مر بعض الوقت منذ ذلك الحين

but the boy remained a stranger and in a gloomy disposition

لكن الصبي ظل غريبًا وفي مزاج كئيب

he displayed a proud and stubbornly disobedient heart

لقد أظهر قلبًا فخورًا وعنيدًا ومتمردًا

he did not want to do any work

لم يكن يريد القيام بأي عمل

he did not pay his respect to the old men

لم يحترم الشيوخ

he stole from Vasudeva's fruit-trees

سرق من أشجار الفاكهة الخاصة بفاسوديفا

his son had not brought him happiness and peace

لم يجلب له ابنه السعادة والسلام

the boy had brought him suffering and worry

لقد جلب له الصبي المعاناة والقلق

slowly Siddhartha began to understand this

بدأ سيدهارثا يفهم هذا الأمر ببطء

But he loved him regardless of the suffering he brought him

لكنه أحبه بغض النظر عن المعاناة التي جلبها له

he preferred the suffering and worries of love over happiness and joy without the boy

فضل معاناة وهموم الحب على السعادة والفرح بدون الولد

from when young Siddhartha was in the hut the old men had split the work

منذ أن كان سيدهارتا الصغير في الكوخ، كان الرجال المسنون يقسمون العمل

Vasudeva had again taken on the job of the ferryman

تولى فاسوديفا مرة أخرى وظيفة سائق العبارة

and Siddhartha, in order to be with his son, did the work in the hut and the field

وسيدهارتا، من أجل أن يكون مع ابنه، قام بالعمل في الكوخ والحقل

for long months Siddhartha waited for his son to understand him

لمدة أشهر طويلة انتظر سيدهارثا ابنه ليفهمه

he waited for him to accept his love

انتظر منه أن يقبل حبه

and he waited for his son to perhaps reciprocate his love

وانتظر أن يبادله ابنه حبه ربما

For long months Vasudeva waited, watching

لمدة أشهر طويلة انتظر فاسوديفا وهو يراقب

he waited and said nothing

انتظر ولم يقل شيئا

One day, young Siddhartha tormented his father very much

ذات يوم، عذب الشاب سيدهارتا والده كثيرًا

he had broken both of his rice-bowls

لقد كسر كلا وعاءي الأرز الخاصين به

Vasudeva took his friend aside and talked to him

أخذ فاسوديفا صديقه جانبًا وتحدث معه

"Pardon me," he said to Siddhartha

"عفوا" قال لسيدهارتا

"from a friendly heart, I'm talking to you"

"من قلب ودود أتحدث إليك"

"I'm seeing that you are tormenting yourself"

"أرى أنك تعذب نفسك"

"I'm seeing that you're in grief"

"أرى أنك في حزن"

"Your son, my dear, is worrying you"

"ابنك يا عزيزي يقلقك"

"and he is also worrying me"

"وهو يقلقني أيضًا"

"That young bird is accustomed to a different life"

"لقد اعتاد هذا الطائر الصغير على حياة مختلفة"

"he is used to living in a different nest"

"لقد اعتاد على العيش في عش مختلف"

"he has not, like you, run away from riches and the city"

"إنه لم يهرب مثلك من الثروة والمدينة"

"he was not disgusted and fed up with the life in Sansara"

"لم يكن يشعر بالاشمئزاز أو الملل من الحياة في سانسارا"

"he had to do all these things against his will"

"كان عليه أن يفعل كل هذه الأشياء ضد إرادته"

"he had to leave all this behind"

"كان عليه أن يترك كل هذا خلفه"

"I asked the river, oh friend"

"سألت النهر يا صديقي"

"many times I have asked the river"

"لقد سألت النهر عدة مرات"

"But the river laughs at all of this"

"لكن النهر يضحك من كل هذا"

"it laughs at me and it laughs at you"

"إنه يضحك علي ويضحك عليك"

"the river is shaking with laughter at our foolishness"

"النهر يهتز من الضحك على حماقتنا"
"Water wants to join water as youth wants to join youth"
"الماء يريد الانضمام إلى الماء كما يريد الشباب الانضمام إلى الشباب"
"your son is not in the place where he can prosper"
"ابنك ليس في المكان الذي يستطيع أن ينجح فيه"
"you too should ask the river"
"يجب عليك أن تسأل النهر أيضًا"
"you too should listen to it!"
"يجب عليك الاستماع إليها أيضًا!"
Troubled, Siddhartha looked into his friendly face
في حالة من الاضطراب، نظر سيدهارثا إلى وجهه الودود
he looked at the many wrinkles in which there was incessant cheerfulness
نظر إلى التجاعيد العديدة التي كانت مليئة بالبهجة المتواصلة
"How could I part with him?" he said quietly, ashamed
"كيف يمكنني أن أفترق عنه؟" قال بهدوء، خجلاً
"Give me some more time, my dear"
"أعطيني المزيد من الوقت يا عزيزتي"
"See, I'm fighting for him"
"انظر، أنا أقاتل من أجله"
"I'm seeking to win his heart"
"أسعى للفوز بقلبه"
"with love and with friendly patience I intend to capture it"
"مع الحب والصبر الودي أعتزم التقاطها"
"One day, the river shall also talk to him"
"يومًا ما، سوف يتحدث النهر معه أيضًا"
"he also is called upon"
"وهو أيضا مدعو"
Vasudeva's smile flourished more warmly
ابتسمت فاسوديفا بحرارة أكبر
"Oh yes, he too is called upon"
"نعم، هو أيضا مدعو"
"he too is of the eternal life"
"فهو أيضا من الحياة الأبدية"
"But do we, you and me, know what he is called upon to do?"

- 225 -

"ولكن هل نحن، أنت وأنا، نعلم ما هو مطلوب منه أن يفعله؟"
"we know what path to take and what actions to perform"
"نحن نعلم ما هو المسار الذي يجب أن نتخذه وما هي الإجراءات التي يجب أن نتخذها"
"we know what pain we have to endure"
"نحن نعلم حجم الألم الذي يتعين علينا أن نتحمله"
"but does he know these things?"
"ولكن هل يعرف هذه الأشياء؟"
"Not a small one, his pain will be"
"ليس صغيرا، ألمه سيكون"
"after all, his heart is proud and hard"
"بعد كل شيء، قلبه فخور وقاس"
"people like this have to suffer and err a lot"
"أشخاص مثل هؤلاء يجب أن يعانوا ويخطئوا كثيرًا"
"they have to do much injustice"
"عليهم أن يرتكبوا الكثير من الظلم"
"and they have burden themselves with much sin"
"وحملوا أنفسهم إثمًا كثيرًا"
"Tell me, my dear," he asked of Siddhartha
"أخبرني يا عزيزتي" سأل سيدهارثا
"you're not taking control of your son's upbringing?"
"أنت لا تتحكم في تربية ابنك؟"
"You don't force him, beat him, or punish him?"
"أنت لا تجبره، ولا تضربه، ولا تعاقبه؟"
"No, Vasudeva, I don't do any of these things"
"لا، فاسوديفا، أنا لا أفعل أيًا من هذه الأشياء"
"I knew it. You don't force him"
"كنت أعلم ذلك، لا تجبره على ذلك"
"you don't beat him and you don't give him orders"
"لا تضربه ولا تعطيه أوامر"
"because you know softness is stronger than hard"
"لأنك تعلم أن اللين أقوى من القسوة"
"you know water is stronger than rocks"
"أنت تعلم أن الماء أقوى من الصخور"
"and you know love is stronger than force"
"وأنت تعلم أن الحب أقوى من القوة"

"Very good, I praise you for this"
"حسنًا، أثني عليك على هذا"

"But aren't you mistaken in some way?"
"ولكن ألا تخطئ بطريقة ما؟"

"don't you think that you are forcing him?"
"ألا تعتقد أنك تجبره؟"

"don't you perhaps punish him a different way?"
"ألا يمكنك معاقبته بطريقة مختلفة؟"

"Don't you shackle him with your love?"
"ألا تقيده بحبك؟"

"Don't you make him feel inferior every day?"
"ألا تجعله يشعر بالنقص كل يوم؟"

"doesn't your kindness and patience make it even harder for him?"
"أليس لطفك وصبرك يجعل الأمر أصعب بالنسبة له؟"

"aren't you forcing him to live in a hut with two old banana-eaters?"
"ألا تجبره على العيش في كوخ مع اثنين من آكلي الموز المسنين؟"

"old men to whom even rice is a delicacy"
"كبار السن الذين يعتبرون حتى الأرز طعامًا شهيًا"

"old men whose thoughts can't be his"
"رجال كبار في السن لا يمكن أن تكون أفكارهم مثل أفكاره"

"old men whose hearts are old and quiet"
"الرجال المسنين الذين قلوبهم قديمة وهادئة"

"old men whose hearts beat in a different pace than his"
"كبار السن الذين تنبض قلوبهم بوتيرة مختلفة عن نبضاته"

"Isn't he forced and punished by all this?""
"أليس مجبرًا ومعاقبًا بكل هذا؟"

Troubled, Siddhartha looked to the ground
في حالة من الاضطراب، نظر سيدهارثا إلى الأرض

Quietly, he asked, "What do you think should I do?"
سأل بهدوء: "ماذا تعتقد أن علي أن أفعل؟"

Vasudeva spoke, "Bring him into the city"
قال فاسوديفا "أحضروه إلى المدينة"

"bring him into his mother's house"
"أدخلوه إلى بيت أمه"

"there'll still be servants around, give him to them"
"سيظل هناك خدم في الجوار، أعطه لهم"
"And if there aren't any servants, bring him to a teacher"
"وإن لم يكن هناك خدم فأتوا به إلى معلم"
"but don't bring him to a teacher for teachings' sake"
"ولكن لا تحضروه إلى المعلم من أجل التعليم"
"bring him to a teacher so that he is among other children"
"أحضروه إلى المعلم ليكون بين الأطفال الآخرين"
"and bring him to the world which is his own"
"وإحضاره إلى العالم الذي هو ملكه"
"have you never thought of this?"
"هل لم تفكر في هذا من قبل؟"
"you're seeing into my heart," Siddhartha spoke sadly
"أنت ترى ما في قلبي" تحدث سيدهارثا بحزن
"Often, I have thought of this"
"لقد فكرت في هذا كثيرًا"
"but how can I put him into this world?"
"ولكن كيف يمكنني أن أضعه في هذا العالم؟"
"Won't he become exuberant?"
"ألن يصبح متفائلًا؟"
"won't he lose himself to pleasure and power?"
"ألن يفقد نفسه للمتعة والسلطة؟"
"won't he repeat all of his father's mistakes?"
"ألن يكرر كل أخطاء والده؟"
"won't he perhaps get entirely lost in Sansara?"
"ألن يضيع تمامًا في سانسارا؟"
Brightly, the ferryman's smile lit up
أضاءت ابتسامة القارب بشكل مشرق
softly, he touched Siddhartha's arm
لمس ذراع سيدهارثا برفق
"Ask the river about it, my friend!"
"اسأل النهر عن ذلك يا صديقي!"
"Hear the river laugh about it!"
"اسمع النهر يضحك عليه!"
"Would you actually believe that you had committed your foolish acts?

هل ستصدق فعلا أنك ارتكبت أفعالك الحمقاء؟
"in order to spare your son from committing them too"
"لكي تنقذ ابنك من ارتكابها أيضًا"
"And could you in any way protect your son from Sansara?"
"وهل تستطيع بأي شكل من الأشكال حماية ابنك من سانسارا؟"
"How could you protect him from Sansara?"
"كيف يمكنك حمايته من سانسارا؟"
"By means of teachings, prayer, admonition?"
"بواسطة التعاليم والصلاة والنصح؟"
"My dear, have you entirely forgotten that story?"
"عزيزتي، هل نسيتِ هذه القصة تمامًا؟"
"the story containing so many lessons"
"القصة تحتوي على الكثير من الدروس"
"the story about Siddhartha, a Brahman's son"
"قصة عن سيدهارتا، ابن البراهمة"
"the story which you once told me here on this very spot?"
"القصة التي أخبرتني بها ذات مرة هنا في هذا المكان بالذات؟"
"Who has kept the Samana Siddhartha safe from Sansara?"
"من الذي أبقى سامانا سيدهارتا في مأمن من سانسارا؟"
"who has kept him from sin, greed, and foolishness?"
"من الذي حفظه من الخطيئة والطمع والجهل؟"
"Were his father's religious devotion able to keep him safe?"
هل كانت تقوى والده الدينية قادرة على حمايته؟
"were his teacher's warnings able to keep him safe?"
"هل كانت تحذيرات معلمه قادرة على الحفاظ على سلامته؟"
"could his own knowledge keep him safe?"
"هل يمكن لمعرفته الخاصة أن تحميه؟"
"was his own search able to keep him safe?"
"هل كان بحثه الخاص قادرًا على الحفاظ على سلامته؟"
"What father has been able to protect his son?"
"أي أب استطاع أن يحمي ابنه؟"
"what father could keep his son from living his life for himself?"
"أي أب يستطيع أن يمنع ابنه من أن يعيش حياته لنفسه؟"
"what teacher has been able to protect his student?"
"ما هو المعلم الذي استطاع حماية تلميذه؟"

"what teacher can stop his student from soiling himself with life?"

"ما هو المعلم الذي يستطيع أن يمنع تلميذه من تلويث نفسه بالحياة؟"

"who could stop him from burdening himself with guilt?"

"من يستطيع أن يمنعه من تحميل نفسه بالذنب؟"

"who could stop him from drinking the bitter drink for himself?"

"فمن يستطيع أن يمنعه من شرب المشروب المر لنفسه؟"

"who could stop him from finding his path for himself?"

"من يستطيع أن يمنعه من العثور على طريقه بنفسه؟"

"did you think anybody could be spared from taking this path?"

هل كنت تعتقد أن أي شخص يمكن أن يتجنب اتخاذ هذا الطريق؟

"did you think that perhaps your little son would be spared?"

هل كنت تعتقد أن ابنك الصغير ربما سوف ينجو من الموت؟

"did you think your love could do all that?"

هل كنت تعتقد أن حبك قادر على فعل كل هذا؟

"did you think your love could keep him from suffering"

هل كنت تعتقد أن حبك يمكن أن يحميه من المعاناة؟

"did you think your love could protect him from pain and disappointment?

هل كنت تعتقد أن حبك يمكن أن يحميه من الألم وخيبة الأمل؟

"you could die ten times for him"

"يمكنك أن تموت من أجله عشر مرات"

"but you could take no part of his destiny upon yourself"

"ولكنك لا تستطيع أن تأخذ جزءًا من مصيره على نفسك"

Never before, Vasudeva had spoken so many words

لم يسبق من قبل أن تحدث فاسوديفا بهذا القدر من الكلمات

Kindly, Siddhartha thanked him

بكل لطف شكره سيدهارتا

he went troubled into the hut

لقد ذهب مضطربا إلى الكوخ

he could not sleep for a long time

لم يتمكن من النوم لفترة طويلة

Vasudeva had told him nothing he had not already thought and known

لم يخبره فاسوديفا بأي شيء لم يفكر فيه ويعرفه بالفعل

But this was a knowledge he could not act upon

لكن هذه كانت معرفة لم يستطع التصرف بناءً عليها

stronger than knowledge was his love for the boy

كان حبه للصبي أقوى من المعرفة

stronger than knowledge was his tenderness

كان حنانه أقوى من المعرفة

stronger than knowledge was his fear to lose him

كان خوفه من فقدان المعرفة أقوى من خوفه من فقدان المعرفة.

had he ever lost his heart so much to something?

هل فقد قلبه من أجل شيء ما إلى هذا الحد؟

had he ever loved any person so blindly?

هل أحب أي شخص بهذه الطريقة العمياء؟

had he ever suffered for someone so unsuccessfully?

هل عانى من أجل شخص ما دون جدوى من قبل؟

had he ever made such sacrifices for anyone and yet been so unhappy?

هل سبق له أن قدم مثل هذه التضحيات لأي شخص ومع ذلك كان تعيسًا إلى هذا الحد؟

Siddhartha could not heed his friend's advice

لم يستطع سيدهارثا أن يستمع لنصيحة صديقه

he could not give up the boy

لم يستطع التخلي عن الصبي

He let the boy give him orders

ترك الصبي يعطيه الأوامر

he let him disregard him

لقد سمح له بتجاهله

He said nothing and waited

لم يقل شيئا وانتظر

daily, he attempted the struggle of friendliness

كان يحاول يوميًا النضال من أجل الصداقة

he initiated the silent war of patience

لقد بدأ حرب الصبر الصامتة

Vasudeva also said nothing and waited

ولم يقل فاسوديفا شيئًا أيضًا وانتظر

They were both masters of patience

كانا كلاهما ماهرين في الصبر

one time the boy's face reminded him very much of Kamala

في إحدى المرات، ذكّره وجه الصبي بكامالا كثيرًا

Siddhartha suddenly had to think of something Kamala had once said

فجأة، كان على سيدهارثا أن يفكر في شيء قالته كامالا ذات مرة

"You cannot love" she had said to him

"لا يمكنك أن تحب" قالت له

and he had agreed with her

وقد وافقها الرأي

and he had compared himself with a star

وكان قد قارن نفسه بنجم

and he had compared the childlike people with falling leaves

وقد شبه الناس الطفوليين بأوراق الشجر المتساقطة

but nevertheless, he had also sensed an accusation in that line

لكن مع ذلك، فقد أحس أيضًا باتهام في هذا السطر

Indeed, he had never been able to love

في الواقع، لم يكن قادرا على الحب أبدا

he had never been able to devote himself completely to another person

لم يكن قادرًا أبدًا على تكريس نفسه بالكامل لشخص آخر

he had never been able to to forget himself

لم يكن قادرا على نسيان نفسه أبدا

he had never been able to commit foolish acts for the love of another person

لم يكن قادرًا أبدًا على ارتكاب أفعال حمقاء من أجل حب شخص آخر

at that time it seemed to set him apart from the childlike people

في ذلك الوقت بدا الأمر وكأنه يميزه عن الأشخاص الذين يشبهون الأطفال

But ever since his son was here, Siddhartha also become a childlike person

ولكن منذ أن كان ابنه هنا، أصبح سيدهارثا أيضًا شخصًا طفوليًا

he was suffering for the sake of another person

كان يعاني من أجل شخص آخر

he was loving another person

كان يحب شخصًا آخر

he was lost to a love for someone else

لقد فقد حبه لشخص آخر

he had become a fool on account of love

لقد أصبح أحمقًا بسبب الحب

Now he too felt the strongest and strangest of all passions

والآن شعر أيضًا بأقوى وأغرب المشاعر على الإطلاق

he suffered from this passion miserably

لقد عانى من هذا الشغف بشدة

and he was nevertheless in bliss

وكان مع ذلك في نعيم

he was nevertheless renewed in one respect

ومع ذلك فقد تجدد في جانب واحد

he was enriched by this one thing

لقد أثرى نفسه بهذا الشيء الواحد

He sensed very well that this blind love for his son was a passion

لقد أحس جيدًا أن هذا الحب الأعمى لابنه كان شغفًا

he knew that it was something very human

لقد عرف أن هذا شيء إنساني للغاية

he knew that it was Sansara

لقد عرف أنها سانسارا

he knew that it was a murky source, dark waters

كان يعلم أن هذا مصدر عكر ومياه مظلمة

but he felt it was not worthless, but necessary

ولكنه شعر أنه ليس بلا قيمة، بل ضروريًا

it came from the essence of his own being

لقد جاء من جوهر وجوده

This pleasure also had to be atoned for

كان لابد من التكفير عن هذه المتعة أيضًا

this pain also had to be endured

كان لا بد من تحمل هذا الألم أيضًا

these foolish acts also had to be committed
كان لا بد من ارتكاب هذه الأفعال الحمقاء أيضًا
Through all this, the son let him commit his foolish acts
ومن خلال كل هذا، تركه الابن يرتكب أفعاله الحمقاء
he let him court for his affection
لقد سمح له بالخطبة من أجل عاطفته
he let him humiliate himself every day
لقد سمح له بإذلال نفسه كل يوم
he gave in to the moods of his son
استسلم لمزاج ابنه
his father had nothing which could have delighted him
لم يكن لدى والده أي شيء يمكن أن يسعده
and he nothing that the boy feared
ولم يكن هناك شيء يخشاه الصبي
He was a good man, this father
لقد كان رجلاً صالحًا، هذا الأب
he was a good, kind, soft man
لقد كان رجلاً طيبًا ولطيفًا وناعمًا
perhaps he was a very devout man
ربما كان رجلاً متديناً جداً
perhaps he was a saint, the boy thought
ربما كان قديسا، فكر الصبي
but all these attributes could not win the boy over
ولكن كل هذه الصفات لم تستطع أن تكسب الصبي
He was bored by this father, who kept him imprisoned
لقد سئم من هذا الأب الذي أبقاه سجينا
a prisoner in this miserable hut of his
سجين في هذا الكوخ البائس
he was bored of him answering every naughtiness with a smile
لقد سئم من رده على كل شقاوة بابتسامة
he didn't appreciate insults being responded to by friendliness
لم يكن يتقبل الرد على الإهانات بالود
he didn't like viciousness returned in kindness
لم يحب الشر فعاد باللطف

this very thing was the hated trick of this old sneak
كان هذا الشيء هو الخدعة المكروهة لهذا المتسلل القديم
Much more the boy would have liked it if he had been threatened by him
كان الصبي سيحب ذلك كثيرًا لو تم تهديده من قبله
he wanted to be abused by him
أراد أن يتعرض للإساءة من قبله

A day came when young Siddhartha had had enough
جاء يوم حيث كان الشاب سيدهارتا قد سئم
what was on his mind came bursting forth
ما كان في ذهنه خرج فجأة
and he openly turned against his father
وانقلب على والده علانية
Siddhartha had given him a task
لقد أعطاه سيدهارتا مهمة
he had told him to gather brushwood
لقد طلب منه أن يجمع الحطب
But the boy did not leave the hut
ولكن الصبي لم يغادر الكوخ
in stubborn disobedience and rage, he stayed where he was
في عصيانه العنيد وغضبه، بقي حيث كان
he thumped on the ground with his feet
كان يضرب الأرض بقدميه
he clenched his fists and screamed in a powerful outburst
قبض على قبضتيه وصرخ في انفجار قوي
he screamed his hatred and contempt into his father's face
صرخ بكراهيته واحتقاره في وجه والده
"Get the brushwood for yourself!" he shouted, foaming at the mouth
"احصل على الحطب لنفسك!" صاح، ورغوة في فمه
"I'm not your servant"
"أنا لست خادمك"
"I know that you won't hit me, you wouldn't dare"
"أعلم أنك لن تضربني، ولن تجرؤ على ذلك"
"I know that you constantly want to punish me"

"أعلم أنك تريد معاقبتي باستمرار"
"you want to put me down with your religious devotion and your indulgence"
"أنت تريد أن تحط من قدري بتدينك وانغماسك في الملذات"
"You want me to become like you"
"تريدني أن أصبح مثلك"
"you want me to be just as devout, soft, and wise as you"
"أنت تريدني أن أكون متدينًا وناعمًا وحكيمًا مثلك"
"but I won't do it, just to make you suffer"
"لكنني لن أفعل ذلك، فقط لأجعلك تعاني"
"I would rather become a highway-robber than be as soft as you"
"أفضل أن أصبح لصًا على أن أكون ضعيفًا مثلك"
"I would rather be a murderer than be as wise as you"
"أفضّل أن أكون قاتلًا على أن أكون حكيمًا مثلك"
"I would rather go to hell, than to become like you!"
"أفضّل أن أذهب إلى الجحيم، على أن أصبح مثلك!"
"I hate you, you're not my father
"أنا أكرهك، أنت لست والدي"
"even if you've slept with my mother ten times, you are not my father!"
"حتى لو نمت مع أمي عشر مرات، فأنت لست والدي!"
Rage and grief boiled over in him
كان الغضب والحزن يغليان بداخله
he foamed at his father in a hundred savage and evil words
لقد غضب من والده بمئة كلمة وحشية وشريرة
Then the boy ran away into the forest
ثم هرب الصبي إلى الغابة
it was late at night when the boy returned
لقد كان الوقت متأخرًا في الليل عندما عاد الصبي
But the next morning, he had disappeared
ولكن في صباح اليوم التالي، كان قد اختفى
What had also disappeared was a small basket
وما اختفى أيضًا هو سلة صغيرة
the basket in which the ferrymen kept those copper and silver coins

السلة التي كان يحفظ فيها العبّارون تلك العملات النحاسية والفضية
the coins which they received as a fare
العملات التي حصلوا عليها كأجرة
The boat had also disappeared
وقد اختفى القارب أيضا
Siddhartha saw the boat lying by the opposite bank
رأى سيدهارثا القارب ملقى على الضفة المقابلة
Siddhartha had been shivering with grief
كان سيدهارثا يرتجف من الحزن
the ranting speeches the boy had made touched him
لقد أثرت الخطب التي ألقاها الصبي عليه
"I must follow him," said Siddhartha
"يجب أن أتبعه" قال سيدهارتا
"A child can't go through the forest all alone, he'll perish"
"لا يستطيع الطفل أن يجتاز الغابة بمفرده، فسوف يموت"
"We must build a raft, Vasudeva, to get over the water"
"يجب علينا بناء طوف، فاسوديفا، للعبور فوق الماء"
"We will build a raft" said Vasudeva
"سوف نبني طوفًا" قال فاسوديفا
"we will build it to get our boat back"
"سنبنيها لاستعادة قاربنا"
"But you shall not run after your child, my friend"
"ولكن لا يجب عليك أن تركض وراء طفلك يا صديقي"
"he is no child anymore"
"إنه لم يعد طفلاً بعد الآن"
"he knows how to get around"
"إنه يعرف كيف يتحرك"
"He's looking for the path to the city"
"إنه يبحث عن الطريق إلى المدينة"
"and he is right, don't forget that"
"وهو على حق، لا تنسى ذلك"
"he's doing what you've failed to do yourself"
"إنه يفعل ما فشلت أنت في فعله بنفسك"
"he's taking care of himself"
"إنه يهتم بنفسه"
"he's taking his course for himself"

"إنه يأخذ مساره الخاص"
"Alas, Siddhartha, I see you suffering"
"آه يا سيدهارتا، أراك تعاني"
"but you're suffering a pain at which one would like to laugh"
"لكنك تعاني من ألم يود المرء أن يضحك عليه"
"you're suffering a pain at which you'll soon laugh yourself"
"إنك تعاني من ألم سوف تضحك منه قريبًا"
Siddhartha did not answer his friend
لم يجب سيدهارثا صديقه
He already held the axe in his hands
لقد كان يحمل الفأس في يديه بالفعل
and he began to make a raft of bamboo
وبدأ في صنع طوف من الخيزران
Vasudeva helped him to tie the canes together with ropes of grass
ساعده فاسوديفا في ربط القصب معًا بحبال من العشب
When they crossed the river they drifted far off their course
عندما عبروا النهر انحرفوا بعيدًا عن مسارهم
they pulled the raft upriver on the opposite bank
سحبوا الطوافة إلى أعلى النهر على الضفة المقابلة
"Why did you take the axe along?" asked Siddhartha
"لماذا أخذت الفأس معك؟" سأل سيدهارتا
"It might have been possible that the oar of our boat got lost"
"ربما كان من الممكن أن يكون مجداف قاربنا قد ضاع"
But Siddhartha knew what his friend was thinking
لكن سيدهارثا عرف ما كان يفكر فيه صديقه
He thought, the boy would have thrown away the oar
كان يعتقد أن الصبي سوف يرمي المجداف
in order to get some kind of revenge
من أجل الحصول على نوع من الانتقام
and in order to keep them from following him
ولكي يمنعهم من اتباعه
And in fact, there was no oar left in the boat
وفي الحقيقة لم يبق في القارب مجداف
Vasudeva pointed to the bottom of the boat

وأشار فاسوديفا إلى قاع القارب

and he looked at his friend with a smile

ونظر إلى صديقه مبتسما

he smiled as if he wanted to say something

ابتسم وكأنه يريد أن يقول شيئا

"Don't you see what your son is trying to tell you?"

ألا ترى ما يحاول ابنك أن يقوله لك؟

"Don't you see that he doesn't want to be followed?"

ألا ترى أنه لا يريد أن يتبعه أحد؟

But he did not say this in words

ولكنه لم يقل هذا بالكلام

He started making a new oar

بدأ في صنع مجداف جديد

But Siddhartha bid his farewell, to look for the run-away

لكن سيدهارثا ودعه، ليبحث عن الهارب

Vasudeva did not stop him from looking for his child

لم يمنعه فاسوديفا من البحث عن طفله

Siddhartha had been walking through the forest for a long time

كان سيدهارثا يمشي في الغابة لفترة طويلة

the thought occurred to him that his search was useless

خطرت له فكرة مفادها أن بحثه كان بلا فائدة

Either the boy was far ahead and had already reached the city

إما أن الصبي كان متقدمًا جدًا وكان قد وصل بالفعل إلى المدينة

or he would conceal himself from him

أو يخفي نفسه عنه

he continued thinking about his son

استمر في التفكير في ابنه

he found that he was not worried for his son

وجد أنه لم يكن قلقا على ابنه

he knew deep inside that he had not perished

كان يعلم في أعماق نفسه أنه لم يهلك

nor was he in any danger in the forest

ولم يكن في أي خطر في الغابة

Nevertheless, he ran without stopping

ومع ذلك، ركض دون توقف

he was not running to save him

لم يكن يركض لإنقاذه

he was running to satisfy his desire

كان يركض لإشباع رغبته

he wanted to perhaps see him one more time

ربما أراد أن يراه مرة أخرى

And he ran up to just outside of the city

وركض حتى وصل إلى خارج المدينة مباشرة

When, near the city, he reached a wide road

وعندما اقترب من المدينة وصل إلى طريق واسع

he stopped, by the entrance of the beautiful pleasure-garden

توقف عند مدخل حديقة المتعة الجميلة

the garden which used to belong to Kamala

الحديقة التي كانت تابعة لكامالا

the garden where he had seen her for the first time

الحديقة التي رآها فيها للمرة الأولى

when she was sitting in her sedan-chair

عندما كانت جالسة على كرسيها المتحرك

The past rose up in his soul

لقد ارتفع الماضي في روحه

again, he saw himself standing there

مرة أخرى، رأى نفسه واقفا هناك

a young, bearded, naked Samana

سامانا شابة، ملتحية، عارية

his hair hair was full of dust

كان شعره مليئا بالتراب

For a long time, Siddhartha stood there

لفترة طويلة، وقف سيدهارثا هناك

he looked through the open gate into the garden

نظر من خلال البوابة المفتوحة إلى الحديقة

he saw monks in yellow robes walking among the beautiful trees

رأى الرهبان يرتدون ثيابا صفراء يتجولون بين الأشجار الجميلة

For a long time, he stood there, pondering

لقد وقف هناك لفترة طويلة وهو يفكر

he saw images and listened to the story of his life

لقد رأى الصور واستمع إلى قصة حياته

For a long time, he stood there looking at the monks

وظل واقفا هناك لفترة طويلة ينظر إلى الرهبان

he saw young Siddhartha in their place

لقد رأى الشاب سيدهارتا في مكانهم

he saw young Kamala walking among the high trees

رأى كامالا الصغيرة تمشي بين الأشجار العالية

Clearly, he saw himself being served food and drink by Kamala

من الواضح أنه رأى نفسه يتلقى الطعام والشراب من كامالا

he saw himself receiving his first kiss from her

رأى نفسه يتلقى قبلته الأولى منها

he saw himself looking proudly and disdainfully back on his life as a Brahman

لقد رأى نفسه ينظر بفخر وازدراء إلى حياته كبراهمي.

he saw himself beginning his worldly life, proudly and full of desire

رأى نفسه يبدأ حياته الدنيوية، بفخر ومليء بالرغبة

He saw Kamaswami, the servants, the orgies

لقد رأى كاماسوامي والخدم والحفلات الجنسية الجماعية

he saw the gamblers with the dice

لقد رأى المقامرين بالنرد

he saw Kamala's song-bird in the cage

لقد رأى طائر كامالا المغرد في القفص

he lived through all this again

لقد عاش كل هذا مرة أخرى

he breathed Sansara and was once again old and tired

تنفس سانسارا وأصبح مرة أخرى عجوزًا ومتعبًا

he felt the disgust and the wish to annihilate himself again

شعر بالاشمئزاز والرغبة في تدمير نفسه مرة أخرى

and he was healed again by the holy Om

وشفي مرة أخرى بواسطة القديس أوم.

for a long time Siddhartha had stood by the gate

لقد وقف سيدهارتا عند البوابة لفترة طويلة

he realised his desire was foolish

أدرك أن رغبته كانت حمقاء

he realized it was foolishness which had made him go up to this place

أدرك أن الحماقة هي التي دفعته إلى الصعود إلى هذا المكان

he realized he could not help his son

أدرك أنه لا يستطيع مساعدة ابنه

and he realized that he was not allowed to cling to him

وأدرك أنه لا يجوز له التشبث به

he felt the love for the run-away deeply in his heart

لقد شعر بحب الهارب بعمق في قلبه

the love for his son felt like a wound

كان حبه لابنه أشبه بالجرح

but this wound had not been given to him in order to turn the knife in it

ولكن هذا الجرح لم يعط له حتى يغرس السكين فيه

the wound had to become a blossom

كان لابد أن يصبح الجرح زهرة

and his wound had to shine

وكان جرحه لابد أن يلمع

That this wound did not blossom or shine yet made him sad

إن هذا الجرح لم يزدهر أو يلمع بعد مما جعله حزينًا

Instead of the desired goal, there was emptiness

بدلاً من الهدف المنشود كان هناك فراغ

emptiness had drawn him here, and sadly he sat down

لقد جذبه الفراغ إلى هنا، وجلس حزينًا

he felt something dying in his heart

شعر بشيء يموت في قلبه

he experienced emptiness and saw no joy any more

لقد شعر بالفراغ ولم يعد يرى أي فرح

there was no goal for which to aim for

لم يكن هناك هدف نسعى لتحقيقه

He sat lost in thought and waited

جلس غارقًا في التفكير وانتظر

This he had learned by the river

لقد تعلم هذا من النهر

waiting, having patience, listening attentively
الانتظار، التحلي بالصبر، الاستماع باهتمام

And he sat and listened, in the dust of the road
وجلس يستمع في غبار الطريق

he listened to his heart, beating tiredly and sadly
كان يستمع إلى نبضات قلبه وهو ينبض بتعب وحزن

and he waited for a voice
وانتظر صوتا

Many an hour he crouched, listening
كان يجلس القرفصاء لساعات طويلة مستمعًا

he saw no images any more
لم يعد يرى أي صور بعد الآن

he fell into emptiness and let himself fall
لقد وقع في الفراغ وسمح لنفسه بالسقوط

he could see no path in front of him
لم يستطع أن يرى أي طريق أمامه

And when he felt the wound burning, he silently spoke the Om
وعندما شعر بالجرح يحترق، تحدث بصمت عن "أوم".

he filled himself with Om
لقد ملأ نفسه بـ أوم

The monks in the garden saw him
لقد رآه الرهبان في الحديقة

dust was gathering on his gray hair
كان الغبار يتجمع على شعره الرمادي

since he crouched for many hours, one of monks placed two bananas in front of him
وبما أنه ظل جالساً لساعات طويلة، فقد وضع أحد الرهبان موزتين أمامه.

The old man did not see him
ولم يره الرجل العجوز

From this petrified state, he was awoken by a hand touching his shoulder
من هذه الحالة المتحجرة، استيقظ على يد تلمس كتفه

Instantly, he recognised this tender bashful touch
على الفور، تعرف على هذه اللمسة الخجولة الرقيقة

Vasudeva had followed him and waited
كان فاسوديفا قد تبعه وانتظر
he regained his senses and rose to greet Vasudeva
استعاد وعيه وقام لتحية فاسوديفا
he looked into Vasudeva's friendly face
نظر إلى وجه فاسوديفا الودود
he looked into the small wrinkles
نظر إلى التجاعيد الصغيرة
his wrinkles were as if they were filled with nothing but his smile
كانت تجاعيده وكأنها لا تحتوي على شيء سوى ابتسامته
he looked into the happy eyes, and then he smiled too
نظر إلى العيون السعيدة، ثم ابتسم أيضًا
Now he saw the bananas lying in front of him
والآن رأى الموز ملقى أمامه
he picked the bananas up and gave one to the ferryman
التقط الموز وأعطى واحدة للقارب
After eating the bananas, they silently went back into the forest
وبعد أن أكلوا الموز، عادوا بصمت إلى الغابة.
they returned home to the ferry
عادوا إلى منزلهم بالعبارة
Neither one talked about what had happened that day
ولم يتحدث أحد منهما عما حدث في ذلك اليوم
neither one mentioned the boy's name
ولم يذكر أحد اسم الصبي
neither one spoke about him running away
لم يتحدث أحد عن هروبه
neither one spoke about the wound
ولم يتحدث أحد عن الجرح
In the hut, Siddhartha lay down on his bed
في الكوخ، استلقى سيدهارثا على سريره
after a while Vasudeva came to him
وبعد فترة جاء إليه فاسوديفا
he offered him a bowl of coconut-milk
قدم له وعاء من حليب جوز الهند

but he was already asleep

ولكنه كان نائما بالفعل

Om
أوم

For a long time the wound continued to burn

لفترة طويلة ظل الجرح يحترق

Siddhartha had to ferry many travellers across the river

كان على سيدهارتا أن ينقل العديد من المسافرين عبر النهر

many of the travellers were accompanied by a son or a daughter

كان العديد من المسافرين برفقة ابن أو ابنة

and he saw none of them without envying them

ولم ير أحداً منهم إلا حسده

he couldn't see them without thinking about his lost son

لم يستطع رؤيتهم دون أن يفكر في ابنه الضائع

"So many thousands possess the sweetest of good fortunes"

"يمتلك الآلاف من الناس أحلى الحظوظ السعيدة"

"why don't I also possess this good fortune?"

"لماذا لا أمتلك هذه الحظوة الطيبة أيضًا؟"

"even thieves and robbers have children and love them"

"حتى اللصوص والقطاع لديهم أطفال ويحبونهم"

"and they are being loved by their children"

"وهم محبوبون من أبنائهم"

"all are loved by their children except for me"

"الجميع محبوبون من أبنائهم إلا أنا"

he now thought like the childlike people, without reason

لقد أصبح الآن يفكر مثل الأطفال، بلا سبب.

he had become one of the childlike people

لقد أصبح واحدا من الناس مثل الأطفال

he looked upon people differently than before

لقد نظر إلى الناس بشكل مختلف عن ذي قبل

he was less smart and less proud of himself
لقد كان أقل ذكاءً وأقل فخرًا بنفسه
but instead, he was warmer and more curious
لكن بدلاً من ذلك، كان أكثر دفئًا وفضولًا
when he ferried travellers, he was more involved than before
عندما كان ينقل المسافرين، كان أكثر مشاركة من ذي قبل
childlike people, businessmen, warriors, women
الناس الطفوليون، رجال الأعمال، المحاربون، النساء
these people did not seem alien to him, as they used to
لم يبدو هؤلاء الناس غرباء عنه، كما اعتادوا أن يكونوا.
he understood them and shared their life
لقد فهمهم وشاركهم حياتهم
a life which was not guided by thoughts and insight
حياة لم تكن موجهة بالأفكار والبصيرة
but a life guided solely by urges and wishes
لكن الحياة موجهة فقط بالرغبات والرغبات
he felt like the the childlike people
لقد شعر وكأنه من الناس الطفوليين
he was bearing his final wound
كان يحمل جرحه الأخير
he was nearing perfection
لقد كان يقترب من الكمال
but the childlike people still seemed like his brothers
لكن الأشخاص الذين يشبهون الأطفال ما زالوا يبدون مثل إخوته
their vanities, desires for possession were no longer ridiculous to him
لم تعد غرورهم ورغباتهم في التملك سخيفة بالنسبة له
they became understandable and lovable
لقد أصبحوا مفهومين ومحبوبين
they even became worthy of veneration to him
حتى أنهم أصبحوا مستحقين التبجيل له
The blind love of a mother for her child
حب الأم الأعمى لطفلها
the stupid, blind pride of a conceited father for his only son
الكبرياء الأعمى الغبي للأب المغرور تجاه ابنه الوحيد

the blind, wild desire of a young, vain woman for jewellery
الرغبة العمياء الجامحة لامرأة شابة مغرورة في الحصول على المجوهرات

her wish for admiring glances from men
رغبتها في الحصول على نظرات إعجاب من الرجال

all of these simple urges were not childish notions
كل هذه الرغبات البسيطة لم تكن مجرد أفكار طفولية

but they were immensely strong, living, and prevailing urges
لكنها كانت قوية للغاية، وحيوية، ورغبات سائدة

he saw people living for the sake of their urges
لقد رأى الناس يعيشون من أجل رغباتهم

he saw people achieving rare things for their urges
لقد رأى الناس يحققون أشياء نادرة لرغباتهم

travelling, conducting wars, suffering
السفر، إدارة الحروب، المعاناة

they bore an infinite amount of suffering
لقد تحملوا قدرًا لا نهائيًا من المعاناة

and he could love them for it, because he saw life
وكان بإمكانه أن يحبهم لذلك، لأنه رأى الحياة

that what is alive was in each of their passions
أن ما هو حي كان في كل من عواطفهم

that what is is indestructible was in their urges, the Brahman
أن ما هو غير قابل للتدمير كان في دوافعهم، البراهمان

these people were worthy of love and admiration
كان هؤلاء الناس يستحقون الحب والإعجاب

they deserved it for their blind loyalty and blind strength
لقد استحقوا ذلك لولائهم الأعمى وقوتهم العمياء

there was nothing that they lacked
لم يكن هناك شيء ينقصهم

Siddhartha had nothing which would put him above the rest, except one thing
لم يكن لدى سيدهارتا أي شيء يجعله متفوقًا على الآخرين، باستثناء شيء واحد

there still was a small thing he had which they didn't
لا يزال هناك شيء صغير لديه ولم يكن لديهم

he had the conscious thought of the oneness of all life
كان لديه فكرة واعية عن وحدة كل أشكال الحياة
but Siddhartha even doubted whether this knowledge should be valued so highly
لكن سيدهارتا شكك حتى في ما إذا كانت هذه المعرفة تستحق التقدير بهذه الدرجة
it might also be a childish idea of the thinking people
قد تكون أيضًا فكرة طفولية من الأشخاص المفكرين
the worldly people were of equal rank to the wise men
وكان أهل الدنيا في مرتبة متساوية مع الحكماء
animals too can in some moments seem to be superior to humans
يمكن للحيوانات أيضًا في بعض اللحظات أن تبدو متفوقة على البشر
they are superior in their tough, unrelenting performance of what is necessary
إنهم متفوقون في أدائهم الصارم الذي لا هوادة فيه لما هو ضروري
an idea slowly blossomed in Siddhartha
فكرة ازدهرت ببطء في سيدهارتا
and the idea slowly ripened in him
ونضجت الفكرة بداخله ببطء
he began to see what wisdom actually was
بدأ يرى ما هي الحكمة في الواقع
he saw what the goal of his long search was
لقد رأى ما هو هدف بحثه الطويل
his search was nothing but a readiness of the soul
لم يكن بحثه سوى استعداد للروح
a secret art to think every moment, while living his life
فن سري للتفكير في كل لحظة أثناء عيش الحياة
it was the thought of oneness
لقد كانت فكرة الوحدة
to be able to feel and inhale the oneness
أن تكون قادرًا على الشعور بالوحدة واستنشاقها
Slowly this awareness blossomed in him
ببطء ازدهر هذا الوعي فيه
it was shining back at him from Vasudeva's old, childlike face

لقد كان يتألق من وجه فاسوديفا القديم الذي يشبه وجه الطفل

harmony and knowledge of the eternal perfection of the world

الانسجام ومعرفة الكمال الأبدي للعالم

smiling and to be part of the oneness

الابتسامة وأن أكون جزءًا من الوحدة

But the wound still burned

ولكن الجرح لا زال يحترق

longingly and bitterly Siddhartha thought of his son

فكر سيدهارثا في ابنه بحنين ومرارة

he nurtured his love and tenderness in his heart

لقد رعى الحب والحنان في قلبه

he allowed the pain to gnaw at him

لقد سمح للألم أن ينخر فيه

he committed all foolish acts of love

لقد ارتكب كل أعمال الحب الحمقاء

this flame would not go out by itself

هذه الشعلة لن تنطفئ من تلقاء نفسها

one day the wound burned violently

ذات يوم احترق الجرح بعنف

driven by a yearning, Siddhartha crossed the river

بدافع الشوق، عبر سيدهارثا النهر

he got off the boat and was willing to go to the city

نزل من القارب وكان على استعداد للذهاب إلى المدينة

he wanted to look for his son again

أراد أن يبحث عن ابنه مرة أخرى

The river flowed softly and quietly

كان النهر يتدفق بهدوء وهدوء

it was the dry season, but its voice sounded strange

لقد كان موسم الجفاف، لكن صوته بدا غريبًا

it was clear to hear that the river laughed

كان من الواضح أن النهر يضحك

it laughed brightly and clearly at the old ferryman

لقد ضحكت بشكل واضح ومشرق على القارب القديم

he bent over the water, in order to hear even better

انحنى فوق الماء، لكي يسمع بشكل أفضل
and he saw his face reflected in the quietly moving waters
ورأى وجهه ينعكس في المياه التي تتحرك بهدوء
in this reflected face there was something
في هذا الوجه المنعكس كان هناك شيء
something which reminded him, but he had forgotten
شيء ذكّره، لكنه نسيه
as he thought about it, he found it
وبينما كان يفكر في الأمر، وجده
this face resembled another face which he used to know and love
كان هذا الوجه يشبه وجهًا آخر كان يعرفه ويحبه
but he also used to fear this face
ولكنه كان يخاف من هذا الوجه أيضًا
It resembled his father's face, the Brahman
كان يشبه وجه والده، البراهمان
he remembered how he had forced his father to let him go
تذكر كيف أجبر والده على تركه يذهب
he remembered how he had bid his farewell to him
تذكر كيف ودعه
he remembered how he had gone and had never come back
تذكر كيف ذهب ولم يعد أبدًا
Had his father not also suffered the same pain for him?
ألم يعاني والده أيضًا نفس الألم من أجله؟
was his father's pain not the pain Siddhartha is suffering now?
ألم يكن ألم والده هو الألم الذي يعاني منه سيدهارتا الآن؟
Had his father not long since died?
هل كان والده قد مات منذ فترة طويلة؟
had he died without having seen his son again?
هل مات دون أن يرى ابنه مرة أخرى؟
Did he not have to expect the same fate for himself?
ألم يكن عليه أن يتوقع نفس المصير لنفسه؟
Was it not a comedy in a fateful circle?
ألم تكن هذه كوميديا في حلقة مصيرية؟
The river laughed about all of this

ضحك النهر من كل هذا

everything came back which had not been suffered

لقد عاد كل شيء لم يكن يعاني منه

everything came back which had not been solved

لقد عاد كل شيء لم يتم حله

the same pain was suffered over and over again

لقد عانى من نفس الألم مرارا وتكرارا

Siddhartha went back into the boat

عاد سيدهارتا إلى القارب

and he returned back to the hut

وعاد مرة أخرى إلى الكوخ

he was thinking of his father and of his son

كان يفكر في والده وفي ابنه

he thought of having been laughed at by the river

كان يعتقد أن النهر يسخر منه

he was at odds with himself and tending towards despair

كان على خلاف مع نفسه ويميل إلى اليأس

but he was also tempted to laugh

ولكنه كان يميل إلى الضحك أيضًا

he could laugh at himself and the entire world

كان بإمكانه أن يضحك على نفسه وعلى العالم أجمع

Alas, the wound was not blossoming yet

يا للأسف الجرح لم يزهر بعد

his heart was still fighting his fate

كان قلبه لا يزال يقاتل مصيره

cheerfulness and victory were not yet shining from his suffering

ولم تكن البهجة والنصر قد تشرق بعد من معاناته

Nevertheless, he felt hope along with the despair

ومع ذلك، فقد شعر بالأمل إلى جانب اليأس.

once he returned to the hut he felt an undefeatable desire to open up to Vasudeva

بمجرد عودته إلى الكوخ، شعر برغبة لا تُقهر في الانفتاح على فاسوديفا

he wanted to show him everything

أراد أن يظهر له كل شيء

he wanted to say everything to the master of listening

أراد أن يقول كل شيء لسيد الاستماع

Vasudeva was sitting in the hut, weaving a basket
كان فاسوديفا جالسًا في الكوخ، ينسج سلة
He no longer used the ferry-boat
لم يعد يستخدم العبارة
his eyes were starting to get weak
بدأت عيناه تضعف
his arms and hands were getting weak as well
كانت ذراعيه ويديه ضعيفتين أيضًا
only the joy and cheerful benevolence of his face was unchanging
لم يتغير إلا الفرح واللطف البهيج في وجهه
Siddhartha sat down next to the old man
جلس سيدهارثا بجانب الرجل العجوز
slowly, he started talking about what they had never spoke about
ببطء، بدأ يتحدث عن ما لم يتحدثا عنه من قبل
he told him of his walk to the city
أخبره عن رحلته إلى المدينة
he told at him of the burning wound
أخبره عن الجرح المحترق
he told him about the envy of seeing happy fathers
أخبره عن الغيرة من رؤية الآباء السعداء
his knowledge of the foolishness of such wishes
معرفته بحماقة مثل هذه الرغبات
his futile fight against his wishes
معركته العبثية ضد رغباته
he was able to say everything, even the most embarrassing parts
كان قادرًا على قول كل شيء، حتى الأجزاء الأكثر إحراجًا
he told him everything he could tell him
لقد أخبره بكل ما استطاع أن يقوله له
he showed him everything he could show him
لقد أظهر له كل ما يمكنه أن يظهره له
He presented his wound to him

قدم له جرحه

he also told him how he had fled today

وأخبره أيضًا كيف هرب اليوم

he told him how he ferried across the water

أخبره كيف عبر الماء

a childish run-away, willing to walk to the city

طفل هارب، على استعداد للسير إلى المدينة

and he told him how the river had laughed

وأخبره كيف ضحك النهر

he spoke for a long time

لقد تحدث لفترة طويلة

Vasudeva was listening with a quiet face

كان فاسوديفا يستمع بوجه هادئ

Vasudeva's listening gave Siddhartha a stronger sensation than ever before

أعطى استماع فاسوديفا لسيدهارتا إحساسًا أقوى من أي وقت مضى

he sensed how his pain and fears flowed over to him

لقد شعر كيف أن آلامه ومخاوفه تدفقت إليه

he sensed how his secret hope flowed over him

لقد أحس كيف أن أمله السري يتدفق عليه

To show his wound to this listener was the same as bathing it in the river

إن إظهار جرحه لهذا المستمع كان بمثابة الاستحمام به في النهر

the river would have cooled Siddhartha's wound

كان النهر ليبرد جرح سيدهارتا

the quiet listening cooled Siddhartha's wound

الاستماع الهادئ يبرد جرح سيدهارتا

it cooled him until he become one with the river

لقد برّدته حتى أصبح واحداً مع النهر

While he was still speaking, still admitting and confessing

بينما كان لا يزال يتحدث، لا يزال يعترف ويعترف

Siddhartha felt more and more that this was no longer Vasudeva

شعر سيدهارتا أكثر فأكثر أن هذا لم يعد فاسوديفا

it was no longer a human being who was listening to him

لم يعد إنسانًا يستمع إليه

this motionless listener was absorbing his confession into himself

كان هذا المستمع الساكن يستوعب اعترافه في داخله

this motionless listener was like a tree the rain

كان هذا المستمع الثابت مثل شجرة المطر

this motionless man was the river itself

كان هذا الرجل الثابت هو النهر نفسه

this motionless man was God himself

هذا الرجل الذي لا يتحرك كان الله نفسه

the motionless man was the eternal itself

كان الرجل الثابت هو الأبدي نفسه

Siddhartha stopped thinking of himself and his wound

توقف سيدهارثا عن التفكير في نفسه وجرحه

this realisation of Vasudeva's changed character took possession of him

لقد استحوذ هذا الإدراك لشخصية فاسوديفا المتغيرة عليه

and the more he entered into it, the less wondrous it became

وكلما دخل فيه أكثر، أصبح أقل عجبًا.

the more he realised that everything was in order and natural

كلما أدرك أن كل شيء كان على ما يرام وطبيعيًا

he realised that Vasudeva had already been like this for a long time

أدرك أن فاسوديفا كان على هذا النحو لفترة طويلة

he had just not quite recognised it yet

لم يكن قد أدرك ذلك بعد تمامًا

yes, he himself had almost reached the same state

نعم، لقد وصل هو نفسه تقريبًا إلى نفس الحالة

He felt, that he was now seeing old Vasudeva as the people see the gods

شعر أنه يرى الآن فاسوديفا العجوز كما يرى الناس الآلهة

and he felt that this could not last

وشعر أن هذا لا يمكن أن يستمر

in his heart, he started bidding his farewell to Vasudeva

في قلبه بدأ يودع فاسوديفا

Throughout all this, he talked incessantly

خلال كل هذا، كان يتحدث بلا انقطاع

When he had finished talking, Vasudeva turned his friendly eyes at him

عندما انتهى من الحديث، وجه فاسوديفا نظراته الودية إليه

the eyes which had grown slightly weak

العيون التي أصبحت ضعيفة قليلا

he said nothing, but let his silent love and cheerfulness shine

لم يقل شيئًا، بل ترك حبه الصامت ومرحه يتألقان

his understanding and knowledge shone from him

أشرق منه فهمه ومعرفته

He took Siddhartha's hand and led him to the seat by the bank

أخذ يد سيدهارتا وقاده إلى المقعد بجوار البنك

he sat down with him and smiled at the river

جلس معه وابتسم للنهر

"You've heard it laugh," he said

"لقد سمعته يضحك" قال

"But you haven't heard everything"

"ولكنك لم تسمع كل شيء"

"Let's listen, you'll hear more"

"دعونا نستمع، سوف تسمع المزيد"

Softly sounded the river, singing in many voices

كان النهر يغني بصوت خافت، بأصوات عديدة

Siddhartha looked into the water

نظر سيدهارتا إلى الماء

images appeared to him in the moving water

ظهرت له صور في الماء المتحرك

his father appeared, lonely and mourning for his son

ظهر والده وحيدًا حزينًا على ابنه

he himself appeared in the moving water

لقد ظهر هو نفسه في الماء المتحرك

he was also being tied with the bondage of yearning to his distant son

كان أيضًا مقيدًا بعبودية الشوق إلى ابنه البعيد

his son appeared, lonely as well

وظهر ابنه وحيدا أيضا

the boy, greedily rushing along the burning course of his young wishes

الصبي يندفع بشراهة على طول المسار المحترق لرغباته الشابة

each one was heading for his goal

كل واحد كان متجها نحو هدفه

each one was obsessed by the goal

كان كل واحد منهم مهووسًا بالهدف

each one was suffering from the pursuit

كل واحد كان يعاني من المطاردة

The river sang with a voice of suffering

غنى النهر بصوت المعاناة

longingly it sang and flowed towards its goal

غنى بحنين وتدفق نحو هدفه

"Do you hear?" Vasudeva asked with a mute gaze

"هل تسمع؟" سأل فاسوديفا بنظرة صامتة

Siddhartha nodded in reply

أومأ سيدهارتا برأسه ردًا على ذلك

"Listen better!" Vasudeva whispered

"استمع بشكل أفضل!" همس فاسوديفا

Siddhartha made an effort to listen better

لقد بذل سيدهارتا جهدًا للاستماع بشكل أفضل

The image of his father appeared

ظهرت صورة والده

his own image merged with his father's

اندمجت صورته مع صورة والده

the image of his son merged with his image

اندمجت صورة ابنه مع صورته

Kamala's image also appeared and was dispersed

كما ظهرت صورة كامالا وتم تفريقها

and the image of Govinda, and other images

وصورة جوفيندا، وصور أخرى

and all the imaged merged with each other

ودمجت كل الصور مع بعضها البعض

all the imaged turned into the river

تحولت كل الصور إلى النهر

being the river, they all headed for the goal
وبما أنهم كانوا النهر، فقد توجهوا جميعًا نحو الهدف.

longing, desiring, suffering flowed together
الشوق والرغبة والمعاناة تدفقوا معًا

and the river's voice sounded full of yearning
وصوت النهر بدا مليئا بالشوق

the river's voice was full of burning woe
كان صوت النهر مليئا بالويل الحارق

the river's voice was full of unsatisfiable desire
كان صوت النهر مليئا بالرغبة التي لا يمكن إشباعها

For the goal, the river was heading
بالنسبة للهدف كان النهر متجها

Siddhartha saw the river hurrying towards its goal
رأى سيدهارثا النهر يسارع نحو هدفه

the river of him and his loved ones and of all people he had ever seen
نهره وأحبائه وكل الناس الذين رآهم على الإطلاق

all of these waves and waters were hurrying
كل هذه الأمواج والمياه كانت تتسارع

they were all suffering towards many goals
كانوا جميعا يعانون من أجل تحقيق أهداف عديدة

the waterfall, the lake, the rapids, the sea
الشلال، البحيرة، المنحدرات، البحر

and all goals were reached
وتم الوصول إلى جميع الأهداف

and every goal was followed by a new one
وكل هدف تبعه هدف جديد

and the water turned into vapour and rose to the sky
وتحول الماء إلى بخار وارتفع إلى السماء

the water turned into rain and poured down from the sky
تحول الماء إلى مطر وهطل من السماء

the water turned into a source
تحول الماء إلى مصدر

then the source turned into a stream
ثم تحول المصدر إلى مجرى مائي

the stream turned into a river

تحول النهر إلى نهر
and the river headed forwards again
والنهر يتجه للأمام مرة أخرى
But the longing voice had changed
لكن صوت الشوق تغير
It still resounded, full of suffering, searching
لا يزال يتردد صداه، مليئًا بالمعاناة، باحثًا
but other voices joined the river
لكن أصوات أخرى انضمت إلى النهر
there were voices of joy and of suffering
كانت هناك أصوات الفرح والمعاناة
good and bad voices, laughing and sad ones
الأصوات الطيبة والسيئة، الضاحكة والحزينة
a hundred voices, a thousand voices
مائة صوت، ألف صوت
Siddhartha listened to all these voices
استمع سيدهارثا إلى كل هذه الأصوات
He was now nothing but a listener
لم يعد الآن سوى مستمع
he was completely concentrated on listening
لقد كان يركز بشكل كامل على الاستماع
he was completely empty now
لقد كان فارغا تماما الآن
he felt that he had now finished learning to listen
شعر أنه قد انتهى الآن من تعلم الاستماع
Often before, he had heard all this
لقد سمع كل هذا من قبل في كثير من الأحيان
he had heard these many voices in the river
لقد سمع هذه الأصوات العديدة في النهر
today the voices in the river sounded new
اليوم بدت الأصوات في النهر جديدة
Already, he could no longer tell the many voices apart
بالفعل، لم يعد بإمكانه التمييز بين الأصوات العديدة
there was no difference between the happy voices and the weeping ones
لم يكن هناك فرق بين الأصوات السعيدة والأصوات الباكية

the voices of children and the voices of men were one
كانت أصوات الأطفال وأصوات الرجال واحدة
all these voices belonged together
كل هذه الأصوات تنتمي إلى بعضها البعض
the lamentation of yearning and the laughter of the knowledgeable one
رثاء الشوق وضحك العارف
the scream of rage and the moaning of the dying ones
صرخة الغضب وأنين المحتضرين
everything was one and everything was intertwined
كان كل شيء واحدا وكان كل شيء متشابكا
everything was connected and entangled a thousand times
كان كل شيء متصلاً ومتشابكًا ألف مرة
everything together, all voices, all goals
كل شيء معًا، كل الأصوات، كل الأهداف
all yearning, all suffering, all pleasure
كل الشوق، كل المعاناة، كل المتعة
all that was good and evil
كل ما كان خيرا وشراً
all of this together was the world
كل هذا معًا كان العالم
All of it together was the flow of events
كل هذا كان في مجموعها تدفق الأحداث
all of it was the music of life
كان كل ذلك موسيقى الحياة
when Siddhartha was listening attentively to this river
عندما كان سيدهارثا يستمع باهتمام إلى هذا النهر
the song of a thousand voices
أغنية ألف صوت
when he neither listened to the suffering nor the laughter
عندما لم يستمع إلى المعاناة أو الضحك
when he did not tie his soul to any particular voice
عندما لم يربط روحه بصوت معين
when he submerged his self into the river
عندما غطس نفسه في النهر

but when he heard them all he perceived the whole, the oneness

ولكن عندما سمعهم جميعًا أدرك الكل والوحدة.

then the great song of the thousand voices consisted of a single word

ثم كانت الأغنية العظيمة للألف صوت تتكون من كلمة واحدة

this word was Om; the perfection

كانت هذه الكلمة هي أوم؛ الكمال

"Do you hear" Vasudeva's gaze asked again

"هل تسمع؟" سأل فاسوديفا مرة أخرى

Brightly, Vasudeva's smile was shining

كانت ابتسامة فاسوديفا مشرقة

it was floating radiantly over all the wrinkles of his old face

لقد كان يطفو بشكل مشع فوق كل تجاعيد وجهه القديم

the same way the Om was floating in the air over all the voices of the river

بنفس الطريقة التي كان بها أوم يطفو في الهواء فوق كل أصوات النهر

Brightly his smile was shining, when he looked at his friend

كانت ابتسامته مشرقة عندما نظر إلى صديقه

and brightly the same smile was now starting to shine on Siddhartha's face

والآن بدأت نفس الابتسامة تشرق على وجه سيدهارثا

His wound had blossomed and his suffering was shining

لقد ازدهر جرحه وكان معاناته تتألق

his self had flown into the oneness

لقد طار ذاته إلى الوحدة

In this hour, Siddhartha stopped fighting his fate

في هذه الساعة، توقف سيدهارثا عن محاربة مصيره

at the same time he stopped suffering

وفي نفس الوقت توقف عن المعاناة

On his face flourished the cheerfulness of a knowledge

وعلى وجهه ازدهرت بهجة المعرفة

a knowledge which was no longer opposed by any will

المعرفة التي لم تعد تعارضها أي إرادة

a knowledge which knows perfection

المعرفة التي تعرف الكمال
a knowledge which is in agreement with the flow of events
المعرفة التي تتفق مع تدفق الأحداث
a knowledge which is with the current of life
المعرفة التي تتماشى مع تيار الحياة
full of sympathy for the pain of others
مليئة بالتعاطف مع آلام الآخرين
full of sympathy for the pleasure of others
مليئة بالتعاطف مع متعة الآخرين
devoted to the flow, belonging to the oneness
مكرس للتدفق، ينتمي إلى الوحدة
Vasudeva rose from the seat by the bank
نهض فاسوديفا من المقعد بجوار البنك
he looked into Siddhartha's eyes
نظر إلى عيني سيدهارتا
and he saw the cheerfulness of the knowledge shining in his eyes
ورأى بهجة المعرفة تلمع في عينيه
he softly touched his shoulder with his hand
لمس كتفه برفق بيده
"I've been waiting for this hour, my dear"
"لقد كنت أنتظر هذه الساعة يا عزيزتي"
"Now that it has come, let me leave"
"الآن وقد حان الوقت، دعني أرحل"
"For a long time, I've been waiting for this hour"
"لقد كنت أنتظر هذه الساعة منذ وقت طويل"
"for a long time, I've been Vasudeva the ferryman"
"لقد كنت لفترة طويلة فاسوديفا العبّارة"
"Now it's enough. Farewell"
"الآن يكفي ذلك. وداعا"
"farewell river, farewell Siddhartha!"
"وداعًا أيها النهر، وداعًا يا سيدهارتا!"
Siddhartha made a deep bow before him who bid his farewell
انحنى سيدهارتا بعمق أمام من ودعه
"I've known it," he said quietly

"لقد عرفت ذلك" قال بهدوء

"You'll go into the forests?"

"هل ستذهب إلى الغابات؟"

"I'm going into the forests"

"سأذهب إلى الغابات"

"I'm going into the oneness" spoke Vasudeva with a bright smile

"سأذهب إلى الوحدة" تحدث فاسوديفا بابتسامة مشرقة

With a bright smile, he left

وبابتسامة مشرقة غادر

Siddhartha watched him leaving

شاهده سيدهارثا وهو يغادر

With deep joy, with deep solemnity he watched him leave

بفرح عميق، وبإجلال عميق شاهده يغادر

he saw his steps were full of peace

رأى خطواته مليئة بالسلام

he saw his head was full of lustre

رأى رأسه ملينا باللمعان

he saw his body was full of light

رأى جسده ملينا بالنور

Govinda
جوفيندا

Govinda had been with the monks for a long time
كان جوفيندا مع الرهبان لفترة طويلة
when not on pilgrimages, he spent his time in the pleasure-garden
عندما لم يكن في الحج، كان يقضي وقته في حديقة المتعة
the garden which the courtesan Kamala had given the followers of Gotama
الحديقة التي أعطتها العاهرة كامالا لأتباع جوتاما
he heard talk of an old ferryman, who lived a day's journey away
سمع حديثاً عن رجل عجوز كان يعيش على مسافة يوم واحد من المدينة.
he heard many regarded him as a wise man
سمع الكثيرين يعتبرونه رجلاً حكيماً
When Govinda went back, he chose the path to the ferry
عندما عاد جوفيندا، اختار الطريق إلى العبارة
he was eager to see the ferryman
كان حريصًا على رؤية العبّارة
he had lived his entire life by the rules
لقد عاش حياته كلها وفقًا للقواعد
he was looked upon with veneration by the younger monks
كان ينظر إليه الرهبان الأصغر سنا باحترام
they respected his age and modesty
لقد احترموا سنه وتواضعه
but his restlessness had not perished from his heart
لكن قلقه لم يزول من قلبه
he was searching for what he had not found
كان يبحث عن ما لم يجده
He came to the river and asked the old man to ferry him over
جاء إلى النهر وطلب من الرجل العجوز أن ينقله عبر النهر.
when they got off the boat on the other side, he spoke with the old man
عندما نزلوا من القارب على الجانب الآخر، تحدث مع الرجل العجوز

"You're very good to us monks and pilgrims"

"أنت جيد جدًا معنا الرهبان والحجاج"

"you have ferried many of us across the river"

"لقد نقلت العديد منا عبر النهر"

"Aren't you too, ferryman, a searcher for the right path?"

"ألست أنت أيضًا، أيها القارب، باحثًا عن الطريق الصحيح؟"

smiling from his old eyes, Siddhartha spoke

ابتسم سيدهارثا من عينيه القديمتين وتحدث

"oh venerable one, do you call yourself a searcher?"

"يا سيدي الجليل، هل تسمي نفسك باحثًا؟"

"are you still a searcher, although already well in years?"

"هل مازلت باحثًا، على الرغم من تقدمك في السن؟"

"do you search while wearing the robe of Gotama's monks?"

"هل تبحث وأنت ترتدي رداء رهبان غوتاما؟"

"It's true, I'm old," spoke Govinda

"هذا صحيح، أنا عجوز"، قال جوفيندا

"but I haven't stopped searching"

"لكنني لم أتوقف عن البحث"

"I will never stop searching"

"لن أتوقف عن البحث أبدًا"

"this seems to be my destiny"

"يبدو أن هذا هو مصيري"

"You too, so it seems to me, have been searching"

"أنت أيضًا، كما يبدو لي، كنت تبحث"

"Would you like to tell me something, oh honourable one?"

"هل تريد أن تخبرني بشيء يا سيدي المحترم؟"

"What might I have that I could tell you, oh venerable one?"

"ما الذي قد أملكه لأخبرك به، أيها الجليل؟"

"Perhaps I could tell you that you're searching far too much?"

"ربما أستطيع أن أخبرك أنك تبحث كثيرًا؟"

"Could I tell you that you don't make time for finding?"

"هل يمكنني أن أخبرك أنك لا تجد الوقت للبحث؟"

"How come?" asked Govinda

"كيف ذلك؟" سأل جوفيندا

"When someone is searching they might only see what they search for"

"عندما يقوم شخص ما بالبحث، فقد لا يرى إلا ما يبحث عنه"

"he might not be able to let anything else enter his mind"

"قد لا يكون قادرًا على السماح لأي شيء آخر بالدخول إلى عقله"

"he doesn't see what he is not searching for"

"إنه لا يرى ما لا يبحث عنه"

"because he always thinks of nothing but the object of his search"

"لأنه لا يفكر دائمًا في شيء سوى هدف بحثه"

"he has a goal, which he is obsessed with"

"لديه هدف وهو مهووس به"

"Searching means having a goal"

"البحث يعني وجود هدف"

"But finding means being free, open, and having no goal"

"لكن العثور يعني أن تكون حرًا ومنفتحًا وليس لديك هدف"

"You, oh venerable one, are perhaps indeed a searcher"

"أنت يا سيدي الجليل ربما تكون باحثاً حقاً"

"because, when striving for your goal, there are many things you don't see"

"لأنه عندما تسعى لتحقيق هدفك، هناك أشياء كثيرة لا تراها"

"you might not see things which are directly in front of your eyes"

"قد لا تتمكن من رؤية الأشياء التي هي أمام عينيك مباشرة"

"I don't quite understand yet," said Govinda, "what do you mean by this?"

"أنا لا أفهم تمامًا بعد"، قال جوفيندا، "ماذا تقصد بهذا؟"

"oh venerable one, you've been at this river before, a long time ago"

"يا سيدي الجليل، لقد كنت في هذا النهر من قبل، منذ زمن طويل"

"and you have found a sleeping man by the river"

"ووجدت رجلاً نائماً بجانب النهر"

"you have sat down with him to guard his sleep"

"لقد جلست معه لتحرس نومه"

"but, oh Govinda, you did not recognise the sleeping man"

"ولكن يا جوفيندا، لم تتعرف على الرجل النائم"

Govinda was astonished, as if he had been the object of a magic spell

لقد اندهش جوفيندا، وكأنه كان موضوع تعويذة سحرية

the monk looked into the ferryman's eyes

نظر الراهب في عيني القارب

"Are you Siddhartha?" he asked with a timid voice

"هل أنت سيدهارتا؟" سأل بصوت خجول

"I wouldn't have recognised you this time either!"

"أنا أيضًا لم أتعرف عليك هذه المرة!"

"from my heart, I'm greeting you, Siddhartha"

"من قلبي، أحييك، سيدهارتا"

"from my heart, I'm happy to see you once again!"

"من قلبي، أنا سعيد لرؤيتك مرة أخرى!"

"You've changed a lot, my friend"

"لقد تغيرت كثيرًا يا صديقي"

"and you've now become a ferryman?"

"وأنت أصبحت الآن سائق العبارة؟"

In a friendly manner, Siddhartha laughed

بطريقة ودية، ضحك سيدهارتا

"yes, I am a ferryman"

"نعم، أنا قارب"

"Many people, Govinda, have to change a lot"

"كثير من الناس، جوفيندا، عليهم أن يتغيروا كثيرًا"

"they have to wear many robes"

"عليهم ارتداء العديد من الملابس"

"I am one of those who had to change a lot"

"أنا من هؤلاء الذين اضطروا إلى التغيير كثيرًا"

"Be welcome, Govinda, and spend the night in my hut"

"مرحبًا بك، جوفيندا، واقضِ الليل في كوخي"

Govinda stayed the night in the hut

بقي جوفيندا طوال الليل في الكوخ

he slept on the bed which used to be Vasudeva's bed

كان ينام على السرير الذي كان سرير فاسوديفا

he posed many questions to the friend of his youth

لقد طرح العديد من الأسئلة على صديق شبابه

Siddhartha had to tell him many things from his life

كان على سيدهارتا أن يخبره بالعديد من الأشياء من حياته

then the next morning came

ثم جاء الصباح التالي

the time had come to start the day's journey

لقد حان الوقت لبدء رحلة اليوم

without hesitation, Govinda asked one more question

دون تردد، سأل جوفيندا سؤالا آخر

"Before I continue on my path, Siddhartha, permit me to ask one more question"

"قبل أن أواصل مسيرتي، سيدهارثا، اسمح لي أن أسأل سؤالاً آخر"

"Do you have a teaching that guides you?"

هل لديك تعليم يرشدك؟

"Do you have a faith or a knowledge you follow"

"هل لديك إيمان أو معرفة تتبعها"

"is there a knowledge which helps you to live and do right?"

"هل هناك معرفة تساعدك على العيش وفعل الصواب؟"

"You know well, my dear, I have always been distrustful of teachers"

"أنت تعرف جيدًا يا عزيزتي أنني كنت دائمًا لا أثق في المعلمين"

"as a young man I already started to doubt teachers"

"عندما كنت شابًا بدأت بالفعل أشك في المعلمين"

"when we lived with the penitents in the forest, I distrusted their teachings"

"عندما كنا نعيش مع التائبين في الغابة، كنت أشك في تعاليمهم"

"and I turned my back to them"

"و أعطيتهم ظهري"

"I have remained distrustful of teachers"

"لقد بقيت متشككا في المعلمين"

"Nevertheless, I have had many teachers since then"

"ومع ذلك، كان لدي العديد من المعلمين منذ ذلك الحين"

"A beautiful courtesan has been my teacher for a long time"

"لقد كانت العاهرة الجميلة معلمتي لفترة طويلة"

"a rich merchant was my teacher"

"كان تاجر غني معلمي"

"and some gamblers with dice taught me"

"وعلمني بعض المقامرين بالنرد"
"Once, even a follower of Buddha has been my teacher"
"في يوم من الأيام، كان أحد أتباع بوذا معلمي"
"he was travelling on foot, pilgering"
"كان مسافرا على الأقدام، حجًّا"
"and he sat with me when I had fallen asleep in the forest"
"وجلس معي عندما نمت في الغابة"
"I've also learned from him, for which I'm very grateful"
"لقد تعلمت منه أيضًا، وأنا ممتن جدًا لذلك"
"But most of all, I have learned from this river"
"ولكن الأهم من كل ذلك أنني تعلمت من هذا النهر"
"and I have learned most from my predecessor, the ferryman Vasudeva"
"ولقد تعلمت الكثير من سلفي، القارب فاسوديفا"
"He was a very simple person, Vasudeva, he was no thinker"
"كان شخصًا بسيطًا للغاية، فاسوديفا، لم يكن مفكرًا"
"but he knew what is necessary just as well as Gotama"
"لكنّه كان يعرف ما هو ضروري تمامًا مثل غوتاما"
"he was a perfect man, a saint"
"لقد كان رجلاً كاملاً وقديسًا"
"Siddhartha still loves to mock people, it seems to me"
"يبدو لي أن سيدهارثا لا يزال يحب السخرية من الناس"
"I believe in you and I know that you haven't followed a teacher"
"أنا أؤمن بك وأعلم أنك لم تتبع معلمًا"
"But haven't you found something by yourself?"
"ولكن ألم تجد شيئًا بنفسك؟"
"though you've found no teachings, you still found certain thoughts"
"على الرغم من أنك لم تجد أي تعاليم، إلا أنك وجدت أفكارًا معينة"
"certain insights, which are your own"
"بعض الأفكار التي تخصك"
"insights which help you to live"
"رؤى تساعدك على العيش"
"Haven't you found something like this?"
"ولم تجد شيئا مثل هذا؟"

"If you would like to tell me, you would delight my heart"
"إذا أردت أن تخبرني، فسوف تسعد قلبي"

"you are right, I have had thoughts and gained many insights"
"أنت على حق، لقد كانت لدي أفكار واكتسبت العديد من الأفكار"

"Sometimes I have felt knowledge in me for an hour"
"أحيانًا أشعر بالمعرفة في داخلي لمدة ساعة"

"at other times I have felt knowledge in me for an entire day"
"في أوقات أخرى، شعرت بالمعرفة بداخلي لمدة يوم كامل"

"the same knowledge one feels when one feels life in one's heart"
"المعرفة نفسها التي يشعر بها المرء عندما يشعر بالحياة في قلبه"

"There have been many thoughts"
"لقد كانت هناك أفكار كثيرة"

"but it would be hard for me to convey these thoughts to you"
"ولكن سيكون من الصعب بالنسبة لي أن أنقل لك هذه الأفكار"

"my dear Govinda, this is one of my thoughts which I have found"
"عزيزي جوفيندا، هذه إحدى أفكاري التي وجدتها"

"wisdom cannot be passed on"
"الحكمة لا يمكن أن تنتقل"

"Wisdom which a wise man tries to pass on always sounds like foolishness"
"إن الحكمة التي يحاول الرجل الحكيم أن ينقلها تبدو دائمًا وكأنها حماقة"

"Are you kidding?" asked Govinda
"هل أنت تمزح؟" سأل جوفيندا

"I'm not kidding, I'm telling you what I have found"
"أنا لا أمزح، أنا أخبرك بما وجدته"

"Knowledge can be conveyed, but wisdom can't"
"المعرفة يمكن نقلها، لكن الحكمة لا يمكن نقلها"

"wisdom can be found, it can be lived"
"يمكن العثور على الحكمة، ويمكن أن نعيشها"

"it is possible to be carried by wisdom"
"من الممكن أن نحمل بالحكمة"

"miracles can be performed with wisdom"
"المعجزات يمكن أن تتم بالحكمة"
"but wisdom cannot be expressed in words or taught"
"ولكن الحكمة لا يمكن التعبير عنها بالكلمات أو تدريسها"
"This was what I sometimes suspected, even as a young man"
"هذا ما كنت أشتبه به أحيانًا، حتى عندما كنت شابًا"
"this is what has driven me away from the teachers"
"هذا ما دفعني بعيدًا عن المعلمين"
"I have found a thought which you'll regard as foolishness"
"لقد وجدت فكرة ستعتبرها حماقة"
"but this thought has been my best"
"ولكن هذه الفكرة كانت الأفضل بالنسبة لي"
"The opposite of every truth is just as true!"
"إن عكس كل حقيقة هو صحيح تمامًا!"
"any truth can only be expressed when it is one-sided"
"لا يمكن التعبير عن أي حقيقة إلا عندما تكون من جانب واحد"
"only one sided things can be put into words"
"لا يمكن التعبير عن الأشياء ذات الجانب الواحد بالكلمات"
"Everything which can be thought is one-sided"
"كل ما يمكن التفكير فيه هو من جانب واحد"
"it's all one-sided, so it's just one half"
"إن الأمر كله من جانب واحد، لذا فهو نصف واحد فقط"
"it all lacks completeness, roundness, and oneness"
"إن كل هذا يفتقر إلى الكمال والاستدارة والوحدة"
"the exalted Gotama spoke in his teachings of the world"
"لقد تحدث غوتاما الرفيع في تعاليمه للعالم"
"but he had to divide the world into Sansara and Nirvana"
"لكن كان عليه أن يقسم العالم إلى سانسارا ونيرفانا"
"he had divided the world into deception and truth"
"لقد قسم العالم إلى خداع وحقيقة"
"he had divided the world into suffering and salvation"
"لقد قسم العالم إلى معاناة وخلاص"
"the world cannot be explained any other way"
"لا يمكن تفسير العالم بأي طريقة أخرى"

"there is no other way to explain it, for those who want to teach"

"لا توجد طريقة أخرى لشرح ذلك، لأولئك الذين يريدون التدريس"

"But the world itself is never one-sided"

"لكن العالم نفسه لا يكون من جانب واحد أبدًا"

"the world exists around us and inside of us"

"العالم موجود حولنا وداخلنا"

"A person or an act is never entirely Sansara or entirely Nirvana"

"الشخص أو الفعل لا يكونان سانسارا أو نيرفانا بالكامل"

"a person is never entirely holy or entirely sinful"

"لا يكون الإنسان مقدسًا تمامًا أو خاطئًا تمامًا"

"It seems like the world can be divided into these opposites"

"يبدو أن العالم يمكن تقسيمه إلى هذه الأضداد"

"but that's because we are subject to deception"

"ولكن هذا لأننا عرضة للخداع"

"it's as if the deception was something real"

"يبدو الأمر وكأن الخداع كان شيئًا حقيقيًا"

"Time is not real, Govinda"

"الوقت ليس حقيقيا، جوفيندا"

"I have experienced this often and often again"

"لقد عشت هذا الأمر مرات ومرات"

"when time is not real, the gap between the world and the eternity is also a deception"

"عندما لا يكون الوقت حقيقيًا، فإن الفجوة بين العالم والخلود هي أيضًا خداع"

"the gap between suffering and blissfulness is not real"

"الفجوة بين المعاناة والنعيم ليست حقيقية"

"there is no gap between evil and good"

"لا يوجد فجوة بين الشر والخير"

"all of these gaps are deceptions"

"كل هذه الفجوات هي خداع"

"but these gaps appear to us nonetheless"

"ولكن هذه الفجوات تظهر لنا على الرغم من ذلك"

"How come?" asked Govinda timidly

"كيف ذلك؟" سأل جوفيندا بخجل

"Listen well, my dear," answered Siddhartha
"استمعي جيدًا يا عزيزتي" أجاب سيدهارثا
"The sinner, which I am and which you are, is a sinner"
"الخاطئ الذي أنا عليه والذي أنت عليه هو خاطئ"
"but in times to come the sinner will be Brahma again"
"ولكن في الأوقات القادمة سوف يكون الخاطئ براهما مرة أخرى"
"he will reach the Nirvana and be Buddha"
"سيصل إلى النيرفانا ويصبح بوذا"
"the times to come are a deception"
"الأوقات القادمة خدعة"
"the times to come are only a parable!"
"إن الأوقات القادمة ليست إلا مثلاً!"
"The sinner is not on his way to become a Buddha"
"الخاطئ ليس في طريقه إلى أن يصبح بوذا"
"he is not in the process of developing"
"إنه ليس في طور التطوير"
"our capacity for thinking does not know how else to picture these things"
"إن قدرتنا على التفكير لا تعرف كيف تتصور هذه الأشياء بطريقة أخرى"
"No, within the sinner there already is the future Buddha"
"لا، داخل الخاطئ يوجد بوذا المستقبلي بالفعل"
"his future is already all there"
"مستقبله موجود بالفعل"
"you have to worship the Buddha in the sinner"
"عليك أن تعبد بوذا في الخاطئ"
"you have to worship the Buddha hidden in everyone"
"عليك أن تعبد بوذا المختبئ في كل شخص"
"the hidden Buddha which is coming into being the possible"
"البوذا الخفي الذي يأتي إلى الوجود الممكن"
"The world, my friend Govinda, is not imperfect"
"العالم، يا صديقي جوفيندا، ليس كاملاً"
"the world is on no slow path towards perfection"
"العالم ليس على طريق بطيء نحو الكمال"
"no, the world is perfect in every moment"
"لا، العالم مثالي في كل لحظة"

"all sin already carries the divine forgiveness in itself"
"إن كل خطيئة تحمل في طياتها المغفرة الإلهية"
"all small children already have the old person in themselves"
"كل الأطفال الصغار لديهم بالفعل شخص عجوز في داخلهم"
"all infants already have death in them"
"كل الأطفال لديهم الموت بالفعل"
"all dying people have the eternal life"
"كل الناس المحتضرين لديهم الحياة الأبدية"
"we can't see how far another one has already progressed on his path"
"لا نستطيع أن نرى مدى التقدم الذي أحرزه شخص آخر على نفس المسار"
"in the robber and dice-gambler, the Buddha is waiting"
"في اللص والمقامر، بوذا ينتظر"
"in the Brahman, the robber is waiting"
"في البراهمان، اللص ينتظر"
"in deep meditation, there is the possibility to put time out of existence"
"في التأمل العميق، هناك إمكانية لإخراج الوقت من الوجود"
"there is the possibility to see all life simultaneously"
"هناك إمكانية لرؤية كل أشكال الحياة في وقت واحد"
"it is possible to see all life which was, is, and will be"
"من الممكن أن نرى كل أشكال الحياة التي كانت، والتي هي، والتي ستكون"
"and there everything is good, perfect, and Brahman"
"وهناك كل شيء جيد وكامل وبراهمي"
"Therefore, I see whatever exists as good"
"لذلك أرى أن كل ما هو موجود هو الخير"
"death is to me like life"
"الموت بالنسبة لي كالحياة"
"to me sin is like holiness"
"إن الخطيئة بالنسبة لي هي مثل القداسة"
"wisdom can be like foolishness"
"الحكمة قد تكون كالحماقة"
"everything has to be as it is"

"كل شيء يجب أن يكون كما هو"

"everything only requires my consent and willingness"

"كل شيء يتطلب فقط موافقتي ورغبتي"

"all that my view requires is my loving agreement to be good for me"

"كل ما يتطلبه وجهة نظري هو موافقتي المحبة على أن يكون الأمر جيدًا بالنسبة لي"

"my view has to do nothing but work for my benefit"

"وجهة نظري لا يجب أن تفعل شيئًا سوى العمل لصالحى"

"and then my perception is unable to ever harm me"

"وبعد ذلك يصبح إدراكي غير قادر على إيذائي أبدًا"

"I have experienced that I needed sin very much"

"لقد شعرت بأنني بحاجة ماسة إلى الخطيئة"

"I have experienced this in my body and in my soul"

"لقد عشت هذا في جسدي وفي روحي"

"I needed lust, the desire for possessions, and vanity"

"كنت بحاجة إلى الشهوة، والرغبة في الممتلكات، والغرور"

"and I needed the most shameful despair"

"وكنت في حاجة إلى اليأس الأكثر خزيًا"

"in order to learn how to give up all resistance"

"من أجل تعلم كيفية التخلي عن كل المقاومة"

"in order to learn how to love the world"

"من أجل أن نتعلم كيف نحب العالم"

"in order to stop comparing things to some world I wished for"

"من أجل التوقف عن مقارنة الأشياء بعالم كنت أتمنى أن أعيش فيه"

"I imagined some kind of perfection I had made up"

"لقد تخيلت نوعًا من الكمال الذي ابتكرته"

"but I have learned to leave the world as it is"

"لكنني تعلمت أن أترك العالم كما هو"

"I have learned to love the world as it is"

"لقد تعلمت أن أحب العالم كما هو"

"and I learned to enjoy being a part of it"

"وتعلمت أن أستمتع بكوني جزءًا منه"

"These, oh Govinda, are some of the thoughts which have come into my mind"

"هذه، يا جوفيندا، بعض الأفكار التي خطرت في بالي"

Siddhartha bent down and picked up a stone from the ground

انحنى سيدهارثا والتقط حجرًا من الأرض

he weighed the stone in his hand

كان يزن الحجر في يده

"This here," he said playing with the rock, "is a stone"

"هذا هنا"، قال وهو يلعب بالصخرة، "حجر"

"this stone will, after a certain time, perhaps turn into soil"

"هذا الحجر قد يتحول بعد فترة معينة إلى تربة"

"it will turn from soil into a plant or animal or human being"

"سوف يتحول من التربة إلى نبات أو حيوان أو إنسان"

"In the past, I would have said this stone is just a stone"

"في الماضي كنت سأقول أن هذا الحجر مجرد حجر"

"I might have said it is worthless"

"ربما كنت قد قلت أنه لا قيمة له"

"I would have told you this stone belongs to the world of the Maya"

"كنت لأخبرك أن هذا الحجر ينتمي إلى عالم المايا"

"but I wouldn't have seen that it has importance"

"لكنني لم أكن لأرى أن الأمر له أهمية"

"it might be able to become a spirit in the cycle of transformations"

"قد يكون من الممكن أن يصبح روحًا في دورة التحولات"

"therefore I also grant it importance"

"لذلك أعطيها أهمية أيضًا"

"Thus, I would perhaps have thought in the past"

"وهكذا ربما كنت قد فكرت في الماضي"

"But today I think differently about the stone"

"لكن اليوم أفكر بشكل مختلف بشأن الحجر"

"this stone is a stone, and it is also animal, god, and Buddha"

"هذا الحجر هو حجر، وهو أيضًا حيوان وإله وبوذا"

"I do not venerate and love it because it could turn into this or that"

"أنا لا أقدسه ولا أحبه لأنه قد يتحول إلى هذا أو ذاك"

"I love it because it is those things"

"أنا أحبه لأنه تلك الأشياء"

"this stone is already everything"

"هذا الحجر هو كل شيء بالفعل"

"it appears to me now and today as a stone"

"يبدو لي الآن واليوم وكأنه حجر"

"that is why I love this"

"لهذا السبب أحب هذا"

"that is why I see worth and purpose in each of its veins and cavities"

"لهذا السبب أرى القيمة والغرض في كل عروقه وتجويفاته"

"I see value in its yellow, gray, and hardness"

"أرى قيمة في لونه الأصفر والرمادي وصلابته"

"I appreciated the sound it makes when I knock at it"

"لقد أعجبتني الصوت الذي يصدره عندما أطرق عليه"

"I love the dryness or wetness of its surface"

"أنا أحب جفاف أو رطوبة سطحه"

"There are stones which feel like oil or soap"

"هناك حجارة تشبه الزيت أو الصابون"

"and other stones feel like leaves or sand"

"والأحجار الأخرى تبدو مثل الأوراق أو الرمال"

"and every stone is special and prays the Om in its own way"

"وكل حجر له خاصيته الخاصة ويصلي الأوم بطريقته الخاصة"

"each stone is Brahman"

"كل حجر هو براهمان"

"but simultaneously, and just as much, it is a stone"

"ولكن في نفس الوقت، وبنفس القدر، فهو حجر"

"it is a stone regardless of whether it's oily or juicy"

"إنه حجر بغض النظر عما إذا كان زيتيًا أو عصيريًا"

"and this why I like and regard this stone"

"وهذا هو السبب الذي يجعلني أحب هذا الحجر وأقدره"

"it is wonderful and worthy of worship"

"إنه رائع ويستحق العبادة"

"But let me speak no more of this"

"ولكن دعني لا أتحدث أكثر عن هذا"

"words are not good for transmitting the secret meaning"

"الكلمات ليست جيدة لنقل المعنى السري"
"everything always becomes a bit different, as soon as it is put into words"
"كل شيء يصبح دائمًا مختلفًا بعض الشيء، بمجرد وضعه في الكلمات"
"everything gets distorted a little by words"
"كل شيء يصبح مشوهاً قليلاً بسبب الكلمات"
"and then the explanation becomes a bit silly"
"وبعد ذلك يصبح التفسير سخيفًا بعض الشيء"
"yes, and this is also very good, and I like it a lot"
"نعم، وهذا جيد جدًا أيضًا، وأنا أحبه كثيرًا"
"I also very much agree with this"
"أنا أيضا أتفق مع هذا تماما"
"one man's treasure and wisdom always sounds like foolishness to another person"
"إن كنز وحكمة رجل ما قد تبدو دائمًا وكأنها حماقة بالنسبة لشخص آخر"
Govinda listened silently to what Siddhartha was saying
استمع جوفيندا بصمت إلى ما كان يقوله سيدهارثا
there was a pause and Govinda hesitantly asked a question
كان هناك توقف وسأل جوفيندا سؤالا مترددا
"Why have you told me this about the stone?"
"لماذا أخبرتني بهذا عن الحجر؟"
"I did it without any specific intention"
"لقد فعلت ذلك دون أي نية محددة"
"perhaps what I meant was, that I love this stone and the river"
"ربما ما قصدته هو أنني أحب هذا الحجر والنهر"
"and I love all these things we are looking at"
"وأنا أحب كل هذه الأشياء التي ننظر إليها"
"and we can learn from all these things"
"ويمكننا أن نتعلم من كل هذه الأشياء"
"I can love a stone, Govinda"
"أستطيع أن أحب حجرًا، جوفيندا"
"and I can also love a tree or a piece of bark"
"وأنا أيضا يمكن أن أحب شجرة أو قطعة من اللحاء"
"These are things, and things can be loved"
"هذه أشياء، والأشياء يمكن أن نحبها"

"but I cannot love words"
"لكنني لا أستطيع أن أحب بالكلمات"
"therefore, teachings are no good for me"
"لذلك، فإن التعاليم ليست جيدة بالنسبة لي"
"teachings have no hardness, softness, colours, edges, smell, or taste"
"التعاليم ليس لها صلابة أو ليونة أو ألوان أو حواف أو رائحة أو طعم"
"teachings have nothing but words"
"ليس للتعاليم سوى الكلمات"
"perhaps it is words which keep you from finding peace"
"ربما تكون الكلمات هي التي تمنعك من إيجاد السلام"
"because salvation and virtue are mere words"
"لأن الخلاص والفضيلة مجرد كلمات"
"Sansara and Nirvana are also just mere words, Govinda"
"سانسارا ونيرفانا مجرد كلمات، جوفيندا"
"there is no thing which would be Nirvana"
"لا يوجد شيء يمكن أن يكون نيرفانا"
"therefore Nirvana is just the word"
" لذلك فإن النيرفانا هي مجرد كلمة"
Govinda objected, "Nirvana is not just a word, my friend"
اعترض جوفيندا قائلاً: "النيرفانا ليست مجرد كلمة يا صديقي"
"Nirvana is a word, but also it is a thought"
"النيرفانا هي كلمة، ولكنها أيضًا فكرة"
Siddhartha continued, "it might be a thought"
وتابع سيدهارتا "قد تكون فكرة"
"I must confess, I don't differentiate much between thoughts and words"
"يجب أن أعترف أنني لا أفرق كثيرًا بين الأفكار والكلمات"
"to be honest, I also have no high opinion of thoughts"
"بصراحة، أنا أيضًا ليس لدي رأي عالٍ في الأفكار"
"I have a better opinion of things than thoughts"
"لدي رأي أفضل في الأشياء من الأفكار"
"Here on this ferry-boat, for instance, a man has been my predecessor"
"هنا على هذه العبارة، على سبيل المثال، كان هناك رجل سلفى"
"he was also one of my teachers"

"لقد كان أيضًا أحد أساتذتي"

"a holy man, who has for many years simply believed in the river"

"رجل مقدس، كان يؤمن بالنهر لسنوات عديدة"

"and he believed in nothing else"

"ولم يؤمن بأي شيء آخر"

"He had noticed that the river spoke to him"

"لقد لاحظ أن النهر تحدث إليه"

"he learned from the river"

"لقد تعلم من النهر"

"the river educated and taught him"

"النهر علمه وعلمه"

"the river seemed to be a god to him"

"يبدو أن النهر كان بمثابة إله بالنسبة له"

"for many years he did not know that everything was as divine as the river"

"لمدة سنوات عديدة لم يكن يعلم أن كل شيء كان إلهيًا مثل النهر"

"the wind, every cloud, every bird, every beetle"

"الريح، كل سحابة، كل طائر، كل خنفساء"

"they can teach just as much as the river"

"إنهم قادرون على التدريس بقدر ما يستطيع النهر"

"But when this holy man went into the forests, he knew everything"

"ولكن عندما ذهب هذا الرجل المقدس إلى الغابات، عرف كل شيء"

"he knew more than you and me, without teachers or books"

"لقد كان يعرف أكثر منك ومني، دون معلمين أو كتب"

"he knew more than us only because he had believed in the river"

"لقد كان يعرف أكثر منا فقط لأنه كان يؤمن بالنهر"

Govinda still had doubts and questions

لا يزال جوفيندا لديه شكوك وأسئلة

"But is that what you call things actually something real?"

"ولكن هل ما تسميه بالأشياء هو في الواقع شيء حقيقي؟"

"do these things have existence?"

هل هذه الأشياء لها وجود؟

"Isn't it just a deception of the Maya"

"أليس هذا مجرد خداع من المايا"

"aren't all these things an image and illusion?"

"أليس كل هذه الأشياء مجرد صورة ووهم؟"

"Your stone, your tree, your river"

"حجرك، شجرتك، نهرك"

"are they actually a reality?"

"هل هم حقيقة فعلاً؟"

"This too," spoke Siddhartha, "I do not care very much about"

"هذا أيضًا،" تحدث سيدهارثا، "لا أهتم به كثيرًا"

"Let the things be illusions or not"

"دع الأشياء تكون أوهامًا أو لا تكون"

"after all, I would then also be an illusion"

"بعد كل شيء، سوف أكون أيضًا وهمًا"

"and if these things are illusions then they are like me"

"وإذا كانت هذه الأشياء أوهامًا فهي مثلي"

"This is what makes them so dear and worthy of veneration for me"

"هذا ما يجعلهم أعزاءً جدًا ويستحقون التبجيل بالنسبة لي"

"these things are like me and that is how I can love them"

"هذه الأشياء تشبهني وهذه هي الطريقة التي أستطيع أن أحبهم بها"

"this is a teaching you will laugh about"

"هذا هو التعليم الذي سوف تضحك عليه"

"love, oh Govinda, seems to me to be the most important thing of all"

"الحب يا جوفيندا يبدو لي أنه أهم شيء على الإطلاق"

"to thoroughly understand the world may be what great thinkers do"

"قد يكون الفهم الشامل للعالم هو ما يفعله المفكرون العظماء"

"they explain the world and despise it"

"إنهم يفسرون العالم ويحتقرونه"

"But I'm only interested in being able to love the world"

"لكنني مهتم فقط بأن أكون قادرًا على حب العالم"

"I am not interested in despising the world"

"أنا لا أهتم باحتقار العالم"

"I don't want to hate the world"

"لا أريد أن أكره العالم"

"and I don't want the world to hate me"

"ولا أريد للعالم أن يكرهني"

"I want to be able to look upon the world and myself with love"

"أريد أن أكون قادرًا على النظر إلى العالم وإلى نفسي بالحب"

"I want to look upon all beings with admiration"

"أريد أن أنظر إلى جميع الكائنات بإعجاب"

"I want to have a great respect for everything"

"أريد أن يكون لدي احترام كبير لكل شيء"

"This I understand," spoke Govinda

"هذا ما أفهمه" تحدث جوفيندا

"But this very thing was discovered by the exalted one to be a deception"

"ولكن هذا الأمر عينه اكتشفه العالي على أنه خديعة"

"He commands benevolence, clemency, sympathy, tolerance"

"يأمر بالخير والرحمة والعطف والتسامح"

"but he does not command love"

"لكنّه لا يأمر بالمحبة"

"he forbade us to tie our heart in love to earthly things"

"نهانا أن نربط قلوبنا في حب الأشياء الأرضية"

"I know it, Govinda," said Siddhartha, and his smile shone golden

"أعلم ذلك يا جوفيندا" قال سيدهارثا وابتسامته تتألق باللون الذهبي

"And behold, with this we are right in the thicket of opinions"

"وإذا نحن بهذا في غابة من الآراء"

"now we are in the dispute about words"

"الآن نحن في نزاع حول الكلمات"

"For I cannot deny, my words of love are a contradiction"

"لأنني لا أستطيع أن أنكر أن كلماتي عن الحب متناقضة"

"they seem to be in contradiction with Gotama's words"

"يبدو أنهم يتناقضون مع كلمات جوتاما"

"For this very reason, I distrust words so much"

"لهذا السبب بالذات، أنا لا أثق بالكلمات كثيرًا"

"because I know this contradiction is a deception"
"لأني أعلم أن هذا التناقض هو خداع"
"I know that I am in agreement with Gotama"
"أعلم أنني متفق مع جوتاما"
"How could he not know love when he has discovered all elements of human existence"
"كيف لا يعرف الحب وهو الذي اكتشف كل عناصر الوجود الإنساني"
"he has discovered their transitoriness and their meaninglessness"
"لقد اكتشف زوالهم وعدم أهميتهم"
"and yet he loved people very much"
"ومع ذلك كان يحب الناس كثيرًا"
"he used a long, laborious life only to help and teach them!"
"لقد قضى حياته الطويلة الشاقة فقط لمساعدتهم وتعليمهم!"
"Even with your great teacher, I prefer things over the words"
"حتى مع معلمك العظيم، فأنا أفضل الأشياء على الكلمات"
"I place more importance on his acts and life than on his speeches"
"أعطي أهمية أكبر لأفعاله وحياته من خطاباته"
"I value the gestures of his hand more than his opinions"
"أقدر حركات يده أكثر من آرائه"
"for me there was nothing in his speech and thoughts"
"بالنسبة لي لم يكن هناك شيء في كلامه وأفكاره"
"I see his greatness only in his actions and in his life"
"أرى عظمته فقط في أفعاله وفي حياته"

For a long time, the two old men said nothing
لفترة طويلة، لم يقل الرجلان العجوزان شيئًا
Then Govinda spoke, while bowing for a farewell
ثم تحدث جوفيندا، بينما كان ينحني للوداع
"I thank you, Siddhartha, for telling me some of your thoughts"
"أشكرك يا سيدهارثا على إخباري ببعض أفكارك"
"These thoughts are partially strange to me"
"هذه الأفكار غريبة بالنسبة لي جزئيا".

"not all of these thoughts have been instantly understandable to me"

"لم تكن كل هذه الأفكار مفهومة لي على الفور"

"This being as it may, I thank you"

"ومع ذلك، أشكرك"

"and I wish you to have calm days"

"وأتمنى لك أيامًا هادئة"

But secretly he thought something else to himself

لكن في سره كان يفكر في شيء آخر لنفسه

"This Siddhartha is a bizarre person"

"هذا سيدهارتا شخص غريب"

"he expresses bizarre thoughts"

"إنه يعبر عن أفكار غريبة"

"his teachings sound foolish"

"تعاليمه تبدو سخيفة"

"the exalted one's pure teachings sound very different"

"إن تعاليم الشخص الرفيع النقية تبدو مختلفة جدًا"

"those teachings are clearer, purer, more comprehensible"

"هذه التعاليم أكثر وضوحًا ونقاءً وأكثر قابلية للفهم"

"there is nothing strange, foolish, or silly in those teachings"

"لا يوجد شيء غريب أو أحمق أو سخيف في هذه التعاليم"

"But Siddhartha's hands seemed different from his thoughts"

"لكن يدي سيدهارتا بدت مختلفة عن أفكاره"

"his feet, his eyes, his forehead, his breath"

"قدميه، عينيه، جبهته، أنفاسه"

"his smile, his greeting, his walk"

"ابتسامته، تحيته، مشيته"

"I haven't met another man like him since Gotama became one with the Nirvana"

"لم أقابل رجلاً مثله منذ أن أصبح غوتاما واحدًا مع نيرفانا"

"since then I haven't felt the presence of a holy man"

"منذ ذلك الحين لم أشعر بوجود رجل مقدس"

"I have only found Siddhartha, who is like this"

"لقد وجدت فقط سيدهارتا، الذي هو مثل هذا"

"his teachings may be strange and his words may sound foolish"
"قد تكون تعاليمه غريبة وكلماته تبدو سخيفة"
"but purity shines out of his gaze and hand"
"لكن النقاء يشرق من نظراته ويده"
"his skin and his hair radiates purity"
"بشرته وشعره يشع بالنقاء"
"purity shines out of every part of him"
"النقاء يشرق من كل جزء منه"
"a calmness, cheerfulness, mildness and holiness shines from him"
"يشرق منه الهدوء والبهجة والوداعة والقداسة"
"something which I have seen in no other person"
"شيء لم أره في أي شخص آخر"
"I have not seen it since the final death of our exalted teacher"
"لم أره منذ الموت الأخير لمعلمنا الجليل"
While Govinda thought like this, there was a conflict in his heart
بينما كان جوفيندا يفكر بهذه الطريقة، كان هناك صراع في قلبه
he once again bowed to Siddhartha
انحنى مرة أخرى لسيدهارتا
he felt he was drawn forward by love
شعر أنه ينجذب إلى الحب
he bowed deeply to him who was calmly sitting
انحنى بعمق للذي كان يجلس بهدوء
"Siddhartha," he spoke, "we have become old men"
"سيدهارتا"، قال، "لقد أصبحنا رجالاً مسنين"
"It is unlikely for one of us to see the other again in this incarnation"
"من غير المحتمل أن يرى أحدنا الآخر مرة أخرى في هذا التجسد"
"I see, beloved, that you have found peace"
"أرى يا حبيبي أنك وجدت السلام"
"I confess that I haven't found it"
"أعترف بأنني لم أجده"
"Tell me, oh honourable one, one more word"

"أخبرني يا سيدي الكريم كلمة أخرى"
"give me something on my way which I can grasp"
"أعطني شيئًا في طريقي يمكنني أن أمسكه"
"give me something which I can understand!"
"أعطني شيئًا أستطيع أن أفهمه!"
"give me something I can take with me on my path"
"أعطني شيئًا أستطيع أن آخذه معي في طريقي"
"my path is often hard and dark, Siddhartha"
"طريقي غالبا ما يكون صعبا ومظلما، سيدهارتا"
Siddhartha said nothing and looked at him
لم يقل سيدهارتا شيئًا ونظر إليه
he looked at him with his ever unchanged, quiet smile
نظر إليه بابتسامته الهادئة التي لا تتغير أبدًا
Govinda stared at his face with fear
حدق جوفيندا في وجهه بخوف
there was yearning and suffering in his eyes
كان هناك شوق ومعاناة في عينيه
the eternal search was visible in his look
كان البحث الأبدي واضحا في نظرته
you could see his eternal inability to find
يمكنك أن ترى عجزه الأبدي عن إيجاد
Siddhartha saw it and smiled
لقد رأى سيدهارتا ذلك وابتسم
"Bend down to me!" he whispered quietly in Govinda's ear
"انحنى نحوي!" همس بهدوء في أذن جوفيندا
"Like this, and come even closer!"
"مثل هذا، واقترب أكثر!"
"Kiss my forehead, Govinda!"
"قبل جبهتي، جوفيندا!"
Govinda was astonished, but drawn on by great love and expectation
لقد اندهش جوفيندا، لكنه انجذب إلى الحب الكبير والتوقعات
he obeyed his words and bent down closely to him
امتثل لكلماته وانحنى إليه عن كثب
and he touched his forehead with his lips
ولمس جبهته بشفتيه

when he did this, something miraculous happened to him
عندما فعل هذا، حدث له شيء عجيب

his thoughts were still dwelling on Siddhartha's wondrous words
كانت أفكاره لا تزال تدور حول كلمات سيدهارتا الرائعة

he was still reluctantly struggling to think away time
كان لا يزال يكافح على مضض للتفكير في الوقت.

he was still trying to imagine Nirvana and Sansara as one
كان لا يزال يحاول تخيل نيرفانا وسانسارا كواحدة

there was still a certain contempt for the words of his friend
كان لا يزال هناك قدر معين من الازدراء لكلمات صديقه

those words were still fighting in him
كانت تلك الكلمات لا تزال تقاتل بداخله

those words were still fighting against an immense love and veneration
كانت تلك الكلمات لا تزال تقاوم حبًا وتبجيلًا هائلين

and during all these thoughts, something else happened to him
وأثناء كل هذه الأفكار حدث له شيء آخر

He no longer saw the face of his friend Siddhartha
لم يعد يرى وجه صديقه سيدهارتا

instead of Siddhartha's face, he saw other faces
بدلاً من وجه سيدهارتا، رأى وجوهًا أخرى

he saw a long sequence of faces
لقد رأى سلسلة طويلة من الوجوه

he saw a flowing river of faces
رأى نهرًا متدفقًا من الوجوه

hundreds and thousands of faces, which all came and disappeared
مئات وآلاف الوجوه، التي جاءت جميعها واختفت

and yet they all seemed to be there simultaneously
ومع ذلك، يبدو أنهم جميعًا كانوا هناك في نفس الوقت

they constantly changed and renewed themselves
لقد تغيروا وتجددوا باستمرار

they were themselves and they were still all Siddhartha's face

لقد كانوا أنفسهم وكانوا لا يزالون جميعًا وجه سيدهارتا

he saw the face of a fish with an infinitely painfully opened mouth

رأى وجه سمكة بفم مفتوح بشكل مؤلم إلى ما لا نهاية

the face of a dying fish, with fading eyes

وجه سمكة تموت، وعيون تتلاشى

he saw the face of a new-born child, red and full of wrinkles

رأى وجه طفل حديث الولادة، أحمر اللون ومليئًا بالتجاعيد

it was distorted from crying

لقد تم تشويهه من البكاء

he saw the face of a murderer

لقد رأى وجه القاتل

he saw him plunging a knife into the body of another person

لقد رآه يطعن بسكين في جسد شخص آخر

he saw, in the same moment, this criminal in bondage

لقد رأى في نفس اللحظة هذا المجرم في العبودية

he saw him kneeling before a crowd

لقد رآه راكعًا أمام حشد من الناس

and he saw his head being chopped off by the executioner

ورأى رأسه يقطعها الجلاد

he saw the bodies of men and women

لقد رأى جثث الرجال والنساء

they were naked in positions and cramps of frenzied love

كانوا عراة في أوضاع وتشنجات الحب المحموم

he saw corpses stretched out, motionless, cold, void

رأى جثثًا ممددة، بلا حراك، باردة، فارغة

he saw the heads of animals

رأى رؤوس الحيوانات

heads of boars, of crocodiles, and of elephants

رؤوس الخنازير، والتماسيح، والفيلة

he saw the heads of bulls and of birds

رأى رؤوس الثيران والطيور

he saw gods; Krishna and Agni

لقد رأى الآلهة؛ كريشنا وأجني

he saw all of these figures and faces in a thousand relationships with one another

لقد رأى كل هذه الشخصيات والوجوه في ألف علاقة مع بعضها البعض

each figure was helping the other

كل شخصية كانت تساعد الأخرى

each figure was loving their relationship

كان كل شخص يحب علاقتهما

each figure was hating their relationship, destroying it

كان كل شخص يكره علاقتهما ويدمرها

and each figure was giving re-birth to their relationship

وكان كل رقم يعيد ميلاد علاقتهما

each figure was a will to die

كل شخصية كانت إرادة الموت

they were passionately painful confessions of transitoriness

لقد كانت اعترافات مؤلمة للغاية بالزوال

and yet none of them died, each one only transformed

ولكن لم يمت أحد منهم، بل تحول كل واحد منهم فقط

they were always reborn and received more and more new faces

لقد ولدوا من جديد دائمًا وتلقوا المزيد والمزيد من الوجوه الجديدة

no time passed between the one face and the other

لم يمر وقت بين الوجه والوجه الآخر

all of these figures and faces rested

كل هذه الشخصيات والوجوه كانت مستريحة

they flowed and generated themselves

لقد تدفقوا وتولدوا أنفسهم

they floated along and merged with each other

لقد طافوا معًا واندمجوا مع بعضهم البعض

and they were all constantly covered by something thin

وكانوا جميعًا مغطون باستمرار بشيء رقيق

they had no individuality of their own

لم تكن لديهم شخصية خاصة بهم

but yet they were existing

لكنهم كانوا موجودين

they were like a thin glass or ice

كانوا مثل الزجاج الرقيق أو الجليد

they were like a transparent skin
لقد كانوا مثل الجلد الشفاف
they were like a shell or mould or mask of water
كانوا مثل صدفة أو قالب أو قناع من الماء
and this mask was smiling
وكان هذا القناع مبتسما
and this mask was Siddhartha's smiling face
وكان هذا القناع هو وجه سيدهارتا المبتسم
the mask which Govinda was touching with his lips
القناع الذي كان جوفيندا يلمسه بشفتيه
And, Govinda saw it like this
ورأى جوفيندا الأمر على هذا النحو
the smile of the mask
ابتسامة القناع
the smile of oneness above the flowing forms
ابتسامة الوحدة فوق الأشكال المتدفقة
the smile of simultaneousness above the thousand births and deaths
ابتسامة التزامن فوق آلاف الولادات والوفيات
the smile of Siddhartha's was precisely the same
كانت ابتسامة سيدهارتا هي نفسها تمامًا
Siddhartha's smile was the same as the quiet smile of Gotama, the Buddha
كانت ابتسامة سيدهارتا هي نفس ابتسامة جوتاما الهادئة، بوذا
it was delicate and impenetrable smile
كانت ابتسامة رقيقة وغير قابلة للاختراق
perhaps it was benevolent and mocking, and wise
ربما كان ذلك خيرًا وسخرية وحكمة
the thousand-fold smile of Gotama, the Buddha
ابتسامة بوذا ذات الألف ضعف
as he had seen it himself with great respect a hundred times
كما رآه بنفسه باحترام كبير مائة مرة
Like this, Govinda knew, the perfected ones are smiling
هكذا عرف جوفيندا، أولئك الذين تم إكمالهم يبتسمون
he did not know anymore whether time existed
لم يعد يعرف ما إذا كان الزمن موجودًا أم لا

he did not know whether the vision had lasted a second or a hundred years

ولم يكن يعلم هل استمرت الرؤية ثانية واحدة أم مائة عام

he did not know whether a Siddhartha or a Gotama existed

لم يكن يعلم ما إذا كان هناك سيدهارتا أو جوتاما

he did not know if a me or a you existed

لم يكن يعلم إن كنت أنا أو أنت موجودًا

he felt in his as if he had been wounded by a divine arrow

شعر في داخله وكأنه أصيب بسهم إلهي

the arrow pierced his innermost self

لقد اخترق السهم أعماق نفسه

the injury of the divine arrow tasted sweet

لقد كان طعم إصابة السهم الإلهي حلوًا

Govinda was enchanted and dissolved in his innermost self

كان جوفيندا مسحورًا ومذابًا في أعماق ذاته

he stood still for a little while

لقد وقف ساكنا لفترة قصيرة

he bent over Siddhartha's quiet face, which he had just kissed

انحنى على وجه سيدهارتا الهادئ، الذي كان قد قبله للتو

the face in which he had just seen the scene of all manifestations

الوجه الذي رأى فيه للتو مشهد كل المظاهر

the face of all transformations and all existence

وجه كل التحولات وكل الوجود

the face he was looking at was unchanged

الوجه الذي كان ينظر إليه لم يتغير

under its surface, the depth of the thousand folds had closed up again

تحت سطحها، انغلق عمق الألف طية مرة أخرى

he smiled silently, quietly, and softly

ابتسم بصمت وهدوء ولطف

perhaps he smiled very benevolently and mockingly

ربما ابتسم بلطف وسخرية

precisely this was how the exalted one smiled

هكذا بالضبط ابتسم السامي

Deeply, Govinda bowed to Siddhartha

انحنى جوفيندا بعمق لسيدهارتا

tears he knew nothing of ran down his old face

دموع لم يكن يعرف عنها شيئًا سالت على وجهه القديم

his tears burned like a fire of the most intimate love

كانت دموعه تحترق مثل نار الحب الأكثر حميمية

he felt the humblest veneration in his heart

لقد شعر بأدنى درجات التبجيل في قلبه

Deeply, he bowed, touching the ground

انحنى بعمق، ولمس الأرض

he bowed before him who was sitting motionlessly

انحنى أمام من كان جالسا بلا حراك

his smile reminded him of everything he had ever loved in his life

ذكّرته ابتسامته بكل ما أحبه في حياته

his smile reminded him of everything in his life that he found valuable and holy

ذكّرته ابتسامته بكل شيء في حياته وجده ثمينًا ومقدسًا

www.ingramcontent.com/pod-product-compliance
Lightning Source LLC
Chambersburg PA
CBHW012003090526
44590CB00026B/3853